Betül Tunç

Turkuaz Kitchen

TRADITIONAL &
MODERN DOUGH
RECIPES FOR SWEET
& SAVORY BAKES

FOOD PHOTOGRAPHY BY BETÜL TUNÇ
LIFESTYLE PHOTOGRAPHY BY GENTL AND HYERS

TEN SPEED PRESS
California | New York

CONTENTS

INTRODUCTION

Allow me to introduce myself: I'm Betül, better known to many of you on social media as Turkuaz Kitchen. From my earliest memories, the kitchen has always been my sanctuary, and I knew that one day I would build my world around it. Whether it was at age twelve daydreaming about my first cookbook signing, or at fourteen trying new recipes and pretending to host a cooking show, I've always been captivated by the culinary arts.

My love affair with dough began when I was just eight years old, with dough given to me by my mother to play with. Dough speaks to some of my favorite things about the kitchen, especially how such an unformed and versatile start can turn into a satisfying payoff. Handling dough forces patience, and the therapeutic nature of kneading is a great way to slow down and be present in your cooking process. As fate would have it, my first viral video and my introduction to the kitchen both revolved around dough. The kitchen has truly shaped my life in remarkable ways! Now, I'm realizing my dreams by publishing my first cookbook filled with treasured dough recipes from my youth and adulthood.

I was born and raised in Erzurum, a quaint and chilly city nestled in northeastern Türkiye. As the youngest of four girls in my family, my upbringing was marked by strict rules, which in retrospect, cultivated my creativity. Erzurum is renowned for its long, snowy winters; during those frosty days, I found solace in cooking with my mother and sisters.

Recognizing my enthusiasm for cooking, my mother gradually involved me more in dough preparation. At age eight, she entrusted me with the entire process of making kete (a Turkish pastry particularly popular in my hometown). I vividly remember the hours spent reveling in each step, my small hands working the dough with sheer delight. Despite our ketes turning out a tad too crispy, we still enjoyed them wholeheartedly. From then on, our shared kitchen adventures continued.

Life took an unexpected turn when, after middle school, I had to take a break from my education. It was a difficult period as I was an extroverted, social kid struggling to come to terms with the situation. To this day, I find it hard to discuss those years. During that time, cooking became my comfort, and the kitchen turned into a haven where I could escape boredom, unhappiness, or even hopelessness.

With my newfound abundance of time, I delved into the world of cake-making, initially using ready-made cake mixes. Though I had spent years creatively adapting my mom's doughs, it wasn't until this period that I started crafting doughs and batters from scratch. My first homemade cake was a Maulwurfkuchen (German mole cake), a simple yet scrumptious delight I still enjoy baking occasionally.

In my quest to master more cake recipes from scratch, I became an avid viewer of cooking shows. Back then, finding recipes or cooking videos online was challenging, so I immersed myself in the limited daytime programs featuring Turkish chefs. As someone raised with strict TV restrictions, the newfound freedom to indulge in these shows was exhilarating. I diligently watched or studied each episode, taking notes on enticing recipes and testing them out immediately. Whenever a recipe fell short, my mother's encouragement pushed me to adjust the steps or ingredients and keep baking until I achieved perfection. Some recipes even required three or four attempts in one day!

Gradually, I began to grasp the chemistry of cooking and baking, deciphering errors and understanding the nuances of ingredients and techniques. At fifteen, I participated in a cooking competition hosted by a TV chef I was following. Though my performance was less than stellar, the experience was transformative and fueled my passion for the culinary arts.

My friends and family can attest to my unwavering determination when I set my sights on a goal; I can work tirelessly, day and night, to achieve it. I vividly recall devoting days to honing my knife skills in the kitchen. Lacking the means to attend culinary school, I fashioned my own training program within my small world. Emulating the chefs I admired, I would conjure up recipes as if I were on a TV show, articulating each step to my imaginary viewers. In hindsight, these may not have been conventional aspirations for a young teenager, but they became second nature to me. After getting married, my husband found this habit endearing and was thoroughly charmed by it.

As I delved deeper into the culinary world, I began to dream of pursuing formal pastry education in France. Though it seemed unattainable at the time, I remained committed to refining my skills in anticipation of professional training someday. Consequently, I adopted a more systematic approach, documenting my recipes and refining my techniques. However, I still enjoy embracing a touch of chaos in the kitchen, as this fosters creativity.

Through consistent experimentation and note-taking, my skills improved dramatically. My creations garnered attention from family and friends, and I soon became a popular pastry baker within my close-knit circle. I even conducted informal workshops on various pastry recipes for those in my orbit. It was a time filled with profiteroles, cakes, and cookies as we celebrated the sweet side of life.

Back in those days, while I focused on crafting cakes and pastries, my sister took charge of cooking meals in our home. My mother, who didn't particularly enjoy cooking, was content to taste our creations and offer critiques. A perfectionist by nature, she could always find something to criticize about the food's texture and taste or the use of certain ingredients. Even today, she spends a few minutes during our evening video chats discussing my social media recipes—some of the most popular recipes on my account still don't meet her exacting standards. While handling criticism isn't always easy, my mother's influence helped me develop a perfectionist streak in the kitchen and is a significant factor in the kind of home cook I have become. This attention to detail, though sometimes exhausting, has contributed to the success of my shared recipes. I won't post a recipe until I've tested and tweaked it multiple times, ensuring it's truly share-worthy.

My older sister was my first cooking mentor and her passion for the craft greatly inspired me. I often joke that she cooked like Remy from the movie *Ratatouille,* creating mouthwatering dishes without a recipe in sight. Her ability to work magic with simple ingredients and her improvisational flair were astonishing. When people requested her recipes, they were disappointed to learn that not only did a recipe not exist but she couldn't even recall every ingredient added. She remains one of my biggest inspirations, having taught me the art of crafting unique recipes amid chaos.

For the three years following my break from school, my sister and I collaborated daily on amazing menus, with her handling the main courses and me taking care of appetizers and desserts. When she got married and left home, I was devastated. While I was so happy for her and my new brother-in-law, adjusting to her absence was difficult as she was my closest friend at the time and I lacked a social outlet. This setback sent me into a brief depression but also reinforced my reliance on the kitchen and the opportunities offered by the culinary world. With my sister's departure, the responsibility of cooking for the family fell upon me. Though I didn't initially love cooking as much as baking, I soon caught her enthusiasm, which has stayed with me ever since.

Upon my sister's departure, I knew I needed to reengage with a more social life. I returned to school. My days became busier, juggling meal preparation, teaching, and attending college in the evenings. Nevertheless, my passion for baking remained undiminished. To accommodate my growing responsibilities, I adapted my working habits, learning to operate at a more intense pace in the kitchen. This invaluable lesson has stayed with me ever since, allowing me to navigate a busy life while still pursuing my culinary dreams.

When I first delved into cooking, I focused on preparing classic Turkish dishes. The foundation of Turkish cuisine includes kebabs, pastries, breads, soups, and salads, with stews and multi-ingredient plates as the primary homemade courses. Fast-food was virtually absent from daily meals—well, at least until recently. My affinity for Mediterranean food likely stems from these early culinary habits. Turkish cuisine shares many similarities with Italian, Greek, Balkan, Russian, and Middle Eastern cuisines. Gradually, I began incorporating nontraditional Turkish dishes into my repertoire, such as homemade pizzas, burgers with homemade buns, and other dishes typically reserved for restaurants.

Cooking for my loved ones has always been one of my greatest joys. There's something indescribably satisfying about lovingly preparing a meal, serving it to family and friends, and watching them savor each bite. As part of a large family, we would gather around the dinner table together, with my sisters frequently joining us when we lived in the same city. Before our weekly family gatherings, I would spend the entire day in the kitchen preparing a diverse array of dishes. Looking back, I marvel at the energy I had, fueled by the rewarding sight of my family bonding over food.

At twenty-four, I met my husband, Sait, the love of my life. He was pursuing his PhD in the United States—so after getting married, we moved to America, marking the beginning of a new chapter in my life. We spent two quiet, peaceful years in the charming city of Madison, Wisconsin, surrounded by a close-knit group of Turkish friends. This serene lifestyle provided a much-needed respite from my previously hectic pace. With our move to the US, the culinary landscape expanded dramatically, exposing me to a vast range of flavors, aromas, spices, and cooking techniques. Although I eagerly embraced new tastes, adjusting to some of the more intense spicy flavors took time.

A few years after marrying and settling in the US, my son, Kerem, was born, and we moved to Chicago for my husband's work. At the time, I couldn't establish a social circle right away, partly because Kerem was very young and we didn't have a significant Turkish community in our neighborhood. My English was limited and I spent my days at home with my young son, cherishing the opportunity to bond with him during his formative years. However, as someone who thrives on an active social life, I eventually grew restless. With my husband's support and encouragement, I started my Instagram page, Turkuaz Kitchen, to connect with others online. Little did I know that this decision would ignite my true passions, fuel my relentless drive, and become my obsession. I began by sharing my favorite recipes on my humble page and capturing photos with my smartphone.

Eventually, I realized that my smartphone photographs failed to do justice to the recipes I spent hours perfecting. This prompted me to explore food photography and hone my skills in this area. As I experimented with new recipes daily, I also practiced photographing them using self-taught techniques. This marked the beginning of another chapter in my life, as I eagerly entered the kitchen each day motivated to try new recipes, create unique food styling, and capture stunning photos. My dual passions—food styling and photography—flourished, giving rise to Turkuaz Kitchen's distinctive style. I firmly believe that presentation is crucial in showcasing a dish's true splendor. Food styling became an incredibly important element of my work and I devoted hours to planning the styling for each recipe, seeking out the perfect pieces, and assembling them harmoniously.

As Instagram evolved from a photo-sharing app to a platform for short videos, I began creating vintage-style videos with my unique aesthetic. One of my first videos, featuring punch-down dough, went viral, amassing nearly two million views—an astounding achievement for a page with fewer than thirty thousand followers. Soon, all my dough recipe videos garnered eight to ten million views each and immense engagement. This marked the inception of a new trend, with countless other punch-down videos mimicking my signature style. For me, this period was a dream come true. My follower count skyrocketed to five million in just a year, propelled by phenomenal growth. My audience loved that I prepared recipes from scratch, allowing them to customize flavors and reduce processed ingredients, while also enjoying the added challenge of mastering each dish. Moreover, my vintage-style videos, featuring antique kitchen items, transported viewers to a cozy, tranquil nineteenth-century kitchen. Through these recipe videos, I share my love of food with the world, and when people express their appreciation, I feel even more inspired to develop new recipes every week.

Reaching millions of people from around the globe, from countries I have never visited and from cultures with which I am unfamiliar, has been an indescribable experience. The love and support I have received through this journey have been extraordinary. It is incredibly special for me and my recipes to play a small part in people's lives during their special occasions, whether it be an anniversary dinner or a meticulously prepared festive table, through my recipes. The thought of it fills my heart with joy. It is heartwarming to know that thousands of people made their first homemade pasta with me, overcame their fear of dough recipes, and discovered the therapeutic nature of working with dough. Some days, I receive heartfelt emails that bring me tears of joy. In one instance,

someone shared that she and her mother, who was battling an illness, enjoyed my videos together. After her mother passed away, she found solace in reconnecting with life through my videos and recipes. Reading these kinds of messages filled with love and support motivates me to work harder.

For a long time, I lived my life to make my loved ones happy, often at the expense of my own dreams. My happiness and comfort always took a back seat. It wasn't until I met my husband that I began to prioritize my passions and reflect on what I truly desired in life. He showed me that the key to making my loved ones happy was to find happiness within myself. He has been my superhero throughout this exhilarating yet exhausting journey, helping me discover my true self and appreciate the worth of my goals. When my dear editor Dervla contacted me, it was truly a dream come true. The day I signed for my book, I was overwhelmed with excitement and happiness. I spent months contemplating how to present the most exceptional and unique book for you. Now, as you read these words, I still can't believe it. My cookbook journey has been a whirlwind of emotions. I hope this book fills your life with hope, luck, and unforgettable memories with your loved ones, and inspires you to chase your passions.

If I could speak to my energetic fourteen-year-old self, who was still searching for her identity, I would tell her that I have finally discovered a piece of myself, accepted who I am, and feel prouder than ever before. Every chapter of my life has led me to this moment, when I can share my journey with you through these pages. If not for those experiences, I wouldn't be here, possibly even joining you in your kitchen during some of your most cherished moments. So, I would tell my younger self, and I tell you now: Never give up, never give up.

Dough is an element of just about every food culture around the world, and it's this fact that spurs my continued love for it. This cookbook represents the culmination of my lifelong love for the kitchen and the countless hours spent perfecting my craft. I am excited to share my favorite dough recipes with you, ranging from traditional Turkish pastries to scrumptious desserts and savory flavors and everything in between. The recipes in this book are preceded by centuries of knowledge, passed down through generations. Some of the recipes in this book are passed down from my own family, while others are newer to me. Regardless of how long I've been making them, my goal in putting together the recipes for this book has been to treat these foods with respect, and I hope that my versions of the recipes I've included can enhance, supplement, or in some cases, provide a new perspective or method in this discourse. I hope you can feel the love I have for each and every one through these photographs and techniques, then further feel it through the delicious results when you try these recipes in your own home.

It is my sincerest hope that these recipes ignite your imagination and empower you to create your own unforgettable memories and culinary adventures in the kitchen. Welcome, and happy cooking!

THE PANTRY

Pantry Essentials

Dough is made with just a few key ingredients, so the ingredients you use are even more important than in other recipes. Though cooking is chemistry dependent and numerous factors can influence the outcome, using high-quality ingredients is one of the most significant factors to making delicious doughs. I recommend reading this section thoroughly before embarking on your cooking journey. I have also included some of the special items in my pantry (see Special Pantry Items, page 11) that you may not already have. First, let's start with my pantry essentials:

YEAST

The key to perfectly puffed dough lies in using high-quality yeast. While I was in Türkiye, I exclusively used fresh yeast. When I moved to the US, I found that fresh yeast was not commonly used, thus prompting me to experiment with other types. After a series of tests, I concluded that Red Star Platinum instant yeast consistently performs the best, and that's what I recommend for the recipes in this book (active dry yeast is a good substitute). It has additional dough enhancers that strengthen the gluten of the dough and make the dough more resilient to over- or under-kneading. Always make sure your yeast is fresh; I personally prefer single-use mini-packs as opposed to a jar of bulk yeast. While you can add instant yeast directly to the dry ingredients for dough, after years of trial and error, I prefer to activate the yeast by mixing it with a liquid, preferably with a sprinkle of sugar to hasten its activation and ensure it's not expired. Keep your liquid (milk or water) between 110° and 115°F and avoid direct contact between yeast and salt, as salt can kill the yeast, hindering the dough's rise. I suggest adding the yeast to warm water (110°F) with a little sugar, stirring with a spoon, and letting it bubble for 5 to 7 minutes before use. At

this point, the yeast should be foamy but will not have come to a full head.

FLOUR

Considered one of the pillars of baking, flour is a vital ingredient. Each flour brand interacts with moisture in a different way, influencing the texture and consistency of the dough you prepare. Throughout the recipes featured in this book, I've used the high-quality flour from the King Arthur Baking Company. When possible, I encourage you to invest in trustworthy, high-grade flour—it makes a world of difference to your baking.

All Purpose Flour: This versatile flour is a blend of hard and soft wheat, making it perfect for a wide range of recipes. If you want only one type of flour in your kitchen, this is it. It is perfect for numerous recipes, including cookies, cakes, pie crusts, and even bread. However, remember that all-purpose flour absorbs less water than bread flour, so control the water addition if using this flour for bread recipes. Many of the recipes in this book have been tested with all-purpose flour. The key to good dough is quality flour, so choose a reputable brand with around 11.7 grams of protein.

❊ **Bread Flour:** Ideal for bread recipes, bread flour is high in protein, lending elastic, stretchy structure and a chewy texture to your bread. Like all-purpose flour, it's essential to choose a trusted brand with high protein content (approximately 12.7 grams). If you replace bread flour with all-purpose flour in recipes, adjust the water quantity accordingly. See each recipe for details.

❊ **Semolina Flour:** Widely used in Turkish and Italian cuisines, the type of semolina flour you use can significantly impact the texture and liquid absorption of your recipe. I recommend using a double-milled flour for the best texture, but I tested all the recipes using the regular version for ease of access as well. If you decide to use double-milled semolina, remember to control the water quantity. I added the relevant notes and suggestions within each recipe when necessary.

❊ **Tipo "00" Pizza/Pasta Flour:** Ideal for pizza and pasta, this finely ground flour lends a unique texture to the end product. Although Italian-style tipo "00" flour is available online and in Italian markets, I've used the easily accessible American Type 00 pizza flour from King Arthur Baking for the recipes in this book, which you can find in your local supermarkets.

DAIRY

❊ **Butter:** I use unsalted butter in my dough recipes for better control over the salt content. Opt for a brand that consistently delivers on taste and texture. Remember, high quality doesn't always equate to high cost; there are plenty of excellent, affordable options out there. European-style butter, with its higher fat content, works best in recipes for croissants and Danish pastries. Several European-style butter brands are now widely available in the US; you can find these brands in most supermarkets. I like to use unsalted Danish Creamery European Style Butter.

❊ **Milk:** I always prefer whole cow's milk for its rich, creamy texture. In all vegan recipes, I've substituted original soy milk for dairy, adjusting the flavor ratio accordingly. If you use unsweetened soy milk, I recommend adjusting the amount of sugar accordingly.

❊ **Yogurt:** An indispensable ingredient in Turkish cuisine, yogurt adds a distinct tang and creaminess to numerous dishes. While my personal preference leans toward homemade yogurt, with its slightly acidic character and thinner, less dense consistency, the recipes in this book have been crafted with convenience in mind. Hence, I've opted for plain whole-milk yogurt to ensure simplicity without compromising on flavor or texture.

VEGETABLE SHORTENING

While I'm not a big fan of shortening, some recipes perform better with it instead of butter, especially those that require lard. For recipes that call for shortening, you can also substitute butter or lard.

OIL

Extra-virgin olive oil is my go-to for many recipes, particularly Mediterranean dishes. It adds a delightful finish to many dishes, including focaccia, pizza, and bruschetta. For recipes where olive oil takes center stage, it's worth investing in a high-quality brand. The superior flavor profile of premium olive oil can make a remarkable difference to a dish. For frying, I typically use corn oil.

EGGS

Most of my recipes call for large eggs, typically weighing around 50 to 52 grams each, with egg yolks around 15 to 16 grams and egg whites around 35 to 36 grams. When medium eggs are mentioned, use eggs at 48g. Consider using a scale for precision, especially for enriched doughs, pastas, and custards where egg weight variances can make a big impact. I prefer high-quality organic eggs, which will have a yolk with much richer color and denser nutrient value. I typically use eggs at room temperature for most recipes, taking the eggs out of the fridge 3 to 4 hours before use—with tart, pie, and quiche doughs being the exceptions.

Special Pantry Items

❀ **High-Quality Double-Concentrated Tomato Paste:** Ever since my first encounter with premium Italian-brand tomato pastes, I've been a staunch advocate for their use. Its deep, rich flavor utterly transforms certain recipes, elevating their taste to another level. Although it might be pricier than ordinary tomato paste, the payoff is well worth it. I strongly encourage you to incorporate this superior ingredient into your culinary repertoire. You will generally find double-concentrated tomato paste in tubes and can find numerous brands at your local grocery store.

❀ **Pomegranate Molasses:** A gem commonly found in Middle Eastern kitchens, pomegranate molasses is an exquisite condiment that deserves a spot in your pantry. With its distinctive flavor profile, it lends a vibrant touch to salads and sauces. Having used it in a number of Turkish recipes, I can assure you it's a worthy addition to your pantry. I urge you to source a high-quality product, available in international markets or online.

❀ **Isot Pepper (Urfa Biber):** This exceptional chile variant hailing from southern Türkiye is a discovery you're bound to adore. Isot pepper, with its smoky, slightly sweet notes and mild heat, is an integral component in many Turkish kebabs and accompanying dishes. It can be found in international markets or sourced online and will be the distinguishing flavor in many recipes.

❀ **Vanilla and Other Extracts:** Vanilla is the unsung hero of the dessert world. A whiff of vanilla is indispensable in a patisserie, infusing an irresistible aroma into every dessert it graces. For me, it's a nonnegotiable ingredient in nearly all my dessert recipes, from brioche dough to pastry cream. I prefer vanilla bean paste due to the scarcity and expense of authentic vanilla beans, but pure vanilla extract works just as well. Also, consider stocking up on fruit extracts to add a dash of zest to your desserts. Certainly, using the zest of citrus fruits like lemons or oranges can infuse your dishes with a delightful fruitiness. However, I find that adding a touch of fruit extract enhances the flavor profile even further, providing an unparalleled depth of taste. But use caution—extracts are meant to be used in small quantities and can be very powerful.

❀ **Red Pepper Paste:** Frequently used in Türkiye and its neighboring regions, red pepper paste is one of my kitchen's prized possessions. Available in mild and hot varieties, I recommend the spicy version for those who appreciate a little heat. We'll be using it in several recipes in this book. Look for it in international markets or online.

❀ **Turkish Pistachios:** Ask me the secret ingredient that sets genuine Turkish baklava apart and I'll say pistachios without hesitation. The distinctive aroma and vibrant green hue of Turkish pistachios (which in Turkish hilariously translates to "bird poop pistachio") are what truly define this legendary dessert. As these pistachios are somewhat pricey and difficult to find, I advise you to specifically look for Turkish pistachios online. If you are unable to have them on hand, I recommend substituting walnuts in recipes that utilize Turkish pistachios rather than using generic pistachios.

❀ **Mushroom Powder:** Another secret weapon in my kitchen, mushroom powder brings an incredible umami and unique depth of flavor to homemade soups, especially noodle-based ones. Its subtle influence can make even the simplest of dishes taste extraordinary. You can find it in the international aisle of most grocery stores.

❀ **Tahini:** The quality of tahini can make or break your dish. Poor-quality tahini can be bitter or overly thick and detract from taste and texture. Invest in Middle Eastern tahini from international markets.

HOW TO USE
THIS COOKBOOK

Ever find yourself wistfully staring at the perfectly crafted dough from your favorite bakery or restaurant, thinking such feasts are impossible to achieve in your humble home kitchen? Well, brace yourself for a revelation: You, too, can re-create the magic of dough at home. This book is your compass, guiding you through the labyrinth of dough-making techniques, demystifying them, and revealing that the magic is indeed achievable with just the right techniques, precise timing, quality ingredients, and a dash of effort.

The secret is that there's no secret. It's just passion and hard work. However, this book is not just about dough. It's also your ticket to myriad delicious recipes, providing you a path to becoming a masterful home chef.

We'll start at the beginning, discussing all the critical techniques and key points that have guided my own culinary journey. This book is not just about becoming a baker; it's about embracing the madness of cooking, understanding the science and chemistry behind it, and recognizing the various factors that influence the end result: the quality of your ingredients, the temperature and humidity in your home, and even your patience and attention to detail.

I've tried to make each recipe accessible even for beginners, providing thorough guidance every step of the way. Yes, making dough requires adherence to certain principles. Some recipes are easy; others will test your patience and culinary dexterity. Yet, remember, one of the tricks of successful cooking and baking is patience and never rushing the process.

Our lives are busy, and that propels us toward quick, easy recipes for our daily meals. We seek dishes that require minimal time and readily available ingredients—and there's no fault in that. However, time in the kitchen can be therapeutic and meditative, an opportunity for relaxation and connection, rather than just a means to an end. Take, for instance, a situation where you decide to prepare the Schiacciata (page 65), which is crispy pizza dough and a favorite recipe of mine. You start your dough on a Tuesday, using a minimal amount (2g) of yeast. As the preparation is straightforward, you'll find it enjoyable rather than tiresome. Once the dough is ready, you wrap it tightly in plastic wrap and place it in the refrigerator. This dough is designed to rest, improving in taste and texture, over a 48- to 72-hour period. This means that come Friday night or the weekend, you have a beautifully fermented dough ready to create an Italian-style sandwich for a family pizza night. It's almost like discovering a surprise gift you'd left for yourself earlier in the week. A sense of anticipation develops throughout the week, making the eventual meal a culmination of your thoughtful planning and effort.

So consider the recipes in this book not just ways to prepare meals but as a gateway to enjoyable, enriching experiences. These can be family activities where you bond over cooking or solitary times of relaxation where you're in the kitchen alone, immersing yourself in the satisfying process of preparing food from scratch. I can assure you that every time you engage with the dough or taste the delectable results of your efforts, shared with loved ones or savored alone, you'll find yourself enveloped in a profound sense of joy and accomplishment. The act of creating something tangible and delicious from simple ingredients provides an escape from negative energy and everyday stresses, transporting you to a state of pure contentment and positivity.

As you embark on your cooking journey, here are some pointers:

Understand and prepare your ingredients: Before diving into the actual process of cooking, take a moment to thoroughly read through the entire recipe. Understand every step, the sequence they follow, and the role each ingredient plays. This helps you visualize the process and grasp how the dish will come together. For example, there are instances where certain steps might need to be prepared in advance. If you are making a rough puff pastry, the butter needs to be sufficiently chilled to maintain the layers in the dough. If you're baking cookies, some recipes call for ingredients that are at room temperature. This kind of information is crucial for the success of your dish.

The temperature of your ingredients can significantly impact the end result, particularly when preparing dough. Yeast used in bread making for example, reacts best at warmer temperatures. These are details that can make or break your culinary outcome. Additionally, before you start, make sure that you have gathered all the ingredients needed for the recipe. There's nothing more frustrating than realizing you are missing a key ingredient halfway through the cooking process. After you've completely understood the recipe and assembled your ingredients, you can then begin to prepare them as directed. This might mean chopping vegetables, measuring out spices, or allowing certain ingredients to come to room temperature. Doing this prep work up front—often called mise en place, or "everything in place"—helps the cooking process go smoothly and ensures you're ready to proceed without unnecessary pauses or interruptions.

Weigh your ingredients: I cannot emphasize enough how important measurements are when it comes to baking. Cooking and baking are two completely different realms for me. In cooking, I find freedom in improvisation—I'm never too strict with sticking to a recipe. The thrill of creativity and the chance to whip up various unique flavors with subtle alterations each time is exhilarating. Whether it's adding a bit more yogurt to a sauce or sprinkling in additional spices, minor deviations often lead to unexpected and delightful results.

However, when it comes to baking, precision is paramount. Unlike cooking, baking is a process where the ingredients interact in specific ways. That's why I've crafted each dough recipe in this book with precise gravimetric measurements. I know that meticulously weighing each ingredient may sound tedious and less spontaneous, but trust me, the resulting consistency in your doughs will make the extra effort worthwhile.

So, if your aim is to elevate your baking skills or produce more consistent, perfect doughs, you must adhere to the exact measurements. If you don't already own a kitchen scale, I strongly recommend you get one immediately. Remember, baking isn't just about following a recipe—it's about understanding the science behind it. Only then can you start playing with the rules. Start your baking journey with precision, making sure you become comfortable with how the dough should feel and look as per the recipe.

Once you've made a recipe a few times and are comfortable with it, you can begin experimenting by adding or subtracting ingredients, adjusting quantities, or tweaking the method. At this point you should understand how the recipe works and what each ingredient contributes, thus making informed modifications less likely to spoil the outcome.

Understand your oven's true temperature: As an individual who's shifted residences around five times since I moved to the US, I've had the opportunity to experiment with a variety of ovens. From these experiences, I can confidently say that each oven has its own unique cooking temperature, which might differ from the setting shown on the dial. To ensure the accuracy of your oven's setting, I recommend using an oven thermometer, if available.

In addition to understanding the overall temperature, it's equally important to note the specific heat distribution inside your oven. For instance, if you observe that your oven tends to cook faster at the top than at the bottom, you should adjust your baking by placing your baking sheet on a rack nearer to the oven's bottom and/or covering it with aluminum foil if the top is browning faster than the bottom. On the other hand, if your oven cooks faster at the bottom, you can even out the heat distribution by placing an empty baking sheet on a rack underneath the one with your baking sheet. These adjustments will ensure that your baked goods cook evenly and turn out just right.

Monitor your baking closely in your own oven to be sure you remove your pastries at the ideal time. In my book, I've provided baking times that worked best with my oven, but it's essential that you adjust these timings based on your oven and past baking experiences.

Consider your ambient temperature when fermenting dough: Every yeast dough needs a rest period to allow it to rise, or ferment. When I was developing the recipes for the book, I included specific resting periods for all the recipes. However, my personal ambient temperature at home is usually between 74° and 76°F, which I acknowledge is warmer than many people might keep their homes. As someone who was born in one of the coldest cities in Türkiye, you would expect me to develop a good resistance to cold, but on the contrary, I tend to keep my home warmer than others might.

Bringing the conversation back to the dough, it's crucial to adjust your dough's fermenting time based on the temperature of your own home. Many recipes simply advise letting the dough ferment until it has doubled in size, but sometimes it's not easy to visually gauge this. If you want to confirm that your dough is adequately fermented and ready to be shaped, you can perform a Poke Test (see page 22).

Make sure your ingredients are at the correct temperature: The temperature of the ingredients used in a recipe can significantly impact the final product. For dough-based foods like pies, scones, tarts, biscuits, and rough puff pastry, the ingredients, especially butter, need to be very cold. If the butter is too warm, it will melt during the mixing process and disrupt the texture of the dough, causing it to become similar to a cookie dough.

On the other hand, when making a pastry cream, the butter you add to the cold cream should be softened and at room temperature. If the butter is too hard or cold, it will not mix well with the cold cream. Hard butter separates into chunks instead of blending smoothly into the cream.

Know your dough by feel and sight: As the cook or baker, you're the only person who has an up-close, firsthand view and feel of your dough. Even with precise measurements, there may be instances where the dough turns out too sticky or too dry due to myriad factors like humidity, flour type, ingredient temperature, and so on. Especially if you are measuring ingredients by volume rather than weight (which is less accurate), these discrepancies in dough consistency might be more likely.

When such situations occur, you're encouraged to make adjustments as needed. For instance, if the dough seems too sticky, you can add a bit more flour, or if it's too dry, incorporate more water. This should be done with care, though, adding small amounts at a time, because too much could negatively affect the dough. Remember that it's important to know how the dough should feel and look as per the recipe, and to make adjustments based on that. This skill often comes with practice and experience. Essentially, while measurements are important, don't forget to use your senses and intuition when baking.

Persistence is key: Cooking is an art that comes with its fair share of trials and tribulations. It is essential to understand that experiencing failure when attempting new recipes or techniques is a completely normal part of the journey. In fact, these missteps are not just common, they are the stepping stones to mastering the art of cooking. I urge you to never let setbacks discourage you from trying again. Remember, every failure presents an opportunity to learn and improve. It's through these mishaps that you can refine your techniques and perfect your dishes. One of the most valuable lessons I learned from my mother was to embrace, not fear, failure in the kitchen. She instilled in me the understanding that the journey to culinary mastery is not a straight path but, rather, a winding road with inevitable obstacles. With every attempt, even if unsuccessful, you are a step closer to your goal. The key to success lies in your ability to assess where things went awry, learn from these errors, and apply these lessons to your next cooking endeavor. So, regardless of how many attempts it takes, persevere. Your persistence will pay off in the form of delectable dishes and an improved skill set.

As someone who has found solace in the kitchen, I assure you that the joy of creating something delicious from scratch is an incomparable delight. I encourage you to enjoy the process of cooking, whether it's spending a cozy winter weekend making homemade pasta with the family or simply kneading dough.

I can't wait to see you enjoy the fruits of your labor. Let's embark on this exciting culinary journey together.

Bon appétit!

BASIC DOUGHS

Embark on a culinary adventure with the simplicity and versatility of basic yeast doughs, which are often made with only flour, water, salt, and yeast. These friendly introductions to the baking world aren't just easy to master; they're a canvas for your creativity. Picture your kitchen, stocked with nothing more than everyday staples, transforming into a boutique bakery. And it all begins with the humble union of flour and yeast. Imagine: golden-brown loaves, soft pretzels, and even rustic pizzas. The absence of fermentation-slowing ingredients means that these doughs rise quickly, eager to take on whatever form your heart desires. This is where your baking journey begins—a place where simplicity meets endless possibility.

KEY TECHNIQUES

SPECIAL EQUIPMENT

❀ **Baking Steel:** If you're a fan of home-made pizza, lahmacun, pita, or schiacciata, a baking steel will revolutionize your baking game. After numerous disappointing experiences with pizza stones, my husband gifted me a baking steel—it's an investment I strongly recommend. This will dramatically change the crusts of your goods and will have you baking restaurant-quality foods in no time.

❀ **Dough Whisk:** A dough whisk is a special tool for mixing doughs by hand that you do not want to overmix. Generally, they have a long wooden handle and a sturdy wire head of circular loops that allows you to combine ingredients in both doughs and batters.

❀ **Kitchen Scale:** The key to perfect dough and culinary success lies in accurate measurements. Regrettably, cup measurements can be inconsistent—hence I recommend using a kitchen scale, especially for baking. From kitchen to kitchen, the definition of a cup of flour or liquid will change. With the ratios of wet and dry ingredients so essential to beautiful baked goods, failing to use a scale for some of these recipes will make for an entirely different experience. When I was creating the recipes for the book, I meticulously tested each one using gram measurements, and I strongly recommend that you follow the weight measurements when making dough recipes. While choosing a scale, make sure it is sensitive enough for precise measurements, especially to the gram. A reliable kitchen scale should cost between $20 and $50.

Working with Yeast Dough

Yeast-based doughs require a certain level of mastery, especially when it comes to kneading and time management. Kneading is crucial in creating a strong gluten network. With minimal kneading, the dough won't expand properly because a robust gluten network can't form. Without that network, the yeast won't activate, leading to a dense, hard, or nonfluffy end product.

Conversely, well-kneaded dough allows for even and easy gas production by the yeast. The result? Deliciously soft breads and pastries! But it's not just about vigorous kneading—timing is just as important. As the dough rests, the proteins in the flour merge with water to form gluten. So, by coupling effective kneading with patience, we can create perfect yeast doughs with relative ease.

Let's look at basic yeast doughs. They typically consist of a few primary ingredients and form a gluten network faster due to the absence of additives that may slow the process. With the right technique, creating these doughs becomes a breeze. I personally prefer using the "slap and fold" method, also known as the Bertinet Method or French fold. This method is particularly beneficial for sticky doughs where a standard kneading approach wouldn't work.

SLAP AND FOLD METHOD

This technique isn't solely for highly hydrated doughs like ciabatta or focaccia. I've applied it to various pizza, bread, and pastry recipes, most of which involve softer dough. I credit this technique for creating the perfectly smooth doughs that you may be familiar with from my videos.

Let's delve into the method:

1. Combine your dough ingredients in a suitable bowl. Use a bowl scraper or your hands to lift and mix the ingredients, making sure they're well combined. Spend 3 to 4 minutes kneading the dough until it attains the desired consistency.

2. Once your dough comes together, cover it with plastic wrap and let rest for 15 to 30 minutes as per the recipe's instructions. This relaxation period makes the dough easier to work with.

3. After resting, transfer the dough to a lightly floured work surface. Firmly hold the dough at the top with both hands and slap it onto the table. Then fold it in the middle, rotate your hands, and repeat the slap and the fold as indicated in the recipe. If needed, reflour your counter and hands from time to time.

4. When the dough reaches a smooth and consistent texture, shape it into a ball. Lift it carefully and return it to the bowl with the seam-side down. Cover with plastic wrap again.

5. At this point, your dough should appear smooth and elastic and have a pleasing consistency. Let it rest, covered, for as long as the recipe states, and perform the Poke Test (see page 22) to know if it's ready to be shaped.

BASIC KNEADING TECHNIQUE

If your dough isn't excessively soft or sticky, you can apply the basic kneading method post-mixing. This technique is often the most comprehensible and straightforward for beginner bakers.

Here is the method:

1. Start by combining the required dough ingredients using a bowl scraper or your hands, as explained in the first step of the Slap and Fold Method on page 21.

2. Transfer the dough to a lightly floured work surface. Gently press the dough using the heel of your palm, pushing it away from you, then draw it back toward yourself using the inner surface of your fingers, folding it over itself. Periodically rotate the dough about 45 degrees and repeat this kneading process for 5 to 10 minutes, depending on the specific recipe instructions. Remember to refrain from using excessive flour during this process. As you knead the dough, the gluten network starts to develop, and the stickiness of the dough will naturally diminish over time. This technique not only ensures your dough is well-kneaded but also keeps the dough's consistency intact, preventing it from becoming overly dense due to the addition of extra flour.

3. Once the kneading process is completed, it's essential to verify that the dough has rested sufficiently before shaping it for baking. This is where the Poke Test comes into play (see below).

THE POKE TEST

To determine if the dough is ready for shaping or baking, lightly press a floured finger into the dough and observe the reaction. If the indentation fills up slowly, the dough is ready; if it springs back quickly, the dough requires more resting time.

ROUNDING DOUGH

After kneading, rounding dough into a ball is important in allowing for a nice, smooth surface as well as creating necessary tension on the outside of the dough so it expands evenly during the rising process.

For a large single portion of dough:

1. Place your hands on either side of the dough with the edges of your palms against the surface.

2. Holding your left hand as a guide, use your right hand to push the outer edges of the dough lightly underneath while turning slightly.

3. Continue this motion until the dough is a smooth ball with a nice round top.

4. Carefully lift the ball onto your left hand, maintaining the round shape, and place in the bowl with the open edge down.

For smaller portions (such as for rolls or buns):

1. Pinch the edges of the portion of dough together to make a rough ball with a tucked underside.

2. With the pinched side of the dough in the palm of your hand, place the dough ball on the work surface and shape the fingers of your other hand into a cage. Roll the dough on the work surface into a smooth ball.

Note

❦ *Remember, practice makes perfect. The more you use these techniques, the better your results will be. With the right amount of patience, precision, and love for the art of baking, you'll master the yeast dough techniques in no time.*

Khachapuri

Makes 4 pieces

As a native Türk, it was a pleasant surprise when a recent genetic test revealed that I shared a significant number of genes with people from Georgia and its neighboring countries. This quirky connection might explain my fervent love for khachapuri, and I joke that it's why I excel at making this delicious bread. Once you get a taste of it, I promise it will earn a top spot on your brunch or breakfast menu. A perfect blend of comfort and flavor, khachapuri might well be one of the first dishes on our menu if my team and I ever open a restaurant.

DOUGH

1 cup (220g) warm water (110°F)

2¼ teaspoons (7g) instant (quick-rise) yeast

2 teaspoons (8g) granulated sugar

4 cups (520g) bread flour

1½ teaspoons (9g) kosher salt

½ cup (110g) milk

3 tablespoons (41g) extra-virgin olive oil

FILLING AND TOPPING

2 cups shredded mozzarella cheese

1½ cups crumbled feta cheese

½ cup crumbled blue cheese

½ cup grated Parmesan cheese

Egg wash: 1 egg, beaten with 1 teaspoon extra-virgin olive oil

¼ cup sesame seeds

4 large eggs

FOR SERVING

Butter, sliced

Fresh dill

Red pepper flakes

Make the dough: In a small bowl, combine the water, yeast, and 1 teaspoon of the sugar. Stir together and let rest for 5 to 7 minutes, until foamy.

In a large bowl (or bowl of a stand mixer), whisk together the bread flour, salt, and remaining 1 teaspoon sugar. Add the milk, yeast mixture, and oil to the dry ingredients. While still in the bowl, using your hands, perform the basic kneading technique (see page 22) and knead for 4 to 5 minutes, until the dough is elastic and no longer sticky. (Alternatively, snap on the dough hook and mix on medium speed for 4 to 5 minutes.) Cover the dough with plastic wrap and let rest for 20 minutes.

Transfer the dough to a lightly floured work surface. Continue to knead for an additional 4 to 5 minutes, until smooth. Shape the dough into a ball and return to the bowl. Cover the dough with plastic wrap and let rest at room temperature, until almost doubled in size, for 50 to 60 minutes.

Line a baking sheet with parchment paper and set aside. Transfer the dough to a lightly floured work surface. Using a sharp knife or bench scraper, divide the dough into 4 equal pieces. Round each piece of dough into a smooth ball (see page 22). Place the balls on the prepared baking sheet and cover with a clean kitchen towel. Let rest for 15 to 20 minutes at room temperature.

continued

continued

Khachapuri

Fill the breads: In a medium bowl, combine the mozzarella, feta, blue cheese, and Parmesan. Set aside.

Cut off four 12-inch-square pieces of parchment paper. On a floured work surface, using a rolling pin roll a piece of dough into an 8 × 10-inch oval. Transfer the dough to a piece of parchment paper. Leaving a 1-inch edge around the dough, arrange ⅓ cup of the cheese mixture in the middle in 2 rows along the long sides of the oval. Roll the edges of the dough up over the cheese. Twist the smaller ends of the dough to form the khachapuri shape (like a small canoe). Add another ⅔ cup of the cheese mixture to the center of the dough and spread evenly. Carefully transfer the parchment paper to a baking sheet. Gently stretch the pointy ends of the oval to lengthen the khachapuri. Cover with a clean kitchen towel. Repeat to make the rest of the khachapuri, placing 2 khachapuri on each of two baking sheets and leaving some space between them. Cover with a clean kitchen towel and let rise for 15 to 20 minutes.

Preheat the oven to 400°F.

Brush the outsides of the dough with the egg wash and sprinkle with the sesame seeds.

Bake for 17 to 20 minutes, until golden brown. Remove from the oven, make a well in the center of the khachapuri, and crack an egg inside each well, but hold back about half of the egg white in the shell (see Notes).

Return to the oven and bake for 2 to 3 minutes, or until the egg white is cooked to your preference.

To serve: Serve hot with butter, fresh dill, and red pepper flakes.

Notes

▼ *The reason for not adding all of the egg white on top of the khachapuri is that it can spread and cover the whole top. I like to save the extra bits of egg white to add to omelets.*

▼ *If you know you won't finish all the khachapuri in one day, only crack the eggs over those you will be able to eat. Store the cooled khachapuri (without egg) in an airtight storage container in the fridge for 2 to 3 days. To serve, crack an egg over the khachapuri and then warm by baking in a 350°F oven for 5 to 7 minutes, until the cheese is melty, the egg is cooked, and the bread is warm.*

Whole-Grain Sandwich Bread

Makes 1 loaf

This bread is one of my go-to recipes for my son's, Kerem, lunchbox. Once baked and thoroughly cooled, I slice it into thin portions and freeze. Come morning, they easily transform into mouthwatering grilled cheeses, peanut butter and jam sandwiches, or just about any sandwich you'd fancy.

Owing to our hectic schedules, my husband, Sait, and I seldom get the chance to enjoy leisurely breakfasts. So our weekend breakfasts, which usually morph into brunches after morning exercise and farmers' market visits, have become a cherished ritual. On toast and sandwich days, everyone gets their own breakfast masterpiece. Sait opts for muhammara egg salad sandwich, Kerem goes for avocado toast, and I savor Brie toast topped with fig or apricot marmalade. While everyone has their favorite, I always sneak in a bite from each plate, for the love of variety!

DOUGH

¼ cup (25g) plus
1 tablespoon quick oats

2¼ teaspoons (7g) instant
(quick-rise) yeast

½ cup (110g) warm water
(110°F)

1 teaspoon (4g)
granulated sugar

2¼ cups (293g) bread flour

2 tablespoons (14g)
flaxseed meal

¼ cup (32g) whole wheat
bread flour

1 tablespoon (12g) light
brown sugar

1 teaspoon (6g) kosher salt

½ cup (110g) whole milk

4 tablespoons (2 oz/56g)
unsalted butter, melted

2 tablespoons (18g)
sunflower seeds

1½ teaspoons (5g) whole
flaxseeds

TOPPINGS

1 tablespoon
sunflower seeds

½ tablespoon quick oats

½ teaspoon poppyseeds

Egg wash: 1 egg, beaten

Make the dough: In a blender, grind ¼ cup of the oats into a fine powder and set aside. In a small bowl, whisk together the yeast, warm water, and sugar. Let rest 5 to 7 minutes, until foamy.

In the bowl of a stand mixer, whisk together the flour, ground oats, flaxseed meal, whole wheat bread flour, brown sugar, and salt. Using your hands, make a well in the center of the flour mixture. Add the yeast mixture, milk, and melted butter to the well. Snap on the dough hook and beat on low speed for 1 to 2 minutes to bring everything together. Increase the speed to medium and knead for 3 to 4 minutes. Cover the bowl with a kitchen towel and let rest for 5 to 10 minutes.

In a small bowl, mix together the sunflower seeds, 1 tablespoon of the oats, and the flaxseeds. Add the seed mixture to the dough and continue to knead the dough on medium speed for 4 to 5 minutes, until smooth and no longer sticking to the sides of the bowl. Lightly grease a large bowl and transfer the dough into it. Cover with plastic wrap or a kitchen towel. Let rest at room temperature until almost doubled in size, 45 minutes to 1 hour.

continued

continued

Whole-Grain Sandwich Bread

Place the dough on a lightly floured work surface. Using a rolling pin, roll into a 7½ × 14-inch rectangle. Starting with a short side, roll the dough into a log. Line an 8½ × 4½ × 2½-inch nonstick loaf pan with parchment paper and place the dough log in it seam-side down. Cover loosely with plastic wrap or a kitchen towel and let rest at room temperature until the dough rises ½ to 1 inch above the loaf pan, 45 minutes to 1 hour.

Preheat the oven to 350°F.

Top the loaf: In a small bowl, mix the sunflower seeds, oats, and poppyseeds. Brush the top of the loaf with the egg wash. Sprinkle the seed mixture over the top of the bread.

Bake until golden brown and the internal temperature reaches 195°F, 45 to 50 minutes. If the top is browning too quickly, tent a piece of aluminum foil over the top while baking.

Using a kitchen towel, carefully remove the bread from the pan and transfer to a cooling rack. Let cool to room temperature before slicing. Use for any of your sandwich bread needs.

Note

♦ *Store in an airtight storage bag at room temperature for 3 to 4 days or (with parchment paper between the slices) in the freezer for 3 months. Toast the bread before serving.*

Ciabatta

Makes 4 loaves

Enter the world of ciabatta, one of the finest breads that can be crafted with just a speck of yeast—two grams to be precise. I have a hunch that this will rank among your top picks from this cookbook. It's the epitome of simplicity with a guarantee of stellar results. Thanks to the slow and prolonged fermentation, the aroma and flavor it develops are simply divine. Here's a bonus tip: You can transform this dough into easy French baguettes using the same dimensions and techniques. But if you're on the hunt for a quick and tasty recipe for your sandwiches or toasts, look no further. These breads are a dream come true—they skip the shaping stage entirely and go straight from the mixing bowl to the oven, just for you.

1½ cups plus 1 tablespoon (344g) room temperature water (75° to 80°F)

⅔ teaspoon (2g) instant (quick-rise) yeast

½ teaspoon (2g) granulated sugar

3⅔ cups (476g) bread flour

1¼ teaspoons (8g) kosher salt

In a large bowl (or in the bowl of a stand mixer), whisk together the water, yeast, and sugar. Add the flour and salt. Using a spatula (or the dough hook), mix until everything is just incorporated. The dough will still be sticky and not yet smooth, but it will come together after the folding process. Cover the bowl with plastic wrap and let rest for 30 to 40 minutes at room temperature.

While still in the bowl, lift and stretch the edges of the dough and fold them into the middle, turning the bowl until each side has been folded in two times. Cover it and let rest for 30 to 40 minutes before performing another set of stretches and folds. Repeat this resting and folding process two more times.

After the final stretch and fold, lightly oil an 8 × 8-inch baking dish and transfer the dough to the dish. Cover with plastic wrap and keep it in the refrigerator at least 10 hours or up to 16 hours.

Transfer the dough to a lightly floured work surface. Using your hands, gently stretch the dough into a 9-inch square. Using a dough scraper, cut the dough into 4 equal rectangles. With a fine-mesh sieve, lightly flour the tops of the dough pieces. Place a large kitchen towel on a clean work surface and generously flour the top. Holding a piece of dough by the short ends, gently lift and stretch the dough as you place it on the kitchen towel. Scrunch the towel around the long sides of the ciabatta to

continued

continued

Ciabatta

hold it in place. Repeat this process with each piece of dough, so each loaf has its own little towel cradle. Place plastic wrap over the loaves and then cover fully with another kitchen towel. Let the dough rest for 35 to 45 minutes.

Preheat the oven to 450°F with a baking steel on the left side of the middle rack and a small cast-iron skillet on the bottom right side for at least 15 to 20 minutes. Perform a water drop test (see page 172) to ensure the baking steel is properly heated. It is important that the two pans be placed on opposite sides to allow for even heat flow through the oven. Holding a loaf by the short sides, gently stretch just a little while carefully transferring the first two pieces of dough onto a pizza paddle. Be careful not to hurt or press the dough or it will ruin your beautiful proof and affect the texture. Place the two loaves onto the hot baking steel and throw 6 to 8 ice cubes into the cast-iron pan.

Bake until golden brown, 15 to 17 minutes.

Remove from the oven and place on a cooling rack. Repeat to bake the remaining loaves. Let the loaves cool for 45 minutes to 1 hour before slicing.

Notes

♦ *Alternatively, you can make mini loaves by dividing the dough into 8 pieces and baking them for 13 to 15 minutes.*

♦ *Once fully cooled, place ciabatta in an airtight plastic bag. Keep at room temperature for 2 to 3 days and toast before serving. Alternatively, you can store in the freezer for up to 3 months. To serve, let sit at room temperature for 10 minutes while the oven preheats to 350°F and then bake for 4 to 7 minutes, until soft and spongy.*

Roasted Veggie Sandwiches

Makes 2 medium ciabatta sandwiches (serves 4)

Tomatoes were my snack-time staple as a kid. Yes, you heard it right! When I was around three or four, my mom would hand me a juicy tomato and I'd munch on it like it was an apple. My childhood love for tomatoes naturally progressed into an obsession with shakshuka during my middle school years. Every day, before heading off to my afternoon classes, I'd whip up a shakshuka for brunch. Soon, I found myself experimenting with the classic recipe, adding in bits and pieces of leftovers—sometimes last night's meatballs or grilled chicken, other times a smattering of different cheeses from the fridge. The magic happened when I tossed in some leftover fried eggplant, crowned with a melted cheese layer, just before adding the egg. It was pure bliss! Now, I bring you this recipe as my homage to those cherished memories.

TOMATO SAUCE

20 ounces cherry tomatoes

7 to 8 medium garlic cloves

2 shallots, peeled and quartered

1 teaspoon kosher salt, or more to taste

6 tablespoons extra-virgin olive oil

¼ cup chopped fresh basil

ROASTED VEGGIES

1 medium American eggplant, peeled, halved, and cut crosswise into ¼-inch-thick half-moons

2 medium zucchini, cut into ¼-inch-thick slices

¼ cup extra-virgin olive oil

½ teaspoon kosher salt

½ teaspoon freshly ground black pepper

SANDWICHES

2 medium loaves Ciabatta (page 31)

Extra-virgin olive oil, for drizzling (optional)

⅓ cup Basil Pesto (page 35)

2 balls burrata cheese or stracciatella

1 cup microgreens

Make the tomato sauce: Preheat the oven to 500°F. Line a baking sheet with parchment paper.

Spread the cherry tomatoes, garlic cloves, and shallots on the baking sheet. Sprinkle with the salt and olive oil and toss together using your hands. Roast until the tomatoes are tender, collapsed, and lightly charred, 20 to 25 minutes.

Remove from the oven and let cool for 15 to 20 minutes. Leave the oven on. Peel the garlic and then transfer the ingredients to a medium bowl and use a fork or potato masher to mash the vegetables into a chunky sauce. Add the chopped basil and mix well. Taste, adjust seasoning to your preference, and set aside.

Roast the veggies: Line a baking sheet with parchment paper. Arrange the eggplant and zucchini slices on separate halves of the baking sheet and drizzle each with olive oil, salt, and pepper. Toss with your hands to fully coat, keeping the vegetables separate. Roast until the vegetables are softened and golden brown, 20 to 25 minutes, checking after 15 minutes and flipping the vegetables to ensure even cooking. Remove from the oven and set aside.

continued

continued

Roasted Veggie Sandwiches

Assemble the sandwiches: Using a sharp knife, cut each ciabatta loaf lengthwise in half. Toast the cut sides of the bread, drizzled with oil if you prefer, in a hot skillet or under the broiler for 2 to 3 minutes, until lightly golden brown. Spread 1 to 1½ tablespoons of the pesto on each piece of bread.

Top one side of each sandwich with some of the tomato sauce and roasted vegetables. Tear ¾- to 1-inch pieces of burrata over the vegetables and finish with microgreens and a little more tomato sauce. Top with the other slice of bread and use a sharp knife to cut each sandwich in half. Serve immediately.

BASIL PESTO

Makes 1 cup

¼ cup pine nuts

2 cups fresh basil (about 3 ounces)

2 garlic cloves, peeled but whole

½ cup freshly grated Parmesan cheese

2 tablespoons grated Pecorino Romano cheese

¼ teaspoon kosher salt, plus more to taste

½ cup extra-virgin olive oil, or to taste

½ teaspoon grated lemon zest (optional)

In a nonstick medium skillet, toast the pine nuts over medium heat until golden brown, 2 to 3 minutes, tossing constantly and keeping an eye on them so they don't burn. Set aside and let cool.

In a blender or a food processor, combine the toasted pine nuts, basil, garlic, Parmesan, Pecorino Romano, and salt. Process until all of the ingredients have been fully incorporated. While blending, slowly drizzle the olive oil in through the top. The pesto is finished when it is fully smooth. Taste and add salt and lemon zest, if using, as desired. Transfer to a small screw-top jar. Store covered in the fridge up to 2 weeks.

Bagels

Makes 8 bagels

When I first moved to the States, the classic American bagel was my saving grace. I tasted it for the first time on the very morning we arrived in the United States and it was love at first bite. You see, I'm a creature of habit, and I tend to cling to the familiar, especially when I'm in a new place. Changing my routines or adapting to new ones isn't something I'm very good at. My husband introduced me to bagels, probably in an attempt to fill the void left by the absence of Turkish simits in our morning meals. And, boy, did it work! I became a bagel enthusiast almost instantly. I'm not sure if it was the comforting routine of a bread product at breakfast or just the fact that bagels are downright delicious, but they quickly became a staple in our household. So, for all you bagel lovers out there, I've got a treat for you. Give this recipe a try and let the simple joy of a well-made bagel grace your breakfast table.

BAGELS

2¼ teaspoons (7g) instant (quick-rise) yeast

1½ cups (330g) warm water (110°F)

2 tablespoons (25g) granulated sugar

3¾ cups (490g) bread flour, plus more as needed

1½ teaspoons (9g) kosher salt

8 cups water, for cooking

2 tablespoons molasses, for cooking

1 teaspoon baking soda, for cooking

TOPPINGS

¼ cup everything bagel seasoning

¼ cup poppy seeds

¼ cup sesame seeds

Make the bagels: In the bowl of a stand mixer (or in a large bowl), combine the yeast, 1 cup (220g) of the warm water, and 1 teaspoon of the sugar. Stir together and let rest 5 to 7 minutes, until foamy. Add the bread flour, remaining sugar, the salt, and the remaining ½ cup water (it's okay if it's cooled down some). Snap on the dough hook and knead the dough on low speed for 2 minutes. (If mixing by hand, bring the dough together using your hands or a bowl scraper. Once everything comes together, turn the mixture out onto a work surface.) Increase the speed to medium-low or medium and knead for an additional 5 to 6 minutes, until the dough is smooth. (If kneading by hand, use the basic kneading technique on page 22 to knead for 4 to 5 minutes.) If the dough is too sticky, you can add 2 to 3 more tablespoons of flour. Cover the dough bowl with a kitchen towel and let rest for 15 to 20 minutes.

Flour a work surface. Uncover and transfer the dough onto the prepared work surface. Using your hands, perform the basic kneading technique (see page 22) and knead for 2 to 4 minutes, until smooth.

Lightly grease a bowl and transfer the dough into it. Cover with plastic wrap or a kitchen towel and let rest until doubled in size, 50 to 60 minutes.

continued

TURKUAZ KITCHEN

continued

Bagels

Lightly flour a work surface and a baking sheet. Turn the dough out onto the prepared surface and roll into a log. Using a sharp knife or bench scraper, divide the dough into 8 equal pieces. Roll each piece of dough into a smooth ball (see Rounding Dough on page 22). Place the ball on the prepared baking sheet and cover with a kitchen towel or plastic wrap. Repeat with each piece of dough. Let rest for 10 to 15 minutes at room temperature.

Lightly oil your hands and a work surface. Take one piece of dough and roll it into a 10-inch rope. Using a rolling pin, flatten about 2 inches of one end of the dough. Connect the two ends by wrapping the flattened end around the other. Place on the baking sheet once again and cover loosely with plastic wrap. Repeat this shaping process with each piece of dough. Let rest for 10 to 15 minutes.

Preheat the oven to 425°F. Line 2 baking sheets with parchment paper.

In a large pot, bring the water to a simmer over medium heat. Add the molasses, then stir in the baking soda, as it will cause the water to foam. Let the water come to a boil, then reduce the heat to medium low. Set all the toppings out in shallow dishes and have ready near the stove.

Take the bagels and use your thumbs to turn and lightly stretch them from the center so the middle hole is not too small. Once the water is boiling, add 2 or 3 bagels at a time, giving enough space so the bagels do not touch. Cook for 30 seconds on each side of the bagel (or 60 seconds if you like them chewier), flipping with a straining spoon. Using a straining spoon, remove the bagels from the water and place on the prepared baking sheets. Allow the water to return to a boil and repeat this process with all of the bagels.

While the bagels are still wet, sprinkle or dip in your preferred topping or leave plain. Transfer to the oven and bake until deep golden brown, 18 to 22 minutes.

Remove from the oven and let cool on a rack.

Serve with your favorite spread or as a breakfast sandwich.

Notes

♥ *You can shape the dough by making a hole in the center of each dough ball rather than by rolling them into logs. After you roll the dough into balls and let rest for 10 to 15 minutes, dip a wooden spoon or your finger in flour and make a hole in the center of a dough ball. Put your thumbs in the hole and stretch and turn the dough until there is a ½-inch hole. Repeat with each ball of dough and let rest while covered for 10 to 15 minutes. Follow the rest of the recipe as written.*

♥ *If you would like your bagels to be a little larger for sandwiches, you can divide the dough into 6 pieces.*

♥ *After the bagels come to room temperature, store them in an airtight storage bag at room temperature for 1 to 2 days and toast lightly before serving. To store in the freezer, let the bagels come to room temperature and slice horizontally in half before placing in an airtight storage bag. Store in the freezer for up to 3 months. Before serving, let come to room temperature and toast in a skillet or toaster. You can also place the bagels in a cold oven and then preheat the oven to 350°F. By the time it reaches temperature, the bagels will be fresh and warm.*

Spinach-Artichoke Stuffed Garlic Knots

Makes 15 garlic knots

This recipe includes the dough for my classic garlic knots, but the addition of the spinach-artichoke filling takes it from a regular delicious side to the star of your table. Garlic-knots-meet-spinach-artichoke-dip is a combination that's destined to be a favorite. Two comfort foods, two powerful flavors, one extraordinary taste. Marinated artichoke hearts are an ingredient that I love; I always make sure to buy those that are marinated in oil.

DOUGH

2 teaspoons (6g) instant (quick-rise) yeast

1 tablespoon (12g) granulated sugar

1⅓ cups (293g) warm water (110°F)

4 cups (520g) bread flour, plus more for dusting

¼ cup (55g) extra-virgin olive oil

1½ teaspoons (9g) kosher salt

SPINACH-ARTICHOKE FILLING

2 tablespoons extra-virgin olive oil

1 small onion, diced

4 ounces spinach, roughly chopped

8 ounces cream cheese, at room temperature

1 cup shredded mozzarella cheese

½ cup shredded Parmesan cheese

1 cup artichoke hearts marinated in oil, chopped

1 teaspoon garlic powder

1 teaspoon kosher salt

GARLIC BUTTER

6 tablespoons unsalted butter, melted

2 garlic cloves, minced

1 teaspoon red pepper flakes

1 teaspoon dried oregano

¼ teaspoon kosher salt

Egg wash: 1 egg beaten with ¼ teaspoon honey or sugar

TOPPINGS

¼ cup shredded Parmesan cheese

1½ teaspoons chopped fresh basil

1 tablespoon chopped fresh parsley

Make the dough: In a medium bowl, whisk together the yeast, 1 teaspoon of the sugar, and the warm water. Stir and let rest 3 to 5 minutes, until foamy. Add the flour, olive oil, remaining sugar, and the salt and use your hands to bring the dough together. If the dough is too dry to come together, you can add 1 to 2 tablespoons additional water. While in the bowl, knead the dough for 3 to 4 minutes. Cover with a kitchen towel and let rest for 10 to 15 minutes.

Transfer the dough to a lightly floured work surface. Flour your hands and use the basic kneading technique (see page 22) to knead for 4 to 5 minutes, until smooth and no longer sticky. Round the dough (see page 22) and place in the bowl with the open edge down. Cover with plastic wrap and let rest at room temperature until doubled in size, about 1 hour. (Alternatively, in a stand mixer fitted with a dough hook, knead the dough on medium speed for 4 to 5 minutes. Cover with plastic wrap and let rest for 10 minutes before kneading for an additional 4 to 5 minutes, until the dough is smooth and no longer sticking to the sides of the bowl. Follow the resting and shaping instructions as listed.)

Make the artichoke filling: In a skillet, heat the olive oil over medium-high heat. Add the onion and cook until lightly caramelized, 2 to 3 minutes. Add spinach and cook, stirring constantly, until the spinach is wilted and the liquid is cooked out, 5 to 7 minutes. Let cool completely at room temperature.

In a bowl, combine the cream cheese, mozzarella, and Parmesan. Use a wooden spoon to mix well. Add the artichokes, garlic powder, salt, and cooled spinach mixture and fold until well combined.

continued

continued

Spinach-Artichoke Stuffed Garlic Knots

Line two baking sheets with parchment paper and set aside.

Place the dough on a lightly floured work surface. Roll the dough into a log and use a sharp knife or bench scraper to cut it into 15 equal portions (about 55g each). Working with one portion at a time, roll into a 10-inch rope. Use a rolling pin or your hands to flatten the dough into a 10 × 2½-inch strip. In a line down the middle, add 2 tablespoons of filling, leaving ½ inch from each edge. Pinch the edges together firmly around the filling. Tie the rope into a knot, tucking the edges underneath and re-pinching the seams to make sure the filling stays sealed inside. Place on a prepared baking sheet with the edges tucked under. Repeat with each piece of dough, leaving 2 inches between them on the baking sheets. Cover with plastic wrap and let rest for 20 to 30 minutes.

Preheat the oven to 400°F.

Make the garlic butter: In a small bowl, stir together the melted butter, garlic, pepper flakes, oregano, and salt. In a separate small bowl, beat together the egg, ½ tablespoon of the garlic butter mixture, and honey. Brush each garlic knot with this egg wash.

Bake until golden brown, 20 to 30 minutes.

Remove from the oven and brush with the garlic butter mixture. Top with the shredded Parmesan and the fresh herbs. Serve while warm.

Plain Garlic Knots

Make the dough as directed. After the dough has doubled in size, preheat the oven to 400°F. Place the dough on a floured surface and cut into 60g to 65g pieces. Roll each piece between your palms and slightly pull it to form a rope 8 to 10 inches long. Tie each strip into a knot and place on the prepared baking sheet. Let rest for 15 to 20 minutes.

Lightly brush with the garlic butter egg wash. Bake just until golden brown, 20 to 30 minutes. Brush the garlic butter over the baked knots as directed.

Notes

♥ *You will have some leftover artichoke filling if using 2 tablespoons for each garlic knot. You can either add a little more to each, or you can use the leftover filling for the most delicious omelet!*

♥ *Before baking, you can brush the garlic knots with the garlic butter mixture instead of the egg wash—I prefer to use egg as well to make shinier tops.*

♥ *Store the leftover garlic knots in an airtight storage bag in the fridge for 2 to 3 days or in the freezer for 3 months. To serve, allow the garlic knots to come to room temperature and then place them in a cold oven and preheat it to 350°F. Once the oven comes to temperature, the garlic knots will be ready to serve.*

Soft Pretzels Three Ways

*Makes 8 pretzels or
11 pretzel buns*

I must confess I don't fully understand American football, but I do enjoy the Super Bowl festivities. These soft pretzels are my go-to recipe for such occasions. I created three different shapes from a single dough, one of which I top with cinnamon sugar in order to offer a versatile menu and also make it the star of the party.

DOUGH

2¼ teaspoons (7g) instant (quick-rise) yeast

1¼ cups (275g) warm water (110°F)

1 teaspoon (4g) granulated sugar

4 cups (520g) all-purpose flour

2 tablespoons (30g) molasses

1½ teaspoons (9g) kosher salt

¼ cup (55g) neutral oil or melted unsalted butter

LYE BATH

4½ cups (990g) room temperature water (75° to 80°F)

2 tablespoons (30g) lye (see Notes)

TO FINISH

Pretzel salt or flaky sea salt, for topping

Make the dough: In a small bowl, combine the yeast, ½ cup (110g) of the warm water, and the sugar. Stir and let rest for 5 to 7 minutes, until foamy.

In a large bowl (or the bowl of a stand mixer), combine the flour, molasses, salt, oil, the yeast mixture, and the remaining ¾ cup (165g) water. Shaping your hand like a claw, bring the ingredients together, mixing and periodically squeezing the dough together. Continue this process for 2 to 4 minutes, until everything is fully incorporated. If the dough looks too dry and is not coming together, add 1 tablespoon additional water.

Lightly flour a work surface and turn the dough out into the middle. Using the basic kneading technique (see page 22), knead for 5 to 7 minutes, until it is smooth and no longer sticky—avoid adding additional flour during this process. (If using a stand mixer, snap on the dough hook and mix on medium speed for 7 to 10 minutes, until the dough is smooth and does not stick to the edges of the bowl. Turn out onto a work surface.)

Pinch the edges of the dough together to form a rough ball. Lightly oil a large bowl and transfer the dough into it with the open edge down. Cover it with plastic wrap and let rest until doubled in size, about 1 hour.

Turn the dough out onto a work surface. Do not use additional flour during the shaping process or the dough will become difficult to roll. Roll the dough into a log and use a sharp knife or bench scraper to cut it into 8 equal portions (110g each) for classic pretzel shapes and pretzel bites or 11 equal portions (88g each) for pretzel buns.

> ## Notes
>
> ♦ *If you prefer not to use lye, you can follow a process using baking soda and boiling water. Lye will make the color and texture of the pretzel much more authentic, but I know it can be intimidating or hard to find. To use a baking soda bath, bring 10 cups of water to a boil with ½ cup baking soda. Add 2 pretzels at a time and cook for 20 to 30 seconds, or 8 to 10 seconds for pretzel bites, then remove from the water, following the rest of the recipe as written.*
>
> ♦ *Store the cooled pretzels in an airtight storage bag at room temperature for 2 to 3 days or in the freezer for up to 3 months. To serve, let thaw at room temperature and then bake at 350°F for 4 to 5 minutes, until soft and warm.*

continued

continued

Soft Pretzels Three Ways

Round each piece of dough into a smooth ball (see page 22). Place onto the work surface and cover with a kitchen towel. Let the dough rest for 10 to 15 minutes.

Shape the pretzels as directed in the shape you have chosen (see end of recipe).

Preheat the oven to 425°F. Line two baking sheets with parchment paper.

Make the lye bath: Place a glass or porcelain baking dish on a large baking sheet to avoid splashing. Using gloves, add the water and lye to the baking dish and stir well. Be sure to wear gloves while dipping or the lye can burn your skin. One at a time, dip each pretzel shape into the lye bath using a skimmer or large spatula. Let it sit for the time specified for each pretzel shape (follows). Transfer to the prepared baking sheets, leaving 2 inches between the pretzels and pretzel buns and 1 inch between the pretzel bites.

To finish: Shape the dough according to the individual directions that follow and bake as directed.

Classic Pretzels

Use your hands to roll each piece of dough into a 24-inch rope. Beginning with the first rope, hold the ends and bring your hands together to form a circle with the top ends crossed. Twist the ends around each other twice, bringing the ends down to the bottom of the circle, leaving about 3 inches of rope on each side. Press the twisted ends of the rope into the bottom edge firmly. Carefully place the pretzels in the lye bath and let them sit for 15 seconds before removing onto a prepared baking sheet as directed. Gently stretch the pretzels with your fingers. Sprinkle with pretzel salt. Using a razor or sharp knife, lightly score a horizontal line across the bottom of the knot. Bake the pretzels until golden brown, 13 to 15 minutes. Remove from the oven and serve while warm.

Pretzel Buns

Divide the dough as directed or into 100g pieces for large buns. Roll each piece into a ball and then firmly flatten the top with your hand. Place the buns in the lye bath, and let them sit in the lye bath for 15 seconds before removing onto a prepared baking sheet as directed. Using a sharp razor, make a shallow crosscut on each bun. Sprinkle with pretzel salt and let sit for 5 minutes. Bake the buns until golden brown, 13 to 15 minutes. Remove from the oven and transfer to a cooling rack. Let cool before slicing.

Pretzel Bites

Working with one piece of dough at a time, use your hands to roll it into a 24-inch rope. Cut it into 1-inch pieces using scissors or a sharp knife. Follow the directions for the lye bath, but dip the bites for 5 to 7 seconds. Place on a prepared baking sheet 1 inch apart. Sprinkle with pretzel salt. Bake for 12 to 13 minutes, until golden brown. For sweet pretzel bites, see the variation that follows.

Cinnamon Sugar Pretzel Bites

Form the pretzel bites as directed, but do not sprinkle with salt before baking. Once baked, remove from the oven. In a shallow bowl, stir together 1 tablespoon ground cinnamon and ¾ cup sugar. Melt 4 tablespoons unsalted butter. Using a pastry brush, brush each pretzel bite with the melted butter and then coat with the cinnamon sugar mixture. Serve with coffee.

Bon appétit!

Basic Pizza Dough

Makes three 9-ounce balls (enough for three 10-inch pizzas)

Seeking the perfect pizza dough? Your quest ends here! This recipe is as simple as it is flawless. I've been using the same dough for years and never tire of it. Follow the steps closely and you'll craft the crispiest, most delectable pizza dough you've ever tasted and created.

But don't let the name limit you—this dough isn't just for pizza! You can repurpose it in a variety of ways, including making fried pizzas, a childhood favorite of mine. Back in the day, my mom would whip up these fried pizzas using a bag of raw dough my dad picked up from the local bakery—a common practice in Türkiye. She'd fill them with an assortment of fillings—heaps of cheese, hearty potato—or simply enjoy them plain, sealing the edges well and then deep-frying in hot oil. My fondest memories are of cold winter mornings, cozying up on my mom's lap with a piece of hot, steaming fried pizza and watching the teakettle billow steam.

1½ teaspoons (5g) instant (quick-rise) yeast

1⅓ cups (293g) warm water (110°F)

1 teaspoon (4g) granulated sugar

1 tablespoon (14g) extra-virgin olive oil

3½ cups (455g) bread flour, plus more for dusting

1½ teaspoons (9g) kosher salt

Double-milled semolina flour, for the work surface

In a medium bowl, combine the yeast, ½ cup (110g) of the water, and the sugar. Stir and let rest for 4 to 5 minutes, until foamy. Add the remaining ½ and ⅓ cup (183g) water, the olive oil, flour, and salt. Using your hands or a bowl scraper, bring the dough together by scraping the ingredients from the bottom and folding them over the top. Repeat this process for 3 to 4 minutes, until everything is just combined. The dough will be a little sticky and not entirely smooth, but don't worry! Cover with plastic wrap and let rest for 30 minutes at room temperature.

Very lightly flour a work surface and flour your hands. Using a dough scraper, gently transfer the dough onto the prepared surface. Slap and fold (see page 21) the dough several times until smooth. Round the dough (see page 22) and place in the bowl with the open edge down. Cover with plastic wrap and let rest for 15 to 20 minutes.

Flour the work surface once again and turn the dough out. Roll it into a small log. Using a sharp knife or bench scraper, divide the dough into 3 equal portions. Working with one piece of dough at a time, use your hands to pinch the cut edges

continued

continued

Basic Pizza Dough

of the dough together to form a ball, being careful not to squeeze the air out of the middle. Flour a baking sheet or work surface. Place the balls onto the prepared surface with at least 5 inches between them. Cover each with a large bowl or flour the top of the dough and loosely cover with plastic wrap. Let rest at room temperature until the dough is relaxed and doubled in size, 1½ to 2 hours.

Preheat a pizza oven to 850°F or a traditional oven to 550°F with a baking steel on the top rack for at least 15 to 20 minutes. Perform a water drop test (see page 172) to ensure the steel is properly heated.

Gently flour a work surface with double-milled semolina flour. Transfer the first piece of dough onto the prepared surface. Using your fingers, press the middle of the dough firmly to expand into a round, leaving a 1-inch rim around the edge. Once the dough is about 6 inches wide, use flat hands to press and stretch the middle of the dough, being sure not to rip it. Turn the dough as you press to evenly stretch each side. Lift the dough on the backs of your fingers to continue to stretch the dough until it reaches 10 inches across. Dress with your favorite toppings, avoiding the edge of the crust.

In a pizza oven: Use a pizza paddle to place the pizza dough in the heated pizza oven. Bake for 1 to 2 minutes, rotating consistently.

In a traditional oven: Use a pizza paddle to place the pizza dough on the hot baking steel. Turn the oven to low broil and broil for 60 to 90 seconds while watching, just until the crust is lightly browned. Carefully move the steel down to the lower rack and turn the oven to 500°F. Bake for an additional 5 to 8 minutes, until the crust is crisp and golden brown on top and underneath, checking at 4 minutes to make sure it does not burn.

Remove from the oven, slice, and serve while warm. Repeat with each piece of dough.

Notes

♥ *DO NOT TOUCH THE DOUGH WITH A ROLLING PIN! This will make for an entirely different texture; please, please, please use your fingers to shape the dough.*

♥ *When using a traditional oven, adding the broiling step makes for a delicious crust much closer to those made in pizza ovens.*

Neapolitan Pizza

Makes three 10-inch pizzas

Selecting the right pizza recipe to feature in this cookbook was a challenge—pizza is serious business, after all. I decided to go with the first pizza that comes to mind: Neapolitan. My version of Neapolitan pizza, however, has my favorite pizza sauce, much to the dismay of my Italian friends. While a good Neapolitan pizza prioritizes the dough, I believe the roasted tomatoes, garlic, and fresh spices add a distinctive character to the pizza. Even though my family and I haven't had the chance to taste pizzas in Italy yet, this surpasses any pizza we've tasted stateside. While I'm usually not one to brag, when it comes to pizza, my humility takes a back seat, especially after we got our wood-fired outdoor pizza oven. Homemade is simply the best!

Basic Pizza Dough (page 45)

PIZZA SAUCE

5 to 6 medium Roma tomatoes, quartered

2 garlic cloves, peeled

1½ cups canned whole peeled San Marzano tomatoes

2 tablespoons extra-virgin olive oil

1½ teaspoons kosher salt

Pinch of granulated sugar

1½ teaspoons chopped fresh oregano

1½ teaspoons chopped fresh basil

PIZZA

8 ounces fresh mozzarella cheese, buffalo or cow's milk

Fresh basil, for serving

Extra-virgin olive oil, for drizzling

Shaved Parmesan cheese, for serving (optional)

Prepare the pizza dough as directed.

Preheat the oven to 500°F.

Make the pizza sauce: Place the quartered Roma tomatoes in a baking dish and roast for 10 minutes. Add the garlic and roast until lightly browned, an additional 15 to 20 minutes. Let cool to room temperature.

Transfer the tomatoes and garlic to a deep bowl and use an immersion blender to puree into a sauce texture. (Alternatively, put through a food mill.) Using your hands, thoroughly crush the tomatoes. Add the crushed San Marzano tomatoes, olive oil, salt, sugar, oregano, and basil. Using a wooden spoon, stir until well combined.

Preheat a pizza oven to 850°F or a traditional oven to 550°F with a baking steel for at least 15 to 20 minutes. Perform the water drop test (see page 172) to ensure the steel is properly heated.

Once the steel is hot, place a ball of dough on a lightly floured work surface. Using your fingers, press the middle of the dough firmly, leaving a 1-inch-wide rim around the edge. Once the dough is about 6 inches wide, use flat hands to press and stretch the middle of the dough, being sure not to rip it. Turn the dough as you press to evenly stretch each side. Lift the dough on the backs of your fingers to continue to stretch the dough until it reaches 10 inches.

continued

continued

Neapolitan Pizza

Spread ⅓ cup of the pizza sauce evenly over the top. Tear the fresh mozzarella with your hands and scatter one-third of it over the sauce.

In a pizza oven: Use a pizza paddle to place the pizza in the heated pizza oven and bake for 1 to 2 minutes, turning consistently. Remove from the pizza oven and immediately top with fresh basil, a drizzle of high-quality olive oil, and shaved Parmesan. Slice and serve while hot.

In a traditional oven: Use a pizza paddle to place the pizza on the pizza steel. Turn the oven to low broil and broil for 60 to 90 seconds while watching, until just the edges of the crust are lightly browned. Move the steel down to the lower rack and turn the oven back to 550°F. Bake until golden brown and melty, an additional 5 to 8 minutes. Remove from the oven and immediately top with fresh basil, a light drizzle of high-quality olive oil, and shaved Parmesan. Slice and serve while hot.

Repeat to make two more pizzas.

Notes

♥ *You can grill rather than roast the Roma tomatoes, if you prefer.*

♥ *Adding the broiling step makes for a delicious crust much closer to those made in pizza ovens.*

♥ *You will have some leftover sauce. It can be stored in a clean jar in the fridge for 5 to 8 days and used for pasta or on sandwiches.*

♥ *If you want to make traditional Neapolitan pizza with just tomatoes rather than sauce, I respect your choice! In a bowl, squeeze and crush high-quality San Marzano tomatoes using your hands. Top the dough with the crushed tomatoes, sprinkle with salt, top with mozzarella and fresh basil, and then drizzle with high-quality olive oil after baking.*

♥ *If you don't have a baking steel or pizza stone, you can heat the oven with an upside-down baking sheet on the middle rack.*

No-Knead Mediterranean-Flavored Brunch Bread

Makes 1 loaf

For pastries and breads to rise beautifully, a gluten network is indispensable. While kneading is one way to create this network, resting the dough without kneading can yield similar results. This recipe is about achieving a sublime loaf of bread with minimal kneading, giving it a consistency that rivals a good sourdough. Once your dough is ready, you're free to let your taste buds guide your flavorings—my Mediterranean version features olives, sun-dried tomatoes, walnuts, and herbs. If you have a preference for savory breakfasts, lunches, or brunches, this recipe is a surefire winner.

3 cups (390g) bread flour, plus more for dusting

1 teaspoon (4g) granulated sugar

1½ teaspoons (9g) kosher salt

1 teaspoon (3g) instant (quick-rise) yeast

½ teaspoon (1.5g) garlic powder

1½ cups (330g) hot water (120°F)

⅓ cup pitted mixed Greek olives, chopped

¼ cup marinated sun-dried tomatoes, chopped

¼ cup chopped walnuts

1 teaspoon chopped fresh rosemary

½ teaspoon fresh thyme

1 tablespoon all-purpose flour

In a large bowl, whisk together the bread flour, sugar, salt, yeast, and garlic powder. Add the hot water and stir using a dough whisk or wooden spoon until everything is just combined. At this point, it will be a shaggy sticky dough, but that's okay. Cover the dough with a clean kitchen towel or plastic wrap and let rest for 30 minutes at room temperature.

Meanwhile, in a medium bowl, combine the olives, sun-dried tomatoes, walnuts, rosemary, thyme, and all-purpose flour. Toss to combine well.

Add the olive mixture to the dough and mix using a dough whisk or wooden spoon until the mixture is evenly distributed through the dough. Cover the dough with plastic wrap and let rest at room temperature for 30 to 45 minutes, then move to the refrigerator and let rest for 6 to 8 hours or overnight.

Transfer the dough to a lightly floured work surface. Flour your hands and very gently stretch the dough into a small square. Fold the right and then the left sides into the middle so you have three layers. Set the rectangle with a short side facing you and again lightly stretching as you pull, roll the dough into a log. Position the dough log seam side down. Shape the dough into a ball by turning the dough while gently pushing the edges under with the sides of

continued

continued

No-Knead Mediterranean-Flavored Brunch Bread

your hands. Dust a bread basket or medium bowl lined with a kitchen towel with bread flour and lightly flip the dough ball into it seam side up. Cover with plastic wrap and let rest for 45 minutes to 1 hour at room temperature.

Preheat the oven to 400°F with a 4-quart Dutch oven on the middle rack. Heat for at least 15 to 20 minutes.

Carefully turn the dough out seam side down onto a large piece of parchment paper and use the paper to lift the dough into the hot Dutch oven. Using a razor held at a 45-degree angle, score the top of the dough all the way, creating a curved line just off-center. Place the lid on the Dutch oven and bake until the dough has risen and the cut opens, 30 to 40 minutes.

Uncover and continue to bake until deeply golden brown, another 15 to 20 minutes, to an internal temperature of 195° to 200°F. Remove from the oven and let it cool on a rack for at least 2 hours or overnight.

Slice and serve with your favorite spread or use for delicious sandwiches or toast!

Notes

♥ *Store the sliced bread in an airtight storage bag at room temperature for 3 to 4 days or sliced in the freezer for 3 months with parchment paper between the slices. Before serving, let the slices come to room temperature and then toast.*

♥ *Instead of using the savory ingredients, you can make a sweet version using cranberries, raisins, walnuts, and chocolate. This dough makes a great base for any ingredients you would like!*

Pitas

Makes 7 pieces

Behind my tranquil Instagram videos lies a whirlwind of creative chaos that leaves me exhausted after filming days. I devote the days following a shoot to relaxation, often treating myself with a delicious homemade pita sandwich, savored at a slow pace. Trust me, a good pita can wipe away all weariness.

2 teaspoons (6g) instant (quick-rise) yeast

½ cup plus 5 tablespoons (180g) warm water (110°F)

1 teaspoon (4g) granulated sugar

2¼ cups (293g) all-purpose flour, plus more as needed

¼ cup (32g) whole wheat flour

¼ cup (55g) whole milk

2 tablespoons (28g) extra-virgin olive oil

1 teaspoon (6g) kosher salt

In the bowl of a stand mixer (or in a large bowl), combine the yeast, ½ cup (110 g) of the water, and the sugar. Stir together and let rest 5 to 7 minutes, until foamy. Add the flours, the remaining 5 tablespoons (70g) water, the milk, olive oil, and salt. Snap on the dough hook and knead the dough on low speed for 2 minutes. (If kneading by hand, bring the dough together using your hands or a bowl scraper.) Increase the speed to medium-low or medium and knead for an additional 5 to 6 minutes, until the dough is smooth. (If kneading by hand, use the basic kneading technique on page 22 to knead for 4 to 5 minutes in the bowl. If the dough is too sticky, you can add 1 to 2 tablespoons more flour.) Cover the dough with a kitchen towel or plastic wrap and let rest for 15 to 20 minutes.

Uncover and transfer the dough to a work surface. Using your hands, perform the basic kneading technique (see page 22) and knead for 2 to 3 minutes, until perfectly smooth. Return the dough to the bowl and cover with plastic wrap. Let rest until doubled in size, 1 to 1½ hours.

Lightly flour a baking sheet and set aside. Place the dough on a lightly floured work surface and roll into a log. Using a sharp knife or bench scraper, divide the dough into 7 equal portions. Round each piece of dough into a smooth ball (see page 22). Place on the prepared baking sheet and loosely cover with plastic wrap. Let rest for 15 to 20 minutes.

Preheat the oven to 500°F with a baking steel on the second to top rack. Ensure the steel heats for at least 10 to 15 minutes; perform the water drop test (see page 172) to ensure it is properly heated.

continued

Pitas

Beginning with 2 or 3 balls of dough, roll each into a 6- to 7-inch rounds ¼ inch thick and place them carefully onto a pizza paddle. Use the paddle to carefully transfer the pitas to the hot baking steel.

Bake for 2 to 3 minutes while watching and remove them to a cooling rack once puffed up and lightly browned. After cooling for 30 to 60 seconds, place the pitas in a tortilla warmer or on a plate covered with a kitchen towel to avoid drying out.

Repeat this process with the next batch of dough balls. Be sure to keep them warm and covered until serving.

Notes

♦ *For flatbread pitas, you can also cook them in a very hot skillet. You'll know the pan is hot enough if, when you drizzle it with water, the water immediately sizzles away. After rolling the dough, place one round of pita in the hot pan and let each side cook for 10 seconds, flipping until each side has been cooked for 60 to 70 seconds. Remove from the heat and keep in the tortilla warmer until ready to use. Cooking them this way will not create the pita pocket, though.*

♦ *Store cooled pitas in an airtight storage bag for 2 to 3 days at room temperature and warm in a 350°F oven for 2 to 3 minutes before serving. You can also store them in the freezer with parchment paper between the pieces for 2 to 3 months.*

Hummus with Caramelized Beef and Pita Chips

Serves 4

As a Turkish woman, I have a special place in my heart for hummus. It's an incredible snack that's versatile and always delicious—whether you serve it as a dip with fresh vegetables or chips, drizzle it on a salad, or slather it on a sandwich. Each way it's used, hummus brings a depth of flavor that's simply amazing. But my ultimate favorite way to enjoy it? Paired with homemade pita chips—it's a crowd-pleaser on my guest tables and a nutritious lunch option for my husband and son.

A pro tip from my kitchen to yours: Invest in Middle Eastern tahini from international markets. The quality of tahini can make or break your hummus. Poor-quality tahini can be bitter or overly thick and can detract from the taste and texture of your dish. So choose your tahini wisely for that smooth, rich hummus we all crave.

PITA CHIPS

3 Pitas (page 55)

¼ cup extra-virgin olive oil

½ teaspoon freshly ground black pepper

½ teaspoon red pepper flakes

½ teaspoon garlic salt, or more to taste

HUMMUS

2 cups chickpeas, canned or cooked, skins removed

1 medium garlic clove, peeled

¼ cup fresh lemon juice

½ cup plus 1 tablespoon tahini

¾ teaspoon ground cumin

1 teaspoon kosher salt, or to taste

6 tablespoons ice water, plus more as needed

2 ice cubes

2 tablespoons extra-virgin olive oil

BEEF

2 tablespoons extra-virgin olive oil

12 ounces sirloin steak, cut into small dice

¼ teaspoon ground cumin

½ teaspoon ground sumac

¼ teaspoon ground paprika

½ teaspoon kosher salt

½ teaspoon freshly ground black pepper

FOR SERVING

Extra-virgin olive oil, for drizzling

Ground sumac, for sprinkling

Chopped fresh parsley, for garnish

Make the pita chips: Preheat the oven to 400°F.

Slice pitas in half through the diameter. Then peel each half apart and tear so you have 4 pieces from each pita. In a small bowl, mix together the olive oil, black pepper, red pepper flakes, and garlic salt. Using a pastry brush, brush both sides of the pita pieces with the olive oil mixture. Slice each piece into 3 or 4 triangles. Place the oiled pieces in a single layer on a baking sheet.

Bake for 3 to 4 minutes. Flip the chips for even cooking and bake until lightly golden brown and crispy on both sides, 3 to 4 minutes longer. Remove from the oven and let cool completely.

Make the hummus: In a food processor, combine the chickpeas and garlic and blend until it becomes a stiff paste. Add the lemon juice, tahini, cumin, and salt and continue to process. Add the ice water, ice cubes, and olive oil and blend until smooth and creamy. Add ½ to 1 tablespoon more water to obtain your desired consistency. Place the hummus on a serving platter and use the back of a spoon to create waves on top.

continued

continued

Hummus with Caramelized Beef and Pita Chips

Prepare the beef: Preheat a medium skillet or saucepan over high heat. Add the olive oil and beef to the hot pan and cook, stirring constantly, until seared and lightly browned, 2 to 3 minutes. Add the cumin, sumac, paprika, salt, and pepper and stir to combine. Continue to cook, while stirring, until caramelized, 2 to 3 minutes. Remove from the heat.

To serve: Top the hummus with the hot beef, a drizzle of olive oil and a sprinkling sumac and fresh parsley. Serve with fresh pita chips on the side.

Notes

❦ *Store the hummus in a jar in the refrigerator for 7 to 10 days. You can remove from the fridge and serve with any toppings you want. I highly recommend serving it with diced giardiniera and lightly drizzled with the pickling liquid.*

❦ *To store the pita chips, place them in a bowl on the countertop. Your household will enjoy a healthy snack every time they walk through the kitchen.*

Garlic Naan

Naan was my first introduction to Indian cuisine. It was love at first bite, and I couldn't wait to create my own version. The dough, enriched with yogurt and brushed with butter and fresh herbs as it comes out of the oven, produces a bread with a unique softness and flavor.

DOUGH

¾ cup (165g) whole milk, warmed, plus more as needed

1½ teaspoons (5g) instant (quick-rise) yeast

1 teaspoon (4g) granulated sugar

¼ cup (62g) whole-milk yogurt

2 tablespoons (28g) neutral oil

2½ cups (325g) all-purpose flour, plus more for dusting

¾ teaspoon (3g) baking powder

1 teaspoon (6g) kosher salt

GARLIC BUTTER

4 tablespoons unsalted butter, melted

2 garlic cloves, minced

2 tablespoons chopped fresh parsley

Extra-virgin olive oil, for cooking the naan

Make the dough: In a large bowl, combine the milk, yeast, and ½ teaspoon of the sugar and let rest for 5 to 7 minutes. Add the yogurt and oil and whisk to combine (see Notes). Add the flour, baking powder, salt, and remaining ½ teaspoon sugar. Combine, using your hands or a dough whisk, periodically squeezing to bring the dough together. While in the bowl, knead for 3 to 5 minutes (see page 22), until almost smooth. Cover the dough with a clean kitchen towel or plastic wrap and let rest for 10 to 15 minutes.

Lightly flour a work surface and use a bench scraper to transfer the dough into the middle. Knead the dough for 4 to 5 minutes, until smooth. Shape the dough into a ball and place in the bowl. Cover and let rest until doubled in size, 1 to 1½ hours.

Make the garlic butter: In a small bowl, whisk together the melted butter, garlic, and parsley.

Lightly flour a work surface and place the dough in the middle. Roll the dough into a log and use a sharp knife or bench scraper to cut it into 6 equal portions (about 98g each). Place the pieces on a baking sheet and cover with plastic wrap to avoid drying.

Heat a nonstick griddle over medium-high heat. Drizzle some olive oil onto a paper towel and lightly wipe the bottom of the heated pan. Using a rolling pin, roll a piece of dough into an oval about 6 × 9 inches and about ¼ inch thick. Immediately place the dough on the griddle and cook for 10 to 15 seconds. Continue flipping and cooking until fully cooked, about 60 to 90 seconds total. Remove it from the pan and immediately brush with the garlic butter. Keep the cooked naan under a kitchen towel or in a covered bread holder to keep warm. Repeat this process with the remaining dough.

Notes

♥ *Store leftover naan in airtight storage bags at room temperature for 1 to 2 days or in the freezer for up to 1 month. Heat in a skillet before serving. If frozen, let thaw at room temperature before warming.*

♥ *If your yogurt is very thick, similar to sour cream, add 1 to 2 tablespoons additional milk to achieve the proper consistency.*

Chicken Shish Kebabs with Cacık

Serves 4 to 6

You might be a bit surprised if you've never come across someone who serves chicken kebabs with naan before, as it is a combination of Turkish and Indian cuisine. I began serving naan with my kebabs because it was my favorite of the available flatbreads and the easiest to find in American grocery stores. I enjoyed the combination so much that I began to make my own naan and continued to serve them together. It may sound odd, but it's worth a shot. I also serve this dish with cacık—a yogurt and cucumber sauce that is served as a side with any kebab recipe.

MARINATED CHICKEN

1 teaspoon mild Turkish red pepper paste

1½ teaspoons tomato paste

2 tablespoons whole-milk yogurt

2 tablespoons buttermilk

2 tablespoons extra-virgin olive oil

1 large garlic clove, minced

1½ teaspoons honey

1 tablespoon kosher salt

½ teaspoon freshly ground black pepper

½ teaspoon ground cumin

½ teaspoon dried oregano

½ teaspoon hot paprika

1 pound boneless, skinless chicken thighs, cut into 1½-inch cubes

½ pound boneless, skinless chicken breast, cut into 1½-inch cubes

VEGETABLES

1 medium green bell pepper, halved crosswise and quartered

1 medium red bell pepper, halved crosswise and quartered

1 small red onion, quartered

¼ cup extra-virgin olive oil

1 teaspoon kosher salt

½ teaspoon garlic powder

2 Roma tomatoes, quartered or 6 ounces cherry tomatoes

TO COOK

¼ cup extra-virgin olive oil

1 teaspoon paprika

FOR SERVING

4 to 6 Garlic Naan (page 60)

Cacık (recipe follows)

Acılı Ezme (page 255)

Marinate the chicken: In a large bowl or airtight storage bag, combine the pepper paste, tomato paste, yogurt, buttermilk, olive oil, garlic, honey, salt, pepper, cumin, oregano, and hot paprika and mix well. Add the chicken to the yogurt mixture and mix well. Cover the bowl with plastic wrap or close the bag and place in the fridge. Marinate the chicken for at least 2 to 3 hours or overnight for best flavor.

Prepare the vegetables: In a medium bowl, combine the bell peppers, onion, olive oil, salt, and garlic powder and stir gently with a spoon to evenly coat. Set aside and toss with the tomatoes just before cooking.

Assemble the skewers: If you are using wooden skewers, soak in water for 30 to 45 minutes before using or they will burn on the grill. Thread the chicken pieces onto wood or metal skewers. Make sure the skewers are not overcrowded, leaving ¼ inch between the pieces. Repeat this process with the vegetables on separate skewers. In a small bowl, mix the olive oil and paprika. Brush this mixture over the chicken kebabs.

Cook the kebabs: Heat a grill to medium-high heat. Add the kebabs and cook for a total of 10 to 14 minutes, flipping every 2 to 3 minutes and watching carefully to make sure the chicken does not burn. (Alternatively, cook on the stovetop in a

continued

continued

Chicken Shish Kebabs with Cacık

hot skillet for 10 to 12 minutes, flipping once halfway through, until golden brown or to your preferred tenderness.) Slice open a piece to see if the chicken is fully cooked before removing from the heat.

Place the cooked chicken on a serving plate, cover with aluminum foil, and let rest for 5 to 10 minutes.

Place the vegetable kebabs on the grill and cook until tender and roasted, 8 to 10 minutes total, flipping once halfway through. (Alternatively, cook on the stovetop in a hot skillet for 5 to 7 minutes per side, flipping in between, until caramelized on both sides.) Remove from the heat.

Serve the kebabs wrapped in warm garlic naan and dressed with cacık and acılı ezme.

Note

♦ *You can thread the raw marinated chicken onto the skewers and then store them uncooked on a plate, wrapped in plastic wrap, in the fridge for up to 2 days until ready to cook.*

Cacık (Turkish Tzatziki)

Makes 1½ cups

½ cup full-fat sour cream

½ cup whole-milk yogurt

½ English cucumber, finely diced or grated

½ teaspoon kosher salt, plus more to taste

1 small garlic clove, minced

2 sprigs fresh dill, chopped, or 1 teaspoon dried mint

¼ cup water

Extra-virgin olive oil, for drizzling

In a medium bowl, mix together the sour cream, yogurt, cucumber, salt, garlic, and dill. Mix until smooth. Add the water and continue to mix until well combined. Taste and add more salt if you desire. Keep in the fridge until ready to use. Serve with a drizzle of olive oil.

Note

♦ *Store the cacık in an airtight jar in the fridge for 1 to 2 days.*

Schiacciata

Makes 3 loaves

This dough recipe has been a constant in my kitchen, perfected over the years and serving as the foundation for crispy, aromatic pizzas. The slow cold fermentation process creates a glorious crust, and then as it bakes a divine scent fills the kitchen. Although this bread is typically baked in a large dish, it wasn't until I stumbled upon a schiacciata sandwich at a renowned shop in Tuscany, via a YouTube channel, that I realized I could transform my beloved dough into a crunchy sandwich loaf. Just remember, for the perfect crispy bread, you need to bake the dough on a well-heated baking steel. This ensures a quick rise and the desired texture in no time at all.

1¼ cups (275g) water, at room temperature (75° to 80°F)

⅔ teaspoon (2g) instant (quick-rise) yeast

½ teaspoon (2g) granulated sugar

3 cups (390g) bread flour, plus more for dusting

1¼ teaspoons (8g) kosher salt

2 tablespoons (28g) extra-virgin olive oil

Semolina flour, for rolling

Extra-virgin olive oil, for baking

In a large bowl, whisk together the water, yeast, and sugar. Add the flour, salt, and olive oil. Shaping your hand like a claw, bring the ingredients together, mixing and periodically squeezing the dough together. Continue this process for 3 to 4 minutes, until everything is fully incorporated. The dough will still be sticky, but it will come together during the folding process. Cover the bowl with plastic wrap and let rest for 30 to 40 minutes at room temperature.

Lightly flour a work surface and your hands. Slap and fold (see page 21) the dough several times until almost smooth. Carefully lift the dough from the middle and place in the bowl. Cover with plastic wrap and let rest for 30 to 40 minutes.

While still in the bowl, lift the dough up from the middle, stretching and folding it over itself. Turn the bowl and repeat this process so each edge is incorporated back into the middle of the dough. Cover the bowl with plastic wrap and let rest at room temperature for 30 minutes, then complete the folding process one more time. Transfer to the fridge and let rest for at least 48 hours and up to 72 hours. It's a long wait, but I promise it will be worth it!

After 2 to 3 days, lightly flour a work surface and place the dough in the middle. Use a sharp knife or bench scraper to divide the dough into 3 equal portions. Using your hands, gather and pinch the edges of each piece to form a ball. Heavily flour your work surface

continued

continued

Schiacciata

or a baking sheet. Place the balls on the flour, leaving lots of space between them. If on the counter, cover each ball with a large bowl. If on the baking sheet, give at least 5 inches of space between the balls and flour the tops before covering with plastic wrap. Let rest until no longer cool to the touch, 3 to 4½ hours at room temperature. You will know the dough is ready when it begins to spread into a flatter circle but is still easy to handle.

Preheat the oven to 450°F with a baking steel on the middle rack. Be sure to heat the steel for at least 15 to 20 minutes so it is fully heated. Perform a water drop test (see page 172) to make sure it's hot enough.

Lightly flour a work surface with semolina flour and gently place a dough ball in the center. Drizzle the top with 1½ teaspoons of olive oil, coating your fingertips as well. Using your fingertips, press the dough firmly to make indentations in the dough and shape it into a 6 × 9-inch rectangle. Lift the dough with your hands and lightly stretch it as you place it onto a pizza paddle. Place the dough onto the hot baking steel.

Bake until golden brown, 13 to 15 minutes, carefully turning the dough once halfway through to ensure even baking. Remove from the oven and brush with olive oil, if desired.

Let rest on a cooling rack for 30 to 40 minutes before slicing, laying a kitchen towel over the top if you prefer the crust a little softer. Repeat with the remaining balls of dough.

Serve with your favorite sandwich toppings or eat on its own while warm.

Notes

♥ *This recipe makes a great pizza dough. For pizza, you can follow all the steps until the shaping and then divide the dough into 2 portions. Follow the shaping method from either of the pizza recipes (page 45 and page 49). This will make two crispy and delicious pizzas.*

♥ *If your baking steel is large enough, you can bake multiple schiacciata at once.*

♥ *If you don't have a baking steel or pizza stone, you can heat the oven with an upside-down baking sheet on the middle rack.*

♥ *This bread is best to eat on the same day it's made as it is thin and meant to be very crispy. If needed, you can store it in an airtight storage bag at room temperature for 2 to 3 days.*

♥ *You can add fresh herbs or garlic to the top of the schiacciata before baking.*

♥ *For a slightly fluffier bread, roll into a 6 x 7-inch rectangle. The baking times should not be affected.*

Eggplant and Artichoke Pecorino Cream Sandwiches

Makes 6 sandwiches

Rest times in my kitchen are usually spent exploring new recipes; even when I'm wiped out, I find energy in learning about global cuisines. I love to tour the world via YouTube vlogs, soaking in the flavors from countries I've yet to visit, and sparking new recipe ideas. This sandwich was inspired by a video from Insider Food of a classic sandwich shop in Florence, All'antico Vinaio, showing a variety of sandwiches made with schiacciata. This eggplant and pecorino combo was a standout, a recipe that screamed deliciousness through the screen, making me eager to re-create and taste it myself. We do not eat any meats with pork in my house, so this is a halal version. You can substitute cured Italian meats, such as salami, pancetta, and prosciutto, for the corned beef or pastrami.

ARTICHOKE PECORINO CREAM

8 ounces cream cheese

4 whole oil-marinated artichoke hearts

½ cup finely grated Pecorino Romano cheese

½ cup water

1 teaspoon freshly ground black pepper

2 tablespoons chopped fresh basil

EGGPLANT

2 medium American eggplants, peeled and cut into 1-inch cubes

¼ cup extra-virgin olive oil

1 teaspoon garlic salt

1 teaspoon red pepper flakes

1 teaspoon freshly ground black pepper

Salt

SANDWICHES

3 loaves Schiacciata (page 65)

3 cups arugula

18 slices cured pastrami or oven-roasted corned beef

Make the artichoke pecorino cream: In a food processor, combine the cream cheese, artichoke hearts, Pecorino, water, pepper, and basil. Process until well combined and creamy. Transfer to a small bowl and set aside.

Roast the eggplant: Preheat the oven to 450°F.

In a bowl, toss the eggplant cubes with the olive oil, garlic salt, red pepper flakes, and black pepper. Spread on a baking sheet and bake for 8 to 10 minutes. Use a spatula to flip the pieces and bake until caramelized outside but soft inside, another 8 to 10 minutes, keeping an eye on them. Remove from the oven and set aside. Season with salt to taste.

Make the sandwiches: Using a sharp bread knife, cut the schiacciata loaves in half and then carefully slice each piece lengthwise to make two thinner slices. Spread 1½ to 2 tablespoons of the artichoke pecorino cream on each slice. On one side of each sandwich, layer roasted eggplant, ¼ cup of arugula, 3 slices of the meat, and then another ¼ cup of the arugula on top. Top with the other piece of bread and serve immediately.

ENRICHED DOUGHS

The realm of enriched doughs is a luxurious one, where buttery indulgence meets a tender crumb and every bite is a celebration. These are not your basic yeasted doughs; they're holiday-worthy creations, rich with eggs, butter, and sometimes sugar or other dairy—ingredients that slow fermentation but heighten flavor and texture. Think of buttery brioche, sweet cinnamon rolls, or divine Danishes. Yes, they demand more time and a trusty stand mixer for perfect integration, but oh, how they give back in texture and taste! Each velvety bite is a reminder of the beauty in patience and the richness that comes from a little extra care.

KEY TECHNIQUES

SPECIAL EQUIPMENT

✽ **Stand Mixer/Hand Mixer:** Anyone passionate about cooking likely owns an electric mixer. These tools can save you substantial time and effort when it comes to mixing and kneading. A hand mixer was my first kitchen purchase, and I use it for almost all my cake, cookie, and cream recipes. A stand mixer with dough, paddle, and whisk attachments is a must-have in my kitchen, especially for kneading dough. However, I recommend against using a 6-quart stand mixer bowl for multipurpose use, especially if you have a small family like mine. For small quantities of dough or cream cake recipes, it may hinder proper mixing due to limited bowl contact. If undecided, I suggest starting with a 4- or 5-quart stand mixer (such as KitchenAid's from the classic series). There are just a few recipes where I recommend not using these tools—be wary of overmixing in certain types of doughs, especially scones and biscuits.

Working with Enriched Dough

Enriched yeast doughs often include ingredients like eggs or butter, which slow down gluten network formation compared to basic yeast doughs. So the secret to obtaining a flawlessly smooth enriched dough is cold fermentation and slow, extensive kneading.

Cold fermentation (often with long rising times in the fridge) is one of the keys to achieving rich taste and complex texture in your enriched doughs. Cold-fermented dough will feel stiff when removed from the fridge as the butter will be solid, allowing for easier handling and shaping of the dough. The dough will soften through handling and bake to a perfectly light and fluffy finish. If you do not have the time for cold fermenting, you can continue the recipe after the dough doubles in size at room temperature, but it can be less flavorful and the shaping process can be a little more difficult.

When it comes to kneading enriched doughs, which are generally softer and harder to knead than regular yeast doughs, I highly recommend using a stand mixer for a fluffy, pillow-like texture. You can knead without a stand mixer, but there's more room for error: you might add too much flour or fail to knead the dough sufficiently due to fatigue, resulting in an inferior dough.

STAND MIXER KNEADING METHOD

1. After mixing the dough, add room temperature butter to the dough and knead it on a medium-low setting for 8 to 10 minutes. Then let the dough and machine rest for 5 to 7 minutes, covered with a kitchen towel. Repeat this process until you've kneaded the dough for at least 15 to 25 minutes.

2. When the dough is ready, it will no longer stick to the bowl and will look glossy and smooth. Continue this kneading/resting process until your dough achieves this consistency.

3. Perform the windowpane test (see opposite). If the dough isn't ready, continue kneading and test again.

4. Once the dough is ready, lightly oil a clean work surface with cooking spray and transfer the dough onto it. To further smooth the dough, use the slap and fold method (see page 21).

HAND KNEADING METHOD

1. Start by combining all the dough ingredients in a suitable bowl using a bowl scraper or your hands. Once the dough starts to come together, transfer it to a lightly floured counter and apply the basic kneading technique (see page 22) for 7 to 10 minutes. Remember not to use too much flour and to keep your work surface clean by using a bench scraper when the dough is sticky.

2. After kneading, cover the dough and rest it for 5 to 7 minutes. Add room-temperature butter and integrate it into the dough completely using the basic kneading method. Your dough will be very soft and sticky at this stage, but resist the temptation to add too much flour. You can lightly oil your hands, if necessary.

3. After the butter is fully incorporated, knead the dough for approximately 10 minutes using the slap and fold method (see page 21). With each fold, you'll see the dough gradually becoming smoother and more pliable. Repeat this kneading-resting process until the dough is exceptionally smooth.

4. Perform the windowpane test (below) to be sure that the dough is ready. Then transfer the dough to a lightly oiled clean work surface and use the slap and fold method (see page 21) to smooth it further. Form it into a smooth ball, place it in a bowl, cover it, and let it rest per the recipe's instructions.

WINDOWPANE TEST

To ensure that your dough is well kneaded, take a small piece of dough and roll it into a ball. Stretch the dough without tearing it and hold it up to a light source. If the light can pass through without the dough tearing, your dough is well-kneaded. If not, continue kneading and test again.

TROUBLESHOOTING YEAST DOUGHS

Dough Not Rising

If your leavened dough, bread, or baked product does not rise despite following all the instructions, and its final texture is hard and not as expected, here are potential causes and their solutions:

Your yeast may be stale: Yeast, as a microorganism, has a lifespan and loses its vitality over time. Stale yeast won't create the necessary air bubbles, leading to a dense and hard bread or dough. To avoid this, always test your yeast if you're unsure of its freshness. Mix 2¼ teaspoons (7g) yeast, 1 teaspoon (4g) granulated sugar, and 1 cup (220g) warm water (110°F) in a bowl and wait 7 to 10 minutes. If the yeast foams and forms a hill, it is not stale and is safe to use. You can preserve the freshness of yeast by using small single-use packets and storing them in a dry and dark place. Avoid using large packets or jars unless you bake daily.

Hot liquid may have killed your yeast: Be cautious when preparing yeast dough—the liquid used to activate your yeast should be a maximum temperature of 110°F. Liquid temperatures of 140°F and above can kill the yeast and prevent the dough from rising.

Cold ingredients and environment: Cold materials and environment can slow down the activation of your yeast and even put it into a form of hibernation. While this is intentional for some cold fermented doughs, it can negatively affect your regular rise. To mitigate this risk, make sure your ingredients are at an appropriate temperature. If you're preparing dough in a cold environment, especially during winter, place your dough in an oven that isn't on and place a bowl of hot water in the lower part of the oven to create a steamy environment. This helps in controlling the dough's fermentation.

Your dough may not be well kneaded: An adequate gluten network forms in the dough when it's kneaded well and with the right technique. Ensure your dough is thoroughly kneaded.

Your yeast has been in direct contact with salt:
Yeast and salt are essential ingredients in baking, but they should not be mixed directly. When yeast and salt come into direct contact, the salt absorbs water molecules from the yeast cells, causing them to break down and die. To prevent this, never mix yeast directly with salt. Always add salt to the flour and mix it a bit to avoid this issue.

Incorrect quantity of ingredients: Following the recipe correctly and using the right weights of ingredients is crucial. Excessive salt or sugar can slow the rise of yeast dough. Using too much flour can make the dough hard and dry as the yeast cannot access the amount of water it needs.

Insufficient humidity for proper rising: The dough must be covered during rest to prevent drying out and retain the necessary humidity. If the dough is left to ferment openly, it will crust over, inhibiting its rise by preventing stretching. For short resting times of 5 to 10 minutes, you can cover your dough with a clean damp kitchen towel, but for long-term fermentation processes, wrap your dough tightly with plastic wrap in a large, deep bowl. You can also cover it with an airtight lid or a plate. My preferred method is to place the dough in a large deep bowl, cover it with another bowl of the same size, and seal the sides with plastic wrap. This technique ensures that no matter how much the dough swells, it won't stick to the cover, resulting in a smooth fermented dough.

Dough Collapsed

If your dough has started to collapse after it has risen during fermentation or baking, here are the potential causes and solutions.

You may have overfermented your dough:
Overfermentation can cause your dough to collapse. To prevent this, start checking your dough 10 to 15 minutes before the specified fermentation time in the recipe. A poke test (see page 22) can help determine readiness; if you poke the dough and it doesn't spring back, your dough is overfermented.

The amount of protein in your flour is low:
Using flour with a lower protein content than was specified in the recipe can lead to dough collapse. Always check the type of flour specified in the recipe and use quality flour that you trust.

You have used too little flour: Dough that is too wet can collapse. Always follow the recipes carefully and use a kitchen scale to ensure accuracy.

You mishandled the ready-to-bake dough: After shaping your fermented dough, handle/lift it gently to avoid releasing trapped gas that could cause it to collapse.

If your dough only collapses during baking, not during fermentation, your oven temperature may be too hot or too low. An oven that's too hot will brown the outside quickly, causing you to remove it from the oven before it's fully baked. As a result, the inside will be undercooked, leading to a collapse during cooling. Conversely, if your oven temperature is too low, the dough won't cook fast enough, and it will start to collapse. Use a temperature gauge to make sure your oven is at the correct temperature.

Notes

✦ *Many recipes advise transferring your bread to a cooling rack immediately after taking it out of the oven. This helps remove moisture and preserves the crispy texture of your loaf, so don't ignore this step.*

✦ *Avoid cutting your bread or pastries while they are hot as this can make them doughy. Let them cool down first and use a sharp bread knife for cutting. If you prefer hot bread and pastries, allow them to cool on a rack after removing them from the oven, then gently break them apart with your hands. Smaller items like croissants or bagels you can enjoy while they're hot without needing to cut them.*

Hazelnut-Chocolate Filled Donuts

Makes 20 donuts

There's something comforting about a fresh, fluffy donut paired with a cup of coffee for breakfast. I have a soft spot for the ones filled with chocolate or apples, but a simple one with a cinnamon sugar coating is just as enjoyable. The secret to great donuts? Make them at home and eat them warm right after frying. Serve with tea or coffee.

DOUGH

2¼ teaspoons (7g) dry yeast

¼ cup (55g) warm water (110°F)

5 tablespoons (62g) granulated sugar

4½ cups (585g) all-purpose flour, plus more for dusting

1 cup (220g) milk

¼ teaspoon (2g) kosher salt

2 large eggs (104g)

1 teaspoon (5g) vanilla extract

6 tablespoons (3 oz/86g) unsalted butter, at room temperature

TO FINISH

1 cup granulated sugar

½ teaspoon ground cinnamon

Neutral oil, for deep-frying

Hazelnut-Chocolate Spread (page 108)

Make the dough: In the bowl of a stand mixer, whisk together the yeast, water, and 1 teaspoon of the sugar. Let it rest 5 to 7 minutes, until foamy. Add the flour, milk, remaining sugar, the salt, eggs, and vanilla. Snap on the dough hook and knead the dough on low speed for 4 to 5 minutes, until well combined. Cover with a kitchen towel and let rest for 10 minutes.

Using your hands, make a hole in the middle of the dough. Add the butter in the middle and close the dough over it. Knead the dough on medium-low speed for 10 minutes, periodically using a bowl scraper to incorporate everything on the sides of the bowl back into the dough. Cover with a kitchen towel and let rest for 5 to 6 minutes. Knead again for 7 to 10 minutes; the dough should look smooth and shiny at this point and no longer stick to the sides of the bowl. To make sure it is fully kneaded, perform a windowpane test (see page 73). If it is not ready at this point, continue to knead and rest periodically until it is ready.

Very lightly flour a work surface. Slap and fold (see page 21) the dough 5 to 7 times, until smooth. Round the dough (see page 22) and place in a large bowl with the open edge down. Cover with plastic wrap and let rest at room temperature for 10 to 15 minutes, then move to the refrigerator to rest overnight. (Alternatively, you can let it rest at room temperature for 30 to 45 minutes, and then in the refrigerator for 2 to 4 hours, until doubled in size.)

Line two baking sheets with parchment paper and set aside. Flour a work surface and place the dough in the middle. Roll the dough into a log and use a sharp knife or bench scraper to cut it into 20 equal

continued

continued

Hazelnut-Chocolate Filled Donuts

portions (about 55g each). Round each piece of dough into a smooth ball (see page 22). Place on the prepared baking sheets and flatten each with your hand until about ½ inch thick. Loosely cover with plastic wrap or a clean kitchen towel and rest again at room temperature until almost doubled in size, 1 hour to 1 hour 15 minutes. (If the dough wasn't in the fridge overnight, rest for 40 to 45 minutes or until almost doubled in size.)

To finish: In a shallow dish, whisk together the sugar and cinnamon. Line a plate with paper towels and have near the stove.

Pour 2½ inches of oil into a medium saucepan and heat the oil over medium heat to 350°F.

Working in batches of a couple of donuts at a time, fry each side until golden brown with an internal temperature of 185° to 190°F, 3 to 4 minutes in total, flipping periodically with a straining spoon. (Monitor the oil temperature to make sure it is not too hot or it will be difficult to cook the donuts evenly.) Transfer the donuts to the paper towels to drain. While still hot, dip the donuts into the sugar and cinnamon mixture.

Fit a pastry bag with a ½-inch round tip and fill the bag with the hazelnut-chocolate spread. Using the end of a wooden spoon, make a hole in the side of each donut. Pipe the filling into the donuts. Serve within a day.

Notes

♦ *If you are filling your donuts with a sweet filling, this sweetness level works perfectly. If you are not adding a filling, you can add 1 tablespoon additional sugar to the dough for a sweeter donut.*

♦ *As an alternate method of shaping the dough, you can divide the dough into 2 equal pieces. Using a rolling pin, roll each piece until it is ½ inch thick. Use a 2½-inch round cookie cutter to cut the dough before placing on the lined parchment paper to rest.*

♦ *You can also fill your donuts with pastry cream (see page 222). In that case, I like to dip the donuts in melted sugar instead of granulated sugar for a caramel shell.*

Chocolate Babka

Makes 2 loaves

Chocolate babka is the star of my first Turkuaz Kitchen viral video and one of our most tried and loved recipes. How could anyone resist a velvety dough with a divine chocolate filling? And the scent? Can a dish make you this happy with its aroma alone? There are certain recipes that you know are delicious just by their look and smell—chocolate babka is definitely one of those.

DOUGH

2¼ teaspoons (7g) instant (quick-rise) yeast

¼ cup (55g) warm water (110°F)

¼ cup plus 1 teaspoon (55g) granulated sugar

1 cup (220g) whole milk

2 large eggs (104g)

1 teaspoon (5g) vanilla extract

4¼ cups (553g) bread flour, plus more for dusting

¼ teaspoon (2g) kosher salt

7 tablespoons (3½ oz/99g) unsalted butter, at room temperature

CHOCOLATE PASTE

1 stick unsalted butter

1 cup semisweet chocolate chips

⅓ cup Dutch-process cocoa powder

½ cup powdered sugar

1½ teaspoons instant coffee

Pinch of kosher salt

CARAMEL SYRUP

½ cup granulated sugar

½ cup water

Make the dough: In the bowl of a stand mixer, whisk together the yeast, warm water, and 1 teaspoon of the sugar. Let it rest 5 to 7 minutes, until foamy. Add the milk, eggs, vanilla, flour, remaining sugar, and the salt. Snap on the dough hook and knead the dough on low speed for 4 to 5 minutes, until well combined. Cover with a kitchen towel and let rest for 10 to 15 minutes.

Using your hands, make a hole in the middle of the dough. Add the butter in the middle and close the dough over it. Knead the dough on medium-low speed for 10 minutes, periodically using a bowl scraper to scrape down the sides of the bowl. Cover with a kitchen towel and let rest for 5 to 6 minutes. Continue to knead for 7 to 10 minutes; the dough should look smooth and shiny at this point and no longer stick to the sides of the bowl. To make sure it is fully kneaded, perform a windowpane test (see page 73). If it is not ready at this point, continue to knead and rest periodically until it is ready.

Very lightly flour a work surface. Slap and fold (see page 21) the dough 5 to 7 times, until smooth. Round the dough (see page 22) and place in a large bowl with the open edge down. Cover the bowl with plastic wrap and let rest at room temperature for 30 to 45 minutes. Then transfer the bowl to the fridge and let rest until doubled in size, 2 to 4 hours.

continued

continued

Chocolate Babka

Meanwhile, make the chocolate paste: In a small bowl, melt the butter and chocolate chips in the microwave (in 30-second bursts) or over a pan of simmering water. Once fully melted, add the cocoa powder, powdered sugar, instant coffee, and salt. Whisk until the ingredients are well combined and let cool to room temperature.

Set the dough on a lightly floured work surface. Using a sharp knife or bench scraper, divide the dough into two equal pieces. Use a rolling pin to roll the first piece into a 14 × 12-inch rectangle. If the chocolate paste is too thick to spread, you can warm it in the microwave for just 10 seconds to soften it slightly. Spread the chocolate paste evenly over the dough with an offset spatula. Starting from a long side, tightly roll the piece of dough into a log. Transfer the roll to a baking sheet and repeat with the second piece of dough. Place the baking sheets in the freezer for 5 to 10 minutes so the dough can be easily cut.

Remove the dough from the freezer and then use a sharp bread knife to cut the first log lengthwise down the center so you have two halves with the chocolate showing. Place both pieces next to each other, chocolate side facing up. Begin twisting the two ropes around each other, stretching slightly and keeping the chocolate side up, until you have a long braid. Using your hands, seal the ends so they do not come apart. Place the braid carefully into an 8½ × 4½ x 2½-inch loaf pan. Repeat the slicing and braiding process for the other 14-inch rope. Cover lightly with plastic wrap and let rest at room temperature for 45 to 60 minutes, until risen by half.

Preheat the oven to 345°F.

Bake until the tops turn brown, 30 to 40 minutes, and reach an internal temperature of 195°F. If the tops are browning too quickly, place a small piece of aluminum foil over them to make sure the tops bake evenly.

Meanwhile, make the caramel syrup: In a small saucepan, heat the sugar over medium-low heat. Watch the pot but do not touch it. Once the sugar is melted and begins to lightly caramelize, add the water and reduce the heat to low. Stirring occasionally, continue to cook for 1 to 2 minutes, until the sugar is fully dissolved. Set aside and let cool completely.

Remove the babka from the oven and let cool in the pan for 10 to 15 minutes. Brush with caramel syrup while still in the pan, then brush once again just before serving if you prefer.

Notes

♦ *You can prepare the dough 1 day before baking and refrigerate overnight. After the dough is fully kneaded and in a large bowl, cover with plastic wrap and let rest at room temperature for 10 to 15 minutes before transferring to the fridge to rest overnight. After shaping, extend the rest time to 1 to 1½ hours to allow the dough to almost double in size before baking.*

♦ *Store the babka in an airtight storage bag at room temperature for 2 to 3 days. You can also slice the loaf and place in airtight storage bags, placing parchment paper between the slices if you desire, and store in the freezer for 1 to 2 months. Warm lightly before serving.*

Betül's Way Croissants or Pains au Chocolat

Makes 12 pastries

Crafting the perfect croissant might seem like climbing a mountain, and truth be told, it's one of the trickiest recipes in the world of pastries. From the quality of the ingredients that you choose to the room's temperature, each step holds a unique importance.

Creating croissants is a journey that calls for patience. It's an adventure filled with trial, error, and more often than not, unexpected outcomes. Among all the recipes I've worked on, I've devoted the most time to mastering this one. You wouldn't believe how many croissants I have stashed in my freezer from my numerous practice rounds! Throughout my journey, I've made croissants that turned out like buns, some that had a super-soft texture, and even a few that could pass as artisanal masterpieces. So let's roll up our sleeves and get started!

¾ cup (165g) warm water (110°F)

2 teaspoons (6g) instant (quick-rise) yeast

¼ cup (50g) granulated sugar

⅔ cup (146g) whole milk

4 cups (520g) bread flour, plus more for dusting

½ teaspoon (3g) kosher salt

4 tablespoons (2 oz/56g) unsalted butter, at room temperature

20 tablespoons (10 oz/285g) unsalted European-style butter, at room temperature

24 dark chocolate baking batons (120g) (if making pain au chocolat)

Egg wash: 1 egg whisked with 1 teaspoon water

In the bowl of a stand mixer, mix together the warm water, yeast, and ½ teaspoon of the sugar. Let it rest for 5 to 7 minutes, until foamy. Add the milk, remaining sugar, the flour, and salt. Snap on the dough hook and knead the dough on low speed for 4 to 5 minutes, until well combined. Cover with a kitchen towel and let rest for 5 to 10 minutes. Using your hands, make a hole in the middle of the dough. Add the 4 tablespoons regular butter in the middle and close the dough over it. Knead the dough on medium-low speed for 10 minutes, periodically using a bowl scraper to incorporate everything on the sides of the bowl back into the dough. Cover with a kitchen towel and let rest for 5 to 6 minutes. Continue to knead for 7 to 10 minutes; the dough should look smooth and shiny at this point and no longer stick to the sides of the bowl. To make sure it is fully kneaded, perform a windowpane test (see page 73). If it is not ready at this point, continue to knead and rest periodically until it is ready.

Slap and fold (see page 21) the dough 5 to 7 times, until smooth. Round the dough (see page 22) and place in the bowl with the open edge down. Cover with plastic wrap and let rest for 5 to 10 minutes, then place in the fridge and let rest for 3 to 4 hours.

Notes

❦ *The most important rule is to use European-style butter (see page 10) for croissants; otherwise, the croissant will have a very bready texture.*

❦ *After making the butter layers in the recipe, the dough should definitely be kept in the refrigerator for at least 7 to 8 hours. Between steps or before shaping, the dough must be cooled again to prevent the butter from melting during the process.*

continued

continued

Betül's Way Croissants or Pains au Chocolat

In a small bowl, using a wooden spoon or whisk, mix the European butter until it is smooth and creamy.

Place the dough in the center of a work surface. Roll the dough into a log and use a sharp knife or bench scraper to cut it into 16 equal portions. Round each piece of dough into a smooth ball (see page 22).

Use a rolling pin to roll a ball of dough into a 6-inch round and lightly flour the top. Repeat for all the dough pieces, stacking the rounds on top of one another. Place a large piece of plastic wrap or parchment paper on a work surface. Begin with the first rolled piece of dough once again and, slightly stretching it, transfer it to your prepared surface. Add 1 heaping tablespoon of the European butter and use a knife or an offset spatula to spread it evenly across the dough. Gently pressing and stretching the dough layers as you add them, add the next piece of dough on top of the butter layer and repeat the butter spreading process. Repeat until all layers of dough have been added, flipping the dough stack after every third or fourth layer to make sure each layer is stretching to a consistent size. By the end of this process, the dough stack should be 8 to 9 inches wide. Cover with plastic wrap and refrigerate for at least 7 hours or overnight.

Flour a work surface. Carefully unwrap the dough, taking care not to rip the sides, and place in the center of the work surface. Using a rolling pin, roll the dough into a 20- to 22-inch round. At this point, you can choose to make traditional croissants or pain au chocolat.

To make croissants: Line two or three baking sheets with parchment paper. Using a sharp knife or pizza cutter, cut the dough in half in both directions for 4 equal quarters. Cut each quarter into three 4-inch triangles, or smaller, according to your preference. Using a sharp knife, make a ½-inch cut in the wide end of each triangle. Place the cut side facing you and stretch the dough in front of you. Pulling the bottom edge apart slightly at the cut, roll the dough toward the point to make the croissant shape, lightly stretching as you roll. Place on a prepared baking sheet with the open edge down. Repeat to make more croissants, leaving 3 inches between them on the baking sheets. Loosely cover with plastic wrap and let rest at room temperature until doubled in size, 2 to 2½ hours.

To make pains au chocolat: Line two or three baking sheets with parchment paper. Trim the curved edges of the dough round to make a rectangle. Cut the rectangle in half and then cut each rectangle crosswise into 5 or 6 pieces, according to your preference. Place one chocolate baton along one of the short sides of the rectangle. Roll the dough over the baton and add a second baton. Continue rolling the dough until you reach the end. Place on a prepared baking sheet with the open edge down. Repeat to make more pains au chocolat, leaving 3 inches between them on the baking sheets. Loosely cover with plastic wrap and let rest at room temperature until doubled in size, 2 to 2½ hours.

Preheat the oven to 400°F. While preheating, refrigerate the pastries for at least 15 minutes.

Lightly brush the flat sides of each croissant or pain au chocolat with egg wash, avoiding the layered edges. Bake until golden brown, 20 to 25 minutes.

Transfer to a rack to cool for at least 30 minutes. Serve with coffee or tea.

Cramique

Makes 2 loaves

This is my signature brioche recipe—the life of any birthday celebration in our family. This versatile dough, prepared a few days ahead, magically transforms into two luscious, pillow-soft loaves of bread. We savor one loaf immediately, relishing it with warm coffee, and it typically vanishes within the first 15 to 20 minutes! The second loaf is set aside for a few days to make the perfect birthday breakfast: the most sumptuous French toast you could ever imagine. A small heads-up, though—this dough takes a little longer to prepare than other enriched doughs, owing to the additional eggs. But trust me, a little patience and persistent kneading will reward you with results worth every extra minute!

2¼ teaspoons (7g) instant (quick-rise) yeast

¼ cup (55g) warm whole milk (110°F)

6 tablespoons (75g) granulated sugar

5 large eggs

3¾ cups (490g) bread flour, plus more for dusting

¼ teaspoon (2g) kosher salt

14 tablespoons (7 oz/198g) unsalted butter, at room temperature

1½ teaspoons (7g) vanilla extract

½ cup (85g) chocolate chips, plus more for decorating (optional)

Egg wash: 1 egg beaten with 1 teaspoon neutral oil

2 tablespoons pearl sugar (optional), for garnish

In the bowl of a stand mixer, combine the yeast, milk, and 1 teaspoon of the sugar. Mix and let rest for 5 to 7 minutes, until foamy. Add the eggs, flour, salt, remaining sugar, 6 tablespoons (84g) of the butter, and the vanilla extract. Snap on the dough hook and knead the dough on medium-low speed for 5 to 7 minutes, until it comes together. Cover with a kitchen towel and let rest for 8 to 10 minutes.

Using your hands, make a hole in the middle of the dough. Add the remaining 8 tablespoons (113g) butter in the middle and close the dough over it. Knead the dough on medium-low speed for 10 minutes, periodically using a bowl scraper to incorporate everything on the sides of the bowl back into the dough. Cover with a kitchen towel and let rest for 5 to 6 minutes. Continue to knead for 7 to 10 minutes; the dough should look smooth and shiny at this point and no longer stick to the sides of the bowl. To make sure it is fully kneaded, perform a windowpane test (see page 73). If it is not ready at this point, continue to knead and rest periodically. This is a richer dough than some other sweet doughs, so it may take 25 to 30 minutes of kneading to be ready.

Very lightly flour a work surface. Slap and fold (see page 21) the dough 5 to 7 times, until smooth. Round the dough (see page 22) and place in the bowl with the open edge down. Cover with plastic wrap and let

continued

Cramique

rest at room temperature for 10 to 15 minutes before transferring to the fridge to rest overnight. (If you are looking to bake the same day, you can let it rest at room temperature for 30 to 45 minutes and then in the fridge for 3 to 4 hours.)

Remove the dough from the fridge. If the dough has been in the fridge overnight, let rest in the bowl for 15 to 20 minutes at room temperature before shaping. Place the dough on a clean work surface and divide into 2 equal portions. With your hands, shape one portion into an 8 × 9-inch rectangle and spread ¼ cup of the chocolate chips evenly over the top. Fold one of the long sides into the middle and then the other long side over the top, so the dough is folded in thirds. Starting at a short side, roll the dough from the bottom to the top. Place the dough so the seam side is underneath, and using the edges of your hands, turn and shape the sides of the dough so it creates a ball with a tight surface on top. Using your palm, press firmly to flatten the top of the loaf. Line a baking sheet with parchment paper and transfer the loaf onto it. Decorate the top with a few extra chocolate chips, if desired. Cover loosely with plastic wrap. Repeat this process with the second ball of dough and place on a separate parchment-lined baking sheet. Let the dough rest at room temperature until doubled in size, 3 to 3½ hours (2 to 2½ hours if it hasn't been left in the fridge overnight).

Preheat the oven to 350°F.

Once the loaves are finished rising, brush each with the egg wash. Then, using a razor or the tip of kitchen scissors, score a circle around the entire top of the loaf. Sprinkle the top evenly with the pearl sugar.

Bake until the loaves are golden brown and have an internal temperature of 190° to 200°F, 30 to 35 minutes. If the tops are browning too quickly, tent a piece of aluminum foil over the bread. If you do not have a probe thermometer, you can gently press the top middle of the loaves. If it springs back immediately, the center is fully baked.

Place on a cooling rack to cool for at least 45 minutes to 1 hour before slicing.

Note

✦ *Once fully cooled, store in an airtight storage bag at room temperature for 3 to 4 days or slice and store in the freezer with parchment paper between the slices for up to 2 months. When stored on the counter in an airtight storage bag for 2 to 3 days, the bread will dry out slightly and make incredible French toast (see opposite).*

Crème Brûlée French Toast with Vanilla Sauce

Serves 4

Each year, as my birthday dawns, I awake not to the sound of an alarm but to the tantalizing aroma of Sait cooking something sweet caramelizing in the kitchen. This scent is my very own birthday present to myself—a breakfast that feels like a feast.

The first time I made this crème brûlée French toast, it was just an attempt to blend my love for French toast with my infatuation with the rich texture of crème brûlée. As the creamy egg mixture met the heat and the aroma filled the air, I knew something extraordinary was about to unfold. And when I took that first bite, it was nothing short of a revelation. The caramelized crust gave way to a soft, custard-soaked bread, the sweetness balanced perfectly with the warm, comforting notes of vanilla.

From that moment, this breakfast dish became a symbol of self-love, a way to kick-start my special day by treating myself to a dish that's as delightful as it is decadent. This is a breakfast that isn't just eaten but experienced, making an ordinary day feel like a celebration. It's my hope that this dish will bring the same joy to your special occasions as it does to mine.

VANILLA SAUCE
½ cup (120g) heavy cream

¾ cup (165g) whole milk

1 vanilla bean or
½ tablespoon (15g) vanilla extract

2 large egg yolks

½ tablespoon (5g) cornstarch

3½ tablespoons (45g) granulated sugar

FRENCH TOAST
2 large eggs

½ cup (110g) whole milk

¼ cup (55g) heavy cream

2 tablespoons (26g) granulated sugar

1 teaspoon (3g) vanilla extract

Pinch of kosher salt

Four 1-inch slices Cramique (page 87)

2 to 3 tablespoons (28g to 42g) butter

TO FINISH
¼ cup granulated sugar

Fresh berries

Powdered sugar

Make the vanilla sauce: In a small saucepan, heat the heavy cream and milk over medium heat (if you are using a vanilla bean, add it at this point). In a small bowl, whisk together the egg yolks, cornstarch, and granulated sugar. Once the milk has just begun to bubble, remove from the heat. Very slowly drizzle ½ cup of the hot milk mixture into the egg yolk mixture, whisking constantly. Continuing to whisk, add the egg mixture to the saucepan. Return the saucepan to the heat. Stir the mixture constantly and let come to a boil, cooking for 10 to 20 seconds before removing from the heat. Add the vanilla extract, if using. Let the sauce rest for 4 to 5 minutes at room temperature. Remove the vanilla bean, if necessary. Cover with plastic wrap and press it into the top of the cream. Let rest at room temperature until completely cool, about 1 to 2 hours.

continued

continued

Crème Brûlée French Toast with Vanilla Sauce

Make the French toast: In a shallow dish, whisk together the eggs, milk, heavy cream, granulated sugar, vanilla, and salt until well combined. Soak 2 slices of cramique in the egg mixture, flipping to coat both sides.

Meanwhile, in a nonstick pan, heat 2 tablespoons of the butter over medium heat. Add the French toast to the hot pan and reduce the heat to medium-low. Cook until one side is golden brown, 4 to 5 minutes, then flip and repeat on the other side. Cook according to your preferred doneness and transfer to a cooling rack. Repeat with the other 2 slices of cramique.

To finish: Coat each slice generously with granulated sugar. Using a kitchen torch, caramelize the sugar. Let cool for a few minutes until the top becomes crunchy. Spread ¼ cup of the vanilla sauce over each of four serving plates. Place a slice of French toast on the vanilla sauce and dress with fresh berries and powdered sugar. Serve immediately.

Note

❧ *This vanilla sauce has a balanced sweetness, to pair well with the crème brûlée and powdered sugar. If you prefer a sweeter sauce, you can add a touch more sugar to your sauce.*

Vegan Brioche Dough

*Makes about
850 grams dough*

Attention all vegan friends who've been eagerly awaiting an eggless enriched dough recipe from me. After relentless experimentation, I've discovered a flawless vegan recipe that's bound to impress. It's a recipe I'm extremely excited to see your reactions to. Try it in my Hazelnut-Chocolate Star Bread (page 106), Burger Buns (page 119), or Chocolate Babka (page 79) and let me know what you think!

2¼ teaspoons (7g) instant (quick-rise) yeast

¼ cup (55g) warm water (110°F)

3½ tablespoons (45g) raw cane sugar

½ cup (120g) original soy milk, at room temperature

½ cup (100g) vegan egg product

3¼ cups (423g) bread flour

¼ teaspoon (2g) kosher salt

6 tablespoons (86g) vegan butter, at room temperature

In the bowl of a stand mixer, stir together the yeast, water, and ½ teaspoon of the raw cane sugar. Mix and let rest for 5 to 7 minutes, until foamy. Add the soy milk, vegan egg, flour, remaining sugar, and the salt. Snap on the dough hook and knead the dough on low speed for 5 to 7 minutes, until well combined. Cover with a kitchen towel and let rest for 8 to 10 minutes.

Using your hands, make a hole in the middle of the dough. Add the vegan butter in the middle and close the dough over it. Knead the dough on medium-low speed for 10 minutes, periodically using a bowl scraper to incorporate everything on the sides of the bowl back into the dough. Cover with a kitchen towel and let rest for 5 to 6 minutes. Continue to knead for 7 to 10 minutes; the dough should look smooth and shiny at this point and no longer stick to the sides of the bowl. To make sure it is fully kneaded, perform a windowpane test (see page 73). If it is not ready at this point, continue to knead and rest periodically until it is ready.

Slap and fold (see page 21) the dough 5 to 7 times, until smooth. Round the dough (see page 22) and place in a large bowl with the open edge down. Cover with plastic wrap and let rest at room temperature for 10 to 15 minutes, then in the fridge overnight. (If you are in a hurry, you can let it rest at room temperature for 30 to 40 minutes and then in the fridge for at least 2 to 3 hours, until doubled in size.)

Remove the dough from the fridge and use in place of any brioche recipe. You can increase or decrease the amount of sugar slightly for sweet or savory recipes.

Swedish Cardamom Buns

Makes 16 buns

If you, like me, dream of sipping coffee and savoring pastries in a bustling New York café, these Swedish cardamom buns are for you. I have never been to Sweden . . . or to New York, but something about these intricately knotted, delicious pastries evoke the image of a beautiful day at a New York coffee shop in the fall. With each bite, you'll feel as though you're sitting streetside in the city that never sleeps, enjoying the ambiance and, of course, the sweet aroma of cardamom.

DOUGH

1¼ cups (275g) warm whole milk (110°F)

2¼ teaspoons (7g) instant (quick-rise) yeast

6 tablespoons (75g) granulated sugar

4 cups (520g) all-purpose flour, plus more for dusting

¼ teaspoon (2g) kosher salt

1 large egg plus 1 egg yolk

1 tablespoon (7g) ground cardamom

7 tablespoons (3½ oz/99g) unsalted butter, at room temperature

FILLING

8 tablespoons unsalted butter, at room temperature

½ cup granulated sugar

1 tablespoon ground cardamom

1½ teaspoons ground cinnamon

Egg wash: 1 egg beaten with 1 teaspoon milk

Make the dough: In the bowl of a stand mixer, whisk together ½ cup (110g) of the milk, the yeast, and 1 teaspoon of the sugar. Let rest for 5 to 7 minutes, until foamy. Add the flour, the remaining ¾ cup (165g) milk, the remaining sugar, the salt, the egg and yolk, and cardamom. Snap on the dough hook and knead the dough on low speed for 3 to 4 minutes, until well combined. Cover with a kitchen towel and let rest for 10 minutes.

Using your hands, make a hole in the middle of the dough. Add the butter in the middle and close the dough over it. Knead the dough on medium-low speed for 10 minutes, periodically using a bowl scraper to incorporate everything on the sides of the bowl back into the dough. Cover with a kitchen towel and let rest for 5 to 6 minutes. Continue to knead for 8 to 10 minutes; the dough should look smooth and shiny at this point and no longer stick to the sides of the bowl. To make sure it is fully kneaded, perform a windowpane test (see page 73). If it is not ready at this point, continue to knead and rest periodically until it is ready.

Very lightly flour a work surface. Slap and fold (see page 21) the dough 5 to 7 times, until smooth. Round the dough (see page 22) and place in a large bowl with the open edge down. Cover with plastic wrap and let rest at room temperature for 10 to 15 minutes and then in the fridge overnight. (Alternatively, you can let it rest at room temperature for 30 to 40 minutes and then in the fridge for 2 to 4 hours, until doubled in size.)

continued

continued

Swedish Cardamom Buns

Make the filling: The next day, in a medium bowl, mix together the butter, sugar, cardamom, and cinnamon.

Make the rolls: Lightly flour a work surface and turn the dough out on it. Use a sharp knife or bench scraper to cut the dough into 2 equal portions. Take the first piece of dough and pinch the edges together to form a ball. Place the open edge of the dough underneath and use your hands to roll the dough into a ball.

Using a rolling pin, roll the dough to a 10 × 16-inch rectangle about ½ inch thick. Use an offset spatula to spread half of the cardamom filling on top. Starting with a short side, fold it over the middle and then fold the other side over the top, so there are three even layers (like folding a letter). Press gently with your hands and then roll the dough into an 8 × 10-inch rectangle. Line two baking sheets with parchment paper.

Use a pizza cutter to slice the dough lengthwise into 8 pieces about 1 inch wide. Take a piece of the dough and hold one end between your second and third fingers. Stretching the dough, wrap it around your fingers three times: once straight, once slightly to the left, and once slightly to the right. Gently slide the dough off your hand and fold the other end into the middle underneath the dough so it appears as an intricate knot with the ends hidden.

Arrange the buns on the prepared baking sheets, leaving 2 inches between them. Cover loosely with plastic wrap and a clean kitchen towel and let rest at room temperature until almost doubled in size, 1 to 1½ hours.

Preheat the oven to 375°F. Brush each bun with the egg wash. Bake until golden brown, 15 to 17 minutes.

When done, transfer the buns to a cooling rack to cool completely.

Notes

♥ *Store in an airtight storage bag at room temperature for 2 to 4 days or in the freezer for up to 2 months. Warm for 3 to 5 minutes at 350°F before serving. If frozen, let thaw at room temperature before warming.*

♥ *After brushing with egg wash, you can sprinkle pearl or turbinado sugar over the tops for a sweet crunch. Alternatively, you can brush with caramel syrup (see Chocolate Babka, page 79) after baking.*

Pistachio Rolls

Makes 8 to 10 rolls

This recipe is a tribute to my husband: His sheer delight in these rolls is one of my life's simplest yet most profound joys. Pistachio Rolls, with their vibrant hue and rich, buttery taste, are his absolute favorites, reminiscent of classic Turkish desserts like baklava that he can never resist. It's this traditional gem that inspired me to bring pistachios into harmony with a pillowy, delicate dough, creating a pastry that's both comforting and a little luxurious; it's like crafting a symphony with Sait's favorite notes.

On our anniversaries, the scent of these rolls baking is a love letter in itself. Like watching snowfall or enjoying the rain, seeing my husband relish these rolls is a heartwarming spectacle. But it's not just about nostalgia; it's about the here and now, the shared glances, the smiles as we relish the complexity of flavors—the way the salty, earthy notes of the pistachios meld with the subtle sweetness of the dough. So, I invite you to make these pistachio rolls your new tradition. They're a celebration of love, of connection, and of the beautifully nuanced dance of flavors that life has to offer. Here's to those heartwarming experiences, wrapped in the guise of a simple yet extraordinary pastry.

DOUGH

½ cup (110g) warm whole milk (110°F)

2 teaspoons (6g) instant (quick-rise) yeast

¼ cup (50g) granulated sugar

2½ cups (325g) bread flour, plus more for dusting

¼ teaspoon (2g) kosher salt

2 large eggs

1 teaspoon (5g) vanilla extract

4 tablespoons (2 oz/56g) unsalted butter, at room temperature

PISTACHIO FILLING

⅓ cup granulated sugar

¾ cup coarsely ground Turkish pistachios

5 tablespoons unsalted butter, at room temperature

CREAM CHEESE FROSTING

4 ounces cream cheese, room temperature

3 tablespoons unsalted butter, at room temperature

1 tablespoon cold mascarpone cheese

1 cup powdered sugar

1 teaspoon vanilla extract

Pinch of kosher salt

¼ cup coarsely ground Turkish pistachios, for garnish

Make the dough: In the bowl of a stand mixer, whisk together the warm milk, yeast, and ½ teaspoon of the granulated sugar. Let rest for 5 to 7 minutes, until foamy. Add the flour, remaining sugar, the salt, eggs, and vanilla. Snap on the dough hook and knead the dough on low speed for 4 to 5 minutes, until well combined. Cover with a kitchen towel and let rest for 7 to 10 minutes.

Using your hands, make a hole in the middle of the dough. Add the butter in the middle and close the dough over it. Knead the dough on medium-low speed for 10 minutes, periodically using a bowl scraper to incorporate everything on the sides of the bowl back into the dough. Cover with a kitchen towel and let rest for 5 to 6 minutes. Continue to knead for 7 to 10 minutes; the dough should look smooth and shiny at this point and no longer stick to the sides of the bowl. To make sure it is fully kneaded, perform a windowpane test (see page 73). If it is not ready at this point, continue to knead and rest periodically until it is ready.

continued

continued

Pistachio Rolls

Lightly grease a large bowl and set aside. Very lightly flour a work surface. Slap and fold (see page 21) the dough 5 to 7 times, until smooth. Round the dough (see page 22) and place in the prepared bowl with the open edge down. Cover with plastic wrap and let sit at room temperature for 25 to 35 minutes. Then transfer the dough to the refrigerator and let rest for 2 to 3 hours, until doubled in size.

Make the pistachio filling: Line a 9-inch square baking dish or 10-inch cast-iron skillet with parchment paper. In a small bowl, mix the granulated sugar and ground pistachios. Lightly flour a work surface and transfer the dough onto it. Using a rolling pin, roll the dough into a 10 × 14-inch rectangle (around ¼ inch thick). With an offset spatula, spread the butter over the dough and then sprinkle the pistachio mixture evenly over the top. Use your hands to gently press the mixture to make sure it sticks to the butter. Starting from a short side, firmly roll the dough into a tight log. Using a thin string or dental floss, cut the dough into 8 to 10 rolls 1 to 1½ inches thick, depending on your preference. Place the buns cut-side down onto your prepared baking dish or in the cast-iron skillet, leaving ¼ inch between the pieces. Loosely cover with plastic wrap and let rest for 30 to 45 minutes at room temperature.

Preheat the oven to 350°F.

Bake the buns until lightly browned for 25 to 30 minutes.

Remove from the oven and let cool in the pan for 10 to 15 minutes.

Make the cream cheese frosting: In a medium bowl, with an electric mixer, beat together the cream cheese, butter, mascarpone, powdered sugar, vanilla, and salt until smooth. Spread on the cooled rolls, sprinkle with ground pistachios, and serve immediately.

Rolls with Cinnamon Sugar Filling

Omit the pistachio filling and combine ¼ cup packed light brown sugar, 5 tablespoons softened unsalted butter, 1½ tablespoons ground cinnamon, a pinch of salt, and ½ teaspoon vanilla extract. Spread over the dough, roll, cut, and bake as directed.

Notes

❦ The Turkish pistachios are the secret to making this recipe extra delicious—if you can't find them, you can use regular pistachios or make classic cinnamon rolls (recipe above).

❦ I grind the pistachios in a food processor until they are just larger than turbinado sugar granules.

❦ Instead of letting the dough rest at room temperature and then in the fridge, you can leave it at room temperature for 1 to 1½ hours, or until doubled in size, before shaping. You can also prepare the dough the night before; let it rest at room temperature for 5 to 10 minutes after kneading and in the fridge overnight. The next day, it will take a little longer to rise before baking.

❦ Store unfrosted rolls, covered with plastic wrap, at room temperature for 1 to 3 days. If you have frosted leftovers, you can cover them with plastic wrap and keep them in the fridge for 2 to 3 days and microwave for 30 seconds before serving.

Chocolate Buns with Caramel Cream

Makes 16 buns

These buns are simply a chocolate rendition of the sweet buns found in many different countries, each with its own name. I always prefer to add a little mascarpone cheese to the cream, as I find the buns made with heavy cream alone a bit dull. The butterscotch chips I use for the filling and the homemade hazelnut-chocolate spread add an extra level of flavor. You have the freedom to experiment with the filling ingredients, but I suggest trying the original recipe first. Perhaps this is what dessert tastes like in heaven!

CHOCOLATE BUNS

2¼ teaspoons (7g) instant (quick-rise) yeast

1 cup (220g) warm whole milk (110°F)

5 tablespoons plus 1 teaspoon (65g) granulated sugar

4 cups (520g) all-purpose flour, plus more for dusting

¼ teaspoon (2g) kosher salt

⅓ cup (74g) room-temperature water (75°F)

¼ cup (30g) Dutch-process cocoa powder

2 large eggs

1 teaspoon (5g) vanilla extract

6 tablespoons (3 oz/86g) unsalted butter, at room temperature

⅓ cup (56g) semisweet chocolate chips, mini or crushed

Egg wash: 1 egg beaten with 1 teaspoon water

CARAMEL CREAM

1 cup creamy, high-quality mascarpone cheese, cold

2 tablespoons Caramel Syrup (page 141)

2 cups cold heavy cream

¾ cup powdered sugar

1 teaspoon vanilla extract

Pinch of kosher salt

TO FINISH

½ cup Hazelnut-Chocolate Spread (page 108)

½ cup butterscotch chips, mini or crushed

Cocoa powder, for dusting

Make the chocolate buns: In the bowl of a stand mixer, combine the yeast, milk, and 1 teaspoon of the sugar. Stir together and let rest for 5 to 7 minutes, until foamy. Add the flour, remaining sugar, the salt, water, cocoa powder, eggs, and vanilla. Snap on the dough hook and knead the dough on low speed for 5 to 7 minutes, until well combined. Cover with a kitchen towel and let rest for 10 minutes.

Using your hands, make a hole in the middle of the dough. Add the butter in the middle and close the dough over it. Knead the dough on medium-low speed for 10 minutes, periodically using a bowl scraper to incorporate everything on the sides of the bowl back into the dough. Cover with a kitchen towel and let rest for 5 to 6 minutes. Continue to knead for 7 to 10 minutes; the dough should look smooth and shiny at this point and no longer stick to the sides of the bowl. To make sure it is fully kneaded, perform a windowpane test (see page 73). If it is not ready at this point, continue to knead and rest periodically until it is ready. Once the dough is fully kneaded, add the chocolate chips and continue to knead just until fully incorporated.

Turn the dough out onto a clean work surface. Slap and fold (see page 21) the dough 5 to 7 times, until smooth. Round the dough (see page 22) and place in the bowl with the open edge down. Cover with plastic wrap. Let rest 10 to 15 minutes at room temperature and then in the fridge overnight. (If you are short on time, you can keep the dough at room temperature for 30 to 45 minutes, and then in the fridge for 2 to 4 hours, until doubled in size.)

continued

continued

Chocolate Buns with Caramel Cream

The next day, transfer the dough to a work surface and roll into a log. Using a sharp knife or bench scraper, divide into 16 equal portions. Round each piece of dough into a smooth ball (see page 22). Line two baking sheets with parchment paper and place the dough balls evenly across both. Use your palm to flatten each piece of dough. Loosely cover with plastic wrap and a kitchen towel and let rest at room temperature until doubled in size, 60 to 75 minutes.

Preheat the oven to 350°F.

Brush the top of each bun with the egg wash.

Bake to an internal temperature of 190°F, 18 to 22 minutes. Remove from the oven and transfer to a rack to cool completely.

Meanwhile, make the caramel cream: In a medium bowl, mix together the mascarpone and caramel until well combined. In a stand mixer fitted with the whisk (or in a medium bowl with a hand mixer), whisk heavy cream and powdered sugar until soft peaks are formed. Gently fold the whipped cream into the mascarpone mixture along with the vanilla and salt. Be careful not to stir or the mixture will lose its stability. Refrigerate for at least 30 minutes and remove just before use.

To finish: Using a sharp knife, slice 1 inch off the tops of the buns. Gently remove some of the inside of each bun or press firmly to create an indent. Add ½ tablespoon of the hazelnut-chocolate spread to each bun and line with butterscotch chips. Fill a piping bag fitted with a ½-inch star tip with the caramel cream. Carefully pipe a layer of cream onto each bun. Cover with the tops of the buns. Dust with cocoa before serving.

Notes

♥ This dessert is similar to the Swedish semlor. This is my chocolate version with hazelnut-chocolate spread, but you can substitute nuts and an almond butter cream or a filling of your choice for the hazelnut-chocolate.

♥ The unfilled buns can be stored in an airtight bag at room temperature for up to 3 days or in the freezer for 2 to 3 months. To serve, place in a 350°F oven for 5 to 7 minutes. If you don't want to fill them, the buns are also delicious just with butter or marmalade.

Bienenstich (German Bee Sting Cake)

*Makes 2 cakes
(8 servings each)*

This delightfully sweet cake comes straight from Germany, and its history is as charming as its taste. Legend has it that the cake was named in the fifteenth century when apprentice bakers thwarted an enemy attack from a neighboring town by hurling beehives at the invaders. In celebration of this clever victory, the townsfolk created this delicious dessert. Imagine a giant sweet bun, topped with crispy, caramelized honey and almonds, and filled with a cloud-like cream that takes each bite to a whole new level of deliciousness. For this recipe, I use a mascarpone cream, but you could also substitute a pastry cream (see page 222). This is Bienenstich—this is your ticket to a sweet celebration above the clouds. Trust me, this is a dessert you won't want to miss.

DOUGH

2¼ teaspoons (7g) instant (quick-rise) yeast

½ cup (110g) warm milk (110°F)

¼ cup (50g) granulated sugar

2½ cups (325g) bread flour, plus more for dusting

¼ teaspoon (2g) kosher salt

2 large eggs

1 teaspoon (5g) vanilla extract

6 tablespoons (3 oz/86g) unsalted butter, at room temperature

ALMOND TOPPING

6 tablespoons unsalted butter, sliced

¼ cup granulated sugar

2 generous tablespoons heavy cream

Pinch of kosher salt

2 tablespoons honey

1 heaping cup sliced almonds

MASCARPONE CREAM

1 cup creamy high-quality mascarpone, cold

1 cup powdered sugar

1 teaspoon vanilla extract or vanilla bean paste

2 cups heavy cream, well chilled

1 teaspoon grated orange zest

3 tablespoons chopped white chocolate

Make the dough: In the bowl of a stand mixer, whisk together the yeast, warm milk, and 1 teaspoon of the sugar. Let rest for 3 to 5 minutes. Add the flour, remaining sugar, the salt, eggs, and vanilla. Snap on the dough hook and knead on low speed for 4 to 5 minutes, until well combined. Cover with a kitchen towel and let rest for 8 to 10 minutes.

Using your hands, make a hole in the middle of the dough. Add the butter and close the dough over it. Knead the dough on medium-low speed for 10 minutes, periodically using a bowl scraper to incorporate everything on the sides of the bowl back into the dough. Cover with a kitchen towel and let rest for 5 to 6 minutes. Continue to knead for 8 to 10 minutes; the dough should look smooth and shiny at this point and no longer stick to the sides of the bowl. To make sure it is fully kneaded, perform the windowpane test (see page 73). If it is not ready at this point, continue to knead and rest periodically until it is ready.

Lightly grease a large bowl and set aside. Very lightly flour a work surface. Slap and fold (see page 21) the dough 5 to 7 times, until smooth. Round the dough (see page 22) and place in the prepared bowl with the open edge down. Cover with plastic wrap and let sit at room temperature for 5 to 10 minutes, then transfer the dough to the refrigerator and let rest overnight. (Alternatively, you can let it rest at

continued

continued

Bienenstich (German Bee Sting Cake)

room temperature for 25 to 35 minutes and then 1 to 3 hours in the fridge, until doubled in size.)

The next day, lightly flour a work surface. Use a bowl scraper to gently release the dough from the bowl, then transfer the dough to the prepared surface. Divide the dough into 2 equal portions (see Notes). Make a quick ball with each piece of dough by gathering the edges and pinching them together, being sure not to squish the air from the dough.

Line two 8-inch springform pans with parchment paper along the sides and bottoms. Using a rolling pin, roll one ball of dough into an 8-inch round and then carefully transfer it to one of the springforms. Press gently to make sure the dough covers the entire bottom of the pan. Repeat with the other piece of dough in the second pan. Cover with plastic wrap and let rest for 30 to 40 minutes at room temperature.

Meanwhile, make the almond topping: In a medium saucepan, melt the butter over medium heat. Add the sugar and heavy cream and cook, stirring with a wooden spoon, just long enough for the mixture to come to a boil. Add the salt and honey and continue to stir and cook for another 15 to 20 seconds, until everything is just incorporated. Add the sliced almonds and stir until fully coated with the mixture. Remove from the heat and let cool to room temperature.

Preheat the oven to 350°F.

Divide the almond topping evenly. Using a spoon, gently spread one half of the almond topping all

over the top of one piece of dough. Taking care not to squish the air out of the dough, use your fingers as needed to separate the almonds from each other and cover the top evenly. Repeat with the rest of the almond mixture and the other piece of dough.

Bake the cakes until deeply golden brown, 27 to 30 minutes, or to an internal temperature of 195°F If the top begins to brown too quickly, tent with a piece of alumnium foil.

Set the cakes on cooling racks and let rest for 15 to 20 minutes before opening the pans and removing the parchment paper. Let cool completely.

Meanwhile, make the mascarpone cream: In a large bowl, with an electric mixer whisk the mascarpone for 20 to 30 seconds, until creamy. Add the powdered sugar and continue to whisk for 30 to 40 seconds, until incorporated. Add the vanilla and heavy cream. Starting on low speed, mix for 1 minute until incorporated, then increase the speed to medium and beat until soft peaks form. Using a spatula, fold in the orange zest and white chocolate. Store in the fridge until ready to use.

Once the cakes have cooled completely, use a sharp bread knife to slice each one horizontally in half. Accomplish this by stabilizing the cake with one hand; with the other hand, insert the bread knife at the halfway point on the side of the cake. Using a gentle sawing motion, periodically turn the cake until you have cut all the way through. Repeat with the second cake.

Transfer half of the cream to a piping bag fitted with a ½-inch round tip. Pipe 1-inch circles evenly over the bottom halves of the cakes. Before replacing the top, use a sharp bread knife to cut each into 8 even wedges. Precutting them will ensure the cream does not squeeze out when slicing the cake. Arrange the wedges over the cream to make a perfect round once again. Slice each piece through to the bottom of the cake and serve immediately.

Notes

❦ *This recipe makes two desserts. If you prefer one, you can either halve the ingredients or make the full portion of enriched dough and then use one half for another recipe, such as cinnamon rolls, sweet buns, or babka.*

❦ *This cake is best served the same day it is prepared but also makes delicious leftovers. If you cannot finish it all in a day, you can cover with plastic wrap and store in the fridge for up to 3 days.*

Vegan Hazelnut-Chocolate Star Bread

Makes one 13-inch star bread

Here's a recipe for infinite happiness: a soft, velvety slice of bread smeared with homemade Nutella, accompanied by a warm cup of coffee on a rainy day. Add to that the scent of rain-drenched earth, the vibrant hues of autumn leaves, and a walk through quiet streets lined with homes emanating a warm glow. Now, blend all these elements into a single moment and invite your loved ones to share this delicious treat. Truly, what more do we need?

Vegan Brioche Dough (page 92)

Bread flour for dusting

⅔ cup Hazelnut-Chocolate Spread (recipe follows)

Egg wash: 1 egg beaten with ½ teaspoon neutral oil

Turbinado sugar (optional), for garnish

Powdered sugar, for serving

Notes

♥ *Instead of one large star bread, you can divide the brioche dough into 8 equal pieces and make two 7-inch star breads.*

♥ *You can also use half of the brioche dough for a 7-inch star bread and use the remaining brioche dough to make any sweet buns or another recipe.*

♥ *If you use store-bought chocolate-hazelnut spread, it will be a little sweeter than ours, so I recommend using only 2 tablespoons between the layers.*

Prepare the vegan brioche dough. Remove from the refrigerator when ready to use.

Place the dough on a lightly floured work surface. Roll the dough into a log and use a sharp knife or bench scraper to cut it into 4 equal portions. Round each piece of dough into a smooth ball (see page 22). Cover the dough with plastic wrap and let rest for 10 to 15 minutes.

Using a rolling pin, roll each ball into a 13-inch round. Cut a piece of parchment paper to the size of your baking sheet. Lay the first round of dough on the parchment paper and use an offset spatula to smooth 3 tablespoons of the hazelnut-chocolate spread evenly over the top. Add the next layer of dough and repeat the process until all the layers have been added, but do not spread the chocolate on top of the last piece of dough. Lightly place a 3-inch-diameter bowl upside down in the middle of the dough to mark the center. Using a pizza cutter, cut from the edge of the dough up to the bowl in 4 quarters. Then use the cutter to divide each of these sections into 4 so you have 16 equal pieces, all joined to the circle in the middle. Take two adjacent sections and twist them away from each other three times so they spiral in different directions. Pinch the ends of the two strands together firmly and repeat this process so you have a star with 8 twisted sections. If the ends begin to come apart, be sure to pinch them together once again.

Very carefully transfer the parchment paper to a baking sheet and cover loosely with plastic wrap. Let rest until almost doubled in size, 1 to 1½ hours. The time will vary based on how long you had the dough in the fridge.

continued

continued

Vegan Hazelnut-Chocolate Star Bread

Preheat the oven to 350°F.

Brush the top of the bread with the egg wash. If desired, sprinkle with turbinado sugar.

Bake until golden brown and the internal temperature reaches 195°F, 25 to 30 minutes.

If the top begins to brown too quickly, tent with a piece of aluminum foil.

Place the pan on a rack and let cool for 45 minutes to 1 hour. Dust with powdered sugar before serving.

Hazelnut-Chocolate Spread

Makes 1½ cups

2 cups skin-on hazelnuts

½ cup skin-on almonds

1 cup powdered sugar

¼ cup Dutch-process cocoa powder

¼ cup semisweet chocolate chips

⅛ teaspoon kosher salt

1 teaspoon vanilla extract

1 teaspoon hazelnut or almond extract

¼ cup peanut or hazelnut oil

Preheat the oven to 380°F.

Place the hazelnuts and almonds on a baking sheet and roast until they are just lightly brown, 8 to 10 minutes.

Remove the nuts from the oven and let them cool. Transfer them to a clean kitchen towel and rub the nuts together in the kitchen towel until the skins come off. Place the nuts in a high-powered food processor or blender and blend them until they turn into a hazelnut/almond butter, 5 to 6 minutes.

Add the powdered sugar, cocoa powder, chocolate chips, salt, vanilla, and hazelnut extract and continue to blend for 2 to 3 minutes. While blending, slowly drizzle in the oil and continue to blend the mixture until smooth, 8 to 10 minutes. Transfer the mixture to a clean jar and let cool in the fridge for 10 minutes before using. Store in the fridge for 20 to 30 days.

Notes

♥ *After adding the cocoa powder and sugar, the spread will solidify, but don't worry and keep running the blender. Do not rush, it will become smooth after a while.*

♥ *The spread will be hot and liquidy after blending. Don't worry; just allow to cool before use.*

Buttermilk Dinner Rolls

Makes 20 to 22 rolls

One of the joys in life for me is watching my loved ones enjoy the food I prepare. I look forward to seeing their reactions, especially when I serve these soft, sometimes cheese-filled, dinner rolls every Thanksgiving and their eyes light up as they bite in. My friends and family have grown accustomed to my gaze, always curious about their culinary experience.

DOUGH

2¼ teaspoons (7g) instant (quick-rise) yeast

¼ cup (55g) warm water (110°F)

1½ tablespoons (19g) granulated sugar

1 cup (240g) buttermilk

3 large eggs

5 cups (650g) bread flour, plus more for dusting

1½ teaspoons (9g) kosher salt

1 stick (4 oz/113g) unsalted butter, at room temperature

Egg wash: 1 egg beaten with 1 teaspoon water

BUTTER TOPPING

3 tablespoons salted butter, melted

¼ teaspoon garlic salt

1 teaspoon minced fresh herbs of your choice, such as rosemary, oregano, thyme, or basil

Make the dough: In the bowl of a stand mixer, combine the yeast, water, and ½ teaspoon of the sugar. Stir and let rest for 5 to 7 minutes, until foamy. Add the buttermilk, eggs, flour, salt, and the remaining sugar. Snap on the dough hook and knead the dough on medium-low speed for 5 to 7 minutes, until it comes together. Cover with a kitchen towel and let rest for 8 to 10 minutes.

Using your hands, make a hole in the middle of the dough. Add the butter in the middle and close the dough over it. Knead the dough on medium-low speed for 10 minutes, periodically using a bowl scraper to incorporate everything on the sides of the bowl back into the dough. Cover with a kitchen towel and let rest for 5 to 6 minutes. Continue to knead for 7 to 10 minutes; the dough should look smooth and shiny at this point and no longer stick to the sides of the bowl. To make sure it is fully kneaded, perform a windowpane test (see page 73). If it is not ready at this point, continue to knead and rest periodically until it is ready.

Very lightly flour a work surface. Slap and fold (see page 21) the dough 5 to 7 times, until smooth. Round the dough (see page 22) and place in the bowl with the open edge down. Cover with plastic wrap. At this point, you can let the dough rise at room temperature for faster results or let the dough rest in the fridge for a richer taste. To prepare sooner, let the dough rest at room temperature until doubled in size, 50 minutes to 1 hour 15 minutes. Otherwise, let the dough rest at room temperature for 30 to 40 minutes and then in the fridge for at least 3 to 4 hours, until doubled in size, for best results.

continued

continued

Buttermilk Dinner Rolls

Once ready, transfer the dough to a work surface. Line two 10-inch cast-iron skillets or one 9 × 14-inch baking dish with parchment paper. Roll the dough into a log and use a sharp knife or bench scraper to cut it into 20 to 22 portions (50g to 55g each). Round each piece of dough into a smooth ball (see page 22). Place the dough balls in the two prepared skillets or the baking dish, leaving ½ inch between them. Cover the pans loosely with plastic wrap. Let rest at room temperature until almost doubled in size, 45 minutes to 1 hour for unrefrigerated dough or 1 hour to 1 hour 15 minutes for chilled dough.

Preheat the oven to 375°F.

Brush the buns with egg wash.

Bake until deeply golden brown, 20 to 25 minutes. If the tops are browning too quickly, you can tent a piece of aluminum foil over the top.

Meanwhile, make the butter topping: In a small bowl, stir together the melted butter, garlic salt, and fresh herbs.

When the buns come out of the oven, brush them immediately with the topping. Serve while warm.

Cheese-Filled Dinner Rolls

For a fun twist on regular dinner rolls, you can prepare this cheese-filled version! In a small bowl, mix ½ cup shredded Parmesan cheese, 1½ cups shredded mozzarella or white cheddar cheese, and ⅔ cup farmer cheese or cream cheese. After shaping the dough into balls, use your hands to lightly press the dough into a 2½- to 3-inch round. Place 1 tablespoon of the filling in the middle of each round and then close the dough around the cheese. Pinch the edges to make sure the dough is sealed. Place them in the prepared skillets or dish seam side down and follow the rest of the recipe as written.

Notes

♥ *You can prepare the dough 1 day before and refrigerate overnight. After the dough is fully kneaded, place it in a large bowl, cover with plastic wrap, and let rest at room temperature for 10 to 15 minutes before transferring to the fridge to rest overnight. After shaping the rolls, let rest 1½ to 2 hours to double in size before baking.*

♥ *Once the rolls have cooled to room temperature, you can store them in an airtight storage bag at room temperature for 1 to 2 days or in the freezer for 2 to 3 months. To serve, let come to room temperature and preheat the oven to 350°F. Cover the rolls with aluminum foil and bake for 5 to 10 minutes, checking periodically after 5 minutes to make sure they are soft and warm but not overbaked.*

Potato Buns

Makes 10 hot dog or burger buns

While introducing my little one to solid food, I used to share small bites and flavors of whatever was on my plate. One day, fresh out of the oven, we both tasted these warm potato buns. His little face lit up after every bite, eagerly clamoring for more. To this day, this remains his favorite bread, a staple in his lunch boxes. When it's hot from the oven, you'll find it hard to resist. This versatile dough can be used for sandwich bread, hot dog buns, or burger buns. In fact, feel free to divide the dough and make some of each!

2¼ teaspoons (7g) instant (quick-rise) yeast

½ cup (110g) warm whole milk (110°F)

1 tablespoon plus 1 teaspoon (17g) granulated sugar

¼ cup (55g) water, at room temperature (75° to 80°F)

1 large egg

3¼ cups (423g) bread flour, plus more if needed

1½ teaspoons (9g) kosher salt

½ cup (100g) mashed potatoes (see Notes, page 114)

4 tablespoons (2 oz/56g) unsalted butter, at room temperature

Egg wash: 1 egg beaten with 1 teaspoon water

1 tablespoon unsalted butter, melted, for topping

In the bowl of a stand mixer, stir together the yeast, milk, and 1 teaspoon of the sugar. Let rest for 5 to 7 minutes, until foamy. Add the water, egg, 3 cups (390g) of the flour, remaining sugar, and the salt. Snap on the dough hook and mix the dough on medium-low speed until just combined, 2 to 3 minutes. Cover with plastic wrap and let rest for 10 minutes. Add the mashed potatoes and knead on medium speed for 3 to 4 minutes, until combined.

Using your hands, make a hole in the middle of the dough. Add the butter in the middle and close the dough over it, then add the remaining ¼ cup flour on top. Knead the dough on medium-low speed for 10 minutes, periodically using a bowl scraper to incorporate everything on the sides of the bowl back into the dough. Cover with a kitchen towel and let rest for 5 to 6 minutes. Continue to knead for 7 to 10 minutes; the dough should look smooth and shiny at this point and no longer stick to the sides of the bowl. If it is sticking at this point, you can add an additional 1 to 1½ tablespoons of flour and continue to knead. Kneading should total 20 to 30 minutes.

Lightly oil a clean work surface (or spray with cooking spray) and transfer the dough onto it. Slap and fold (see page 21) the dough 5 to 7 times until smooth. The potato will make this dough even softer than most of our enriched doughs; it should be perfectly soft and smooth at this point. Round the dough (see page 22) and place in the bowl with the open edge down. Cover with plastic wrap and let rest at room temperature for 10 to 15 minutes and then in the fridge overnight. (Alternatively, you can rest

continued

continued

Potato Buns

it for 30 to 45 minutes at room temperature and then 2 to 3 hours in the fridge, until doubled in size.)

The next day, line two baking sheets with parchment paper. Place the dough on a lightly floured work surface. Roll the dough into a log and use a sharp knife or bench scraper to cut it into 10 equal portions (80g to 85g each). Round each piece of dough into a smooth ball (see page 22).

To shape hot dog buns: Transfer the dough balls to the prepared baking sheets. Cover with plastic wrap or a clean kitchen towel and let rest for 10 minutes. Working with one piece at a time, use your fingers to shape it into a 3 × 5-inch oval and then roll the dough into a log, starting with a long side. Beginning with the first piece of dough, roll lightly into a 5½-inch log, then transfer to a baking sheet. Repeat with the remaining dough pieces. Place 5 logs of dough on each baking sheet with ½ inch between them, which will allow the buns to touch lightly and create that beautiful tear between buns. Cover loosely with plastic wrap and let rest at room temperature until doubled in size, 1 to 1½ hours.

To shape hamburger buns: Transfer the dough balls to the prepared baking sheets at least 5 inches apart. Use your hands to flatten the tops gently. Cover loosely with plastic wrap and let rest at room temperature until doubled in size, 1 to 1½ hours.

To bake either shape: Preheat the oven to 375°F.

Brush each bun with the egg wash.

Bake until deeply golden brown, 20 to 25 minutes for the hot dog buns and 15 to 20 minutes for the hamburger buns.

Remove from the oven and brush the tops with the melted butter. Transfer to a cooling rack and let cool to room temperature.

Notes

♦ *To make mashed potatoes, peel 3 or 4 potatoes and cut into quarters. Place in a saucepan and fill with water so the potatoes are barely covered. Bring to a boil over medium heat and add 1 teaspoon salt and 1 tablespoon olive oil to avoid boiling over. Once boiling, reduce the heat to medium-low and cook for 10 to 12 minutes. Drain the water and cook the potatoes in the dry pan for 1 to 2 minutes over low heat, just until all remaining moisture is soaked up. Remove from the heat and let cool at room temperature. Using a sieve or masher, mash 1 or 2 of the potatoes until very smooth. I often boil 3 or 4 potatoes at a time and then use the leftover potatoes for potato salad or other dinner items.*

♦ *Of course, you can use your own mashed potato recipe as well! The perfect mashed potatoes will be very smooth and room temperature before use. Avoid hot or cold potatoes to get the perfect dough texture.*

♦ *Store any leftover buns in an airtight storage bag at room temperature for 4 to 5 days or in the freezer for 3 months. If frozen, let thaw at room temperature and then toast in a skillet before use.*

Hot Dogs with Crispy Shallots and Potato Chips

Serves 4

As someone who lived in Chicago for years without ever tasting a hot dog, I can safely say it was never high on my list of must-haves. But when it comes to my homemade hot dogs or freshly made ones from the farmers' market, I can't resist. One of my favorite ways to enjoy these hot dogs is with a zesty sauce, crispy shallots, and a generous handful of potato chips. It's an effortlessly delicious lunch you can whip up in no time!

CRISPY SHALLOTS AND POTATO CHIPS

2 large russet potatoes

Neutral oil, for deep-frying

5 to 6 medium shallots, sliced crosswise into ⅛-inch-thick slices

Salt and freshly ground black pepper

HOT DOG SAUCE

¼ cup ketchup

2 tablespoons barbecue sauce

3 tablespoons brine from dill pickles or pickled jalapeños

1 tablespoon apple cider vinegar

1 teaspoon sriracha

½ teaspoon garlic powder

½ teaspoon paprika

2 teaspoons honey

¼ teaspoon kosher salt

ASSEMBLY

4 all-beef hot dogs

4 Potato Buns for hot dogs (page 113), split open

Arugula, for serving

Pickled jalapeños, for serving

Yellow mustard, for serving

Fill a large bowl with ice and water. Wash the potatoes well and slice thinly on a mandoline. Add the potato slices to the ice water, submerge, and stir so the cold water reaches every slice. Let sit at room temperature for 30 minutes to 1 hour. (If you do not have time to soak in cold water, you can rinse and drain the potato slices in cold water 4 to 5 times before cooking.)

Line a large plate with paper towels. Drain the potatoes well and place on the paper towels. Dry very well and set aside.

Meanwhile, make the hot dog sauce: In a small bowl, stir together the ketchup, barbecue sauce, pickle brine, vinegar, sriracha, garlic powder, paprika, honey, and salt. Mix well and adjust seasonings to taste. Set aside.

Prepare the shallots: Line a plate with paper towels. Pour 2½ inches of oil into a medium saucepan and heat to 350°F over medium heat. Gently add the shallots to the hot oil. Fry, turning periodically, until lightly golden brown, 3 to 4 minutes. Remove to the paper towels with a straining spoon and salt immediately. Let rest for 10 minutes, until crispy.

Make the potato chips: Line a second plate with paper towels. Add additional oil to the same pan to bring it back to 2½ inches deep and bring the temperature back up to 350°F.

Once the oil is hot, add the potato slices and fry, turning periodically, until the chips are lightly golden brown, 4 to 5 minutes. Remove from the

continued

continued

Hot Dogs with Crispy Shallots and Potato Chips

oil with a straining spoon and place on the paper towels. Salt immediately and add pepper.

Assemble the dish: Using a sharp knife, score one side of the hot dogs in a crisscross pattern. Heat a grill pan or nonstick skillet over medium-high heat. Add the hot dogs to the hot pan and cook until caramelized and heated through, 1 to 2 minutes per side. Slice each potato bun through the top, being careful not to cut through to the bottom. Add the potato buns to the hot pan and toast the torn sides until golden brown.

Place a bun on each of four serving plates and add a grilled hot dog to each. Coat with the sauce and add arugula and jalapeños. Drizzle with mustard and top with fried shallots. Serve the freshly made potato chips on the side.

Notes

♦ *You can make fried shallots in the microwave! Add 1 cup neutral oil to a microwave-safe bowl. Add the sliced shallots and microwave for 8 to 9 minutes. After the first 5 minutes, stir periodically and check for doneness. Remove when lightly golden brown and drain on paper towels. Salt immediately. This is the easier way, but if you are also preparing potato chips, you can use the same oil for both.*

♦ *If your pot is not large enough to hold all the potato slices, you can fry them in two separate batches.*

Burger Buns

Makes 9 buns

If you're part of my social media family, you know I'm not a big fan of store-bought stuff and love making things at home from scratch, and one of the things I dislike buying the most is burger buns. Nothing brings me down more than serving a carefully prepared burger on a tasteless, stale store-bought bun. That's why I make my own, no matter what. While sometimes I enjoy a potato bun, this burger bun is my go-to. If you're after perfect homemade buns, then this recipe is what you've been waiting for. I'm pretty sure that once you try it, you won't want to buy from the store anymore.

2¼ teaspoons (7g) instant (quick-rise) yeast

½ cup (110g) warm whole milk (110°F)

2 tablespoons plus 1 teaspoon (30g) granulated sugar

¼ cup (55g) water, at room temperature

1 large egg

2½ cups plus 2 tablespoons (340g) bread flour, plus more for dusting

1¼ teaspoons (8g) kosher salt

5 tablespoons (2½ oz/70g) unsalted butter, at room temperature

Egg wash: 1 egg beaten with 1 teaspoon water

White and black sesame seeds (optional), for garnish

In the bowl of a stand mixer, combine the yeast, milk, and 1 teaspoon of the sugar. Stir and let rest for 5 to 7 minutes, until foamy. Add the water, egg, flour, salt, and the remaining sugar. Snap on the dough hook and knead the dough on low speed for 4 to 5 minutes, until well combined. Cover with a kitchen towel and let rest for 10 minutes.

Using your hands, make a hole in the middle of the dough. Add the butter in the middle and close the dough over it. Knead the dough on medium-low speed for 10 minutes, periodically using a bowl scraper to incorporate everything on the sides of the bowl back into the dough. Cover with a kitchen towel and let rest for 5 to 6 minutes. Continue to knead for 7 to 10 minutes; the dough should look smooth and shiny at this point and no longer stick to the sides of the bowl. To make sure it is fully kneaded, perform a windowpane test (see page 73). If it is not ready at this point, continue to knead and rest periodically until it is ready.

Very lightly flour a work surface. Slap and fold (see page 21) the dough 5 to 7 times, until smooth. Round the dough (see page 22) and place in a large bowl with the open edge down. Cover with plastic wrap and let rest at room temperature until doubled in size, 1 hour to 1 hour 15 minutes.

Roll the dough into a log and use a sharp knife or bench scraper to cut it into 9 equal portions (70g to 75g each). Line two baking sheets with parchment paper. Round each piece of dough into a smooth ball (see page 22). Place on the baking sheets and leave

continued

Burger Buns

at least 2 inches between them. Gently flatten each piece with your hands. Cover loosely with plastic wrap and let rest until doubled in size, 1 hour to 1 hour 15 minutes.

Preheat the oven to 375°F.

Brush each bun with the egg wash and sprinkle with sesame seeds, if desired.

Bake until golden brown, 14 to 18 minutes.

Let cool completely on a cooling rack. Serve with your favorite burger or sandwich.

Notes

♥ *You can prepare the dough 1 day before and refrigerate overnight. After the dough is fully kneaded and in a large bowl, cover with plastic wrap and let rest at room temperature for 5 to 10 minutes before transferring to the fridge to rest overnight. After shaping the pieces, let rest 1 to 1½ hours to double in size before baking.*

♥ *To make gourmet black buns, reduce the flour by 1 tablespoon (8g). Add 1 tablespoon (8g) activated charcoal to the flour mixture and follow the recipe. For the egg wash, use egg white only to avoid a yellow glaze on top.*

♥ *I prefer my burger buns to be a little smaller for flexibility with different sandwiches, so that is the size I've written in this recipe. If you prefer a very large bun, you can make each piece 80g to 90g or according to your preference.*

♥ *Store the baked buns in an airtight storage bag at room temperature for 2 to 3 days and slice and toast before serving. You can also store them in the freezer for 1 to 2 months. Before using, bring to room temperature, slice, and toast the buns.*

Fried Chicken Sandwiches with Burger Sauce

Serves 6

Everybody enjoys a fast-food treat now and then. And nothing screams comfort like a crispy fried chicken sandwich on a lazy Friday. But imagine preparing this in your own kitchen, with the ingredients you trust. I'm not advocating against the occasional takeout, but homemade is where my heart is. The key to the perfect fried chicken sandwich lies in marinating the chicken the day before and then patiently frying until it is crispy, tender, and dripping with flavor. Pile it up on a homemade bun, with a generous spread of your favorite sauce. I love adding slaw to my burgers for that pop of color.

BUTTERMILK-MARINATED CHICKEN

6 boneless, skinless chicken thighs

2 cups buttermilk

1 large egg

1½ teaspoons garlic powder

1½ teaspoons kosher salt

1½ teaspoons hot paprika

FLOUR DREDGE

2½ cups all-purpose flour

1 teaspoon baking powder

2 tablespoons hot paprika

2 tablespoons garlic powder

1 tablespoon onion powder

1½ teaspoons dried basil

1½ teaspoons dried oregano

1 teaspoon dried thyme

1 teaspoon celery salt

1 teaspoon freshly ground black pepper

1 teaspoon kosher salt, or more to taste

FRIED CHICKEN SANDWICHES

Neutral oil, for deep-frying

6 Burger Buns (page 119)

Burger Sauce (recipe follows)

6 large lettuce leaves

Red Cabbage Slaw (page 209)

Marinate the chicken: If the chicken thighs are more than ½ inch thick, use a meat tenderizer to pound them to the appropriate size. In a large bowl, mix the buttermilk, egg, garlic powder, salt, and hot paprika. Add the chicken thighs to the mixture and coat well. Cover the bowl with plastic wrap and let rest in the refrigerator for 3 to 4 hours or preferably overnight.

Make the flour dredge: In a large shallow bowl, combine the flour, baking powder, hot paprika, garlic powder, onion powder, basil, oregano, thyme, celery salt, pepper, and kosher salt.

Make the fried chicken: When ready to cook, one at a time, take a piece of chicken from the buttermilk mixture and dredge it in the flour. Use your hands or tongs to coat it well. Shake off the excess flour and transfer it to a rack. Repeat with remaining chicken pieces, making sure they don't touch each other on the rack.

Pour 2½ inches oil into a large pot and heat the oil to 350°F over medium heat. Line a cooking rack with paper towels and have nearby.

Gently add 2 pieces of chicken to the hot oil and fry until golden brown and crispy with an internal temperature of 165° to 170°F, 6 to 8 minutes on each side. Remove the thighs and place on the cooling rack. Test the oil temperature to make sure it stays right around 350°F for even cooking, adjusting

continued

continued

Fried Chicken Sandwiches with Burger Sauce

the heat if necessary. Repeat with the remaining chicken. Let the chicken thighs rest for 5 to 10 minutes before serving.

Assemble the sandwiches: Split the buns in half horizontally and lightly toast the insides. Spread burger sauce generously over each bun. Top with a lettuce leaf, red cabbage slaw, and hot fried chicken. Close with the top bun and serve immediately.

Notes

♥ *You can add dill pickle slices or pickled jalapeños for extra crunch or spice. You can also serve the slaw on the side.*

♥ *Raw chicken is the worst, so if you don't have a meat thermometer be sure to slice and check the inside of the chicken to make sure it is fully cooked.*

♥ *You can serve this recipe with crispy homemade chips (see Hot Dogs with Crispy Shallots and Potato Chips, page 115).*

Burger Sauce

Makes 1 cup

½ cup mayonnaise

¼ cup sriracha

¼ cup sour cream

1 small garlic clove, minced

2 tablespoons chopped dill pickles

1 tablespoon chopped pickled hot chiles

Kosher salt

In a small bowl, combine the mayo, sriracha, sour cream, garlic, dill pickles, and chile peppers. Taste for seasoning and add salt if desired. Transfer to a clean container and store in the fridge for up to 3 days.

QUICK BREADS & SHORT DOUGHS

Who says deliciousness needs to take time? Meet the quick breads and short doughs: your speedy route to baking success. Follow a few golden rules, and they'll never let you down! Perfect for those spur-of-the-moment cravings or unexpected guests, these recipes don't just save time, they're a crash course in baking wizardry. Marvel as baking soda or baking powder work their magic, raising doughs without hours of proofing. From zesty lemon loaves to flaky biscuits or sumptuous scones, these are the treats that make any hour a happy one. Remember: Baking doesn't have to be an all-day affair—sometimes, the fastest treats are the sweetest.

KEY TECHNIQUES

Pie and Tart Doughs

Compared to yeast-based doughs, pie and tart doughs are significantly simpler and less prone to error. There are, however, a few important points to pay attention to when preparing pie and tart dough.

The most crucial consideration is to keep the dough cold. All your ingredients must be thoroughly chilled before you start. The butter and water are especially important. Ensure your butter is very cold by cutting it into cubes and freezing it for a short time before starting the recipe. Also, make sure your water is cold by chilling it with plenty of ice. If the area where you're working is warm, chill the other ingredients you'll be using, like flour, eggs, and even your mixing bowl.

HAND METHOD

If your kitchen and hands are not overly warm, making pie dough by hand is my preferred method:

I. First, add the dry ingredients to a bowl and then add the cold cubed butter. Use your hands like a claw to cover the butter completely with flour and quickly crush it into large, flat pieces with your fingers.

2. Next, add the cold water and mix it into the dough, then gather the dough together and compress it. In some cases, part of the dough may come together nicely while the remaining portion may still look crumbly and dry. When this happens, move the ready part of the dough aside, add a small amount of cold water to the dry portion, and then combine all the dough. The dough should come together without falling apart and should NOT be sticky or wet. A wet dough is hard to work with and can result in a hard crust.

3. When you think the dough is ready, shape it into a ball and then press it into a 1-inch-thick disc. Wrap your dough tightly in plastic wrap and let rest in the refrigerator for at least 30 to 40 minutes. This resting period relaxes the gluten in the dough, preventing a harder-than-desired crust.

FOOD-PROCESSOR METHOD

During summer months when my house is warm, I often prepare the initial stage of my dough in a food processor to prevent transferring heat from my hands to the dough. It's important, however, to never run the food processor for too long. Instead, pulse the ingredients together to prevent overworking the dough, which can result in a tough crust. Once the butter is in large, chickpea-size pieces, transfer the mixture to a large piece of plastic wrap. If there are overly large pieces of butter, simply crush them between your thumb and forefinger. Then drizzle the cold water over the dough, tossing and pressing it together until it forms a cohesive mass. Once the dough is ready, form the dough into a disc, wrap it tightly in plastic wrap, and refrigerate it for at least 30 to 40 minutes.

If you're working in a very hot environment, you can perform the entire process in a food processor. This method requires more care than the others, but it can still work well if done correctly. Pulse the flour and butter a few times in the food processor, then add the cold water and pulse just a few more times until the dough is crumbly. Without waiting for it to completely combine, transfer the mixture to a counter covered with plastic wrap and use your hands to bring the mixture together and form it into a disc. Chill the dough in the refrigerator for at least 30 to 40 minutes or overnight.

After the dough has chilled, take it out of the refrigerator and let rest at room temperature for 4 to 5 minutes if it's been chilling for more than 3 hours. This makes it easier to roll out. Roll out the dough to the size specified in the recipe.

LINING A PIE PLATE

Gently roll the rolled-out dough over the rolling pin to pick it up without misshaping it. Hold the rolling pin over the pie plate and, starting with the open edge of the dough over the edge of the dish, unroll the dough so it fills the dish and falls evenly over the edge. Using your fingers, push the dough into the bottom crevice of the pie plate. Trim off any excess dough around the edges and prick the bottom and sides of the dough with a fork to allow air to escape, preventing the dough from puffing up during baking.

Once your pie or tart base is ready, wrap it in plastic wrap and refrigerate it for at least 30 minutes before baking. This hardens the fat in the dough and helps prevent the crust from warping and shrinking during baking.

Once the dough is chilled, remove it from the refrigerator, line it with a piece of parchment paper larger than your plate, and fill it with pie weights or dried beans. This prevents the dough from puffing up during baking. Bake according to the instructions in your recipe.

TROUBLESHOOTING PIE DOUGH

Here are some common problems you may encounter while making pie dough, along with suggestions on how to fix them.

Dough Crumbles and Breaks During Rolling

If your dough is breaking and falling apart during rolling, it's too dry. While we never want our dough to be wet, an excessively dry dough will be difficult to work with. Add a bit more cold water and gently work it into the dough, just until it holds together.

Pie Crust Shrinks and Deforms During Baking

If your pie crust shrinks and deforms during baking, it means you haven't sufficiently chilled your dough after rolling it out. After rolling out the dough and shaping it in your pie dish, don't forget to cover the dish with plastic wrap and chill it in the refrigerator for at least 30 minutes before baking.

Dough Is Tough Instead of Flaky

If your crust turns out hard, you might have added too much water to your dough or overworked it. To prevent this, always add water in a controlled manner during the mixing process and avoid overworking the dough. Remember that different brands of flour absorb moisture differently, so adjust the amount of water you use based on your specific flour. Unlike other doughs, pie dough should not be kneaded heavily.

Note

❧ *Remember that pie dough loves a hot oven, so preheat your oven sufficiently before placing your pie or tart in it. Ensuring the oven is hot when the pie goes in will help set the crust quickly, leading to a flakier and more tender result.*

Quick Breads, Biscuits, and Scones

Now we are getting into my personal favorite category of baked goods: quick breads, biscuits, and scones. These dough types are wonderfully easy to prepare and don't come with many strict rules. They are quick to make and incredibly tasty, even in their simplest forms.

Here are some key points to remember when making biscuits and scones:

Chill your ingredients: As with pie dough, it's crucial to make sure that your ingredients are cold when making biscuits and scones. Prepare your butter ahead of time by cutting it into pieces and placing it in the freezer for 5 to 10 minutes while you prepare your other ingredients. All other liquid ingredients you use (such as buttermilk, heavy cream, or sour cream) should also be chilled.

Don't overmix: Mix your dry ingredients in a suitable bowl, and then use a pastry cutter or a fork to cut the butter into chickpea-size pieces in the flour mixture, making sure that the butter is evenly distributed. Then add your liquid ingredients to the flour-butter mixture. Use a wooden spoon or fork to mix everything until just combined. Avoid overmixing, which can lead to a tough end result.

Handle with care: Transfer the dough to a clean countertop. Using your hands, shape the dough into a ball. Do not knead it—just press and assemble. Flatten the dough with your hand until it's about 1 inch thick. Then, using a bench scraper or a knife, divide the dough into 4 equal pieces. Stack these pieces on top of one another, press them down with your hand, and flatten them out to a thickness of 2 inches. (Alternatively, you can also fold the dough in thirds, like a letter, and then press it down to a thickness of 2 inches.) This lamination process is an important step in making biscuits or scones and is key to creating quick breads with flaky, perfect layers.

Chill before shaping: Allow the dough to rest in the refrigerator for a few more minutes before shaping your breads.

Bake in a hot oven: Shape your breads according to the recipe instructions and bake in a preheated hot oven for best results.

In short, making delicious biscuits and scones involves careful handling of the dough, maintaining a delicate balance of ingredients, and ensuring the right cooking conditions. With these tips in mind, you'll be on your way to creating baked goods that are sure to impress.

Basic Pie Dough with Variations

*Makes enough for two
9-inch pie crusts*

Don't be intimidated by the thought of making pie dough—it's truly not as daunting as it may seem. The key to a perfect pie dough lies in the details. Keeping the ingredients cold, adding water gradually, and handling the dough gently are critical. Equally important is letting the dough cool after each stage, a step that ensures flaky layers.

The recipe I'm sharing with you is my all-purpose pie dough, tried and true, used in both savory and sweet recipes for many years. Its versatility and reliability make it a staple in my kitchen. I'm confident that once you've given it a shot, this recipe will become your go-to for pie dough. Get ready to impress yourself!

2 sticks (8 oz/226g) cold butter, cut into ½-inch cubes

½ cup (110g) cold water, plus more if needed

2½ cups (325g) all-purpose flour, plus more for dusting

½ teaspoon (2g) granulated sugar

¼ teaspoon (2g) kosher salt

½ teaspoon (2g) cold apple cider vinegar

Place the cubed butter in the freezer for 5 to 10 minutes before using. Place ice cubes in the cold water.

In a food processor, combine the flour, sugar, and salt. Add the cubes of cold butter and pulse 8 to 10 times until the butter is coated with the flour mixture and forms large chickpea-size pieces.

Line a work surface with a large piece of plastic wrap and transfer the dough to it. Squeeze any too-large pieces of butter between your thumb and pointer finger to press them into the flour mixture. In a small bowl, mix the vinegar and ½ cup cold water. Drizzle the vinegar mixture over the top of the dough. Using your hands, toss the mixture together until the liquid has been incorporated. Gather and press the dough together until it comes together. At this point there may be parts that are still dry and crumbly. Set aside the parts of the dough that are fully hydrated and drizzle up to ½ tablespoon of cold water over the dry parts. Continue to press and gather the dough pieces until no longer crumbly. Avoid kneading or overhandling the dough. Combine all the dough, shape into a ball, and then flatten into a disc. At this point the dough should not be crumbly or cracked but should not feel wet. Using a sharp knife or bench scraper, cut the disc into 2 equal portions. Use your hands to quickly shape the 2 pieces into balls and then press each into a 6-inch round. Cover each tightly with plastic wrap and refrigerate for at least 30 to 40 minutes or overnight.

Once it is fully chilled, remove the dough from the fridge and let sit for 3 to 5 minutes, until a little bit softened to allow for easy rolling. Lightly flour a work surface and roll one portion into a 12 to 13-inch round, about ⅛-inch thick, or around 3 inches wider than your pie plate as measured across the top. Carefully move the dough to the pie plate, and press it in gently to line the plate (see page 127) and trim the dough as close to the edges of your pan as you can. Using a fork, pierce holes 1 to 1½ inches apart around the sides and bottom of the crust. Cover with plastic wrap and place in the fridge for at least 30 minutes. Remove from the fridge and proceed according to your pie recipe.

Sweet Pie Dough

To make dough for a sweet pie, increase the sugar to 1 teaspoon (4g) and reduce the salt to a pinch (1g). Follow the rest of the instructions as written. To amp up the flavor, you can also add flavoring extracts (½ teaspoon), citrus zest (1 teaspoon), or ground spices (¼ teaspoon) to the ingredients in the food processor step. One of my favorite versions is to add fresh mint leaves; I find it goes perfectly with berry pies.

Savory Pie Dough

To make pie dough for a savory filling, increase the salt to ¾ teaspoon (5g) and add ½ teaspoon (2g) garlic powder and 1 teaspoon fresh herbs (rosemary, basil, or thyme) in the food processor step.

Note

♥ *The dough can keep in the fridge for up to 2 days or in the freezer for up to 2 months before use. If the dough is frozen, thaw in the fridge overnight before baking with your favorite recipe.*

Rough Puff Pastry

Makes 1 ready-to-use block

My teenage fascination with pastry began with store-bought puff pastry. It was the simplest yet tastiest ingredient for making desserts. I loved preparing a mille-feuille–inspired dessert with a quick pastry cream sandwiched between two layers of crispy puff pastry and topped with sliced strawberries. My father—my childhood hero—was particularly fond of this family favorite. Years later, when he visited me in Chicago, I served the same dessert made with my homemade puff pastry. My father, a man of deep emotions, was moved to tears, reminiscing about the sweet past. To this day, I still whip up this dessert with my homemade puff pastry. While a bit of a process, the result is magical and addictive. I promise you it's not as complicated as it sounds.

1½ sticks (6 oz/170g) cold unsalted butter, unsliced

1½ cups (195g) all-purpose flour, plus more for dusting

1½ tablespoons (19g) granulated sugar

½ teaspoon (3g) kosher salt

¼ cup (55g) cold water, plus more if needed

¼ teaspoon (2g) cold distilled white vinegar

Cut 6 tablespoons of the butter into cubes and place on a cold plate. Grate the remaining 6-tablespoon block of butter onto a separate cold plate. Transfer both to the freezer to chill for 10 to 20 minutes.

In a medium bowl, combine the flour, sugar, and salt and mix well. Place the flour bowl in the fridge to chill for 10 to 20 minutes. Before removing the butter, add the cold water and a few ice cubes to a small bowl.

Once everything is nice and cold, remove the ingredients from the fridge and freezer. To the flour bowl, add the grated butter. Using your hands or a wooden spoon, quickly toss to cover the butter with flour. Add the cubed butter and quickly toss to incorporate the butter. Smush each butter cube between your thumb and forefinger, but do not hold long enough to let the butter melt. Measure out ¼ cup of the ice water and mix in the vinegar. Add to the flour mixture and give it a quick mix.

Transfer the dough to a work surface. Using your hands, bring the dough together and press to combine well. Some of the dough may not come together at this point—remove the properly hydrated dough and drizzle a small amount of water (1 to 3 teaspoons) the dry parts. Continue to press to combine and then bring all the dough back together once ready. It should still look a little bit dry but not too crumbly. Transfer the dough to a piece of plastic wrap and press the dough into a 4 × 5-inch rectangle and cover with plastic wrap. Once in the plastic wrap, you can continue to press the edges of the dough together using your hands and a bench scraper. Place in the fridge and let rest for 2 hours.

Remove the dough from the fridge and let rest for 2 to 3 minutes at room temperature. Unwrap the dough and place on a lightly floured work surface. Using a rolling pin, hit the dough several times evenly over the top of the dough. Some parts of the dough will crack at this point; use your hands and a bench scraper to bring the dough back together. Roll the dough into a 6 × 10-inch rectangle, continuing to press the dough back together at the cracks. It will be a little dry and a little hard to roll at this point—use a bench scraper to help you gather and straighten the edges as you roll. With a short side of the rectangle facing you, fold the top and bottom thirds of the dough to the middle. It will still be a little dry and not a perfect shape, but just do your best. Cover with plastic wrap, place in the fridge, and let rest for 30 to 40 minutes.

Remove the dough from the fridge, unwrap, and once again hit the dough across the top with a rolling pin, pressing the dough back together with your hands at the cracks. Roll the dough into a 6 × 12-inch rectangle, again using the bench scraper as necessary to straighten the edges and press together the cracks. Repeat the folding process. Cover with plastic wrap and refrigerate again for 30 to 40 minutes. Repeat this rolling, folding, and cooling process two more times. On the third fold, the dough should begin to look much more smooth and more similar to store-bought puff pastry dough, though you should still be able to see spots of butter. After completing the final fold, cover the dough with plastic wrap and let rest in the fridge for at least 3 hours or overnight.

This is your basic puff pastry, ready to use like store-bought for any recipe. Keep it in the fridge for up to 2 days or in the freezer for up to 3 months. If frozen, place in the fridge overnight before use.

Food Processor Rough Puff

You can also make a delicious puff pastry using a food processor, which I sometimes prefer in the summer when my home is very warm. Though it'll be much easier, the food processor will cut the butter smaller and affect the texture slightly. Cut all the butter into large cubes, place on a plate, and chill in the freezer for 1 hour. In a medium bowl, combine the flour, sugar, and salt and chill in the fridge. About 10 to 15 minutes before making the dough, add the cold water and a few ice cubes to a small bowl. Once everything is nice and cold, add the flour mixture and half of the cubed butter to a food processor. Pulse for 1 second at a time, 8 to 10 times. Add ¼ cup of the cold water, cold vinegar, and remaining butter and again pulse for 1 second at a time, 8 to 15 times. Transfer the dough to a piece of plastic wrap, smushing any too-large pieces of butter between your thumb and forefinger. Follow the process for bringing the dough together, rolling, folding, and cooling as directed in the main recipe.

Apple Pie with Easy Vanilla Mascarpone Ice Cream

Makes one 9-inch pie

Let's be honest, as someone who just can't get enough of good food, my all-time favorite American holiday has got to be Thanksgiving. Imagine the crisp fall air, the gorgeous leaves changing colors, and every house warming up with delicious smells from the kitchen. It's like stepping into a food lover's dream even as I'm sitting here writing on a rainy day in May.

The prep work starts a day early, beginning with the pie dough. On the big day itself, after a leisurely walk around the neighborhood, I get right to it with the apple pie. It needs a little time to cool, so it's always first up on my cooking schedule. I've always believed that a good meal should end on a sweet note. That's where my apple pie really shines. It has consistently been the star of our Thanksgiving meal, year after year.

I'm sure you've got your own special family recipes that have been handed down through the generations. But I encourage you to give my apple pie a try. With a flaky pie crust and the yummy apple filling, it's a taste that's hard to beat. Serve it with some homemade ice cream and trust me, it'll be the hit of your dinner table.

Basic Pie Dough (page 130)

APPLE FILLING

4 medium Granny Smith apples, peeled and cubed

4 medium Gala apples, peeled and cubed

1½ teaspoons fresh lemon juice

2 tablespoons orange juice

½ cup granulated sugar

½ cup packed light brown sugar

¼ teaspoon kosher salt

4 tablespoons salted butter

1½ tablespoons cornstarch

2 tablespoons water

1½ teaspoons ground cinnamon

1 teaspoon pumpkin pie spice

1 teaspoon grated orange zest

1 teaspoon vanilla extract

ASSEMBLY

Egg wash: 1 egg beaten with 1 teaspoon water

2 tablespoons turbinado sugar, for topping

Easy Vanilla Mascarpone Ice Cream (recipe follows), for serving

Prepare the pie dough as directed. When dividing the dough, split the dough 60/40 so the dough disc for the bottom will be a little larger than the dough for the top. Cover with plastic wrap and refrigerate until well chilled.

Make the apple filling: In a large bowl, combine the apple cubes, lemon juice, orange juice, granulated sugar, brown sugar, and salt. Using your hands or a wooden spoon, toss to combine.

In a large cast-iron skillet or nonstick pan, melt the butter over medium heat. Add the apple mixture and cook, stirring constantly, until the apples are slightly softened, 5 to 7 minutes.

In a small bowl, stir together the cornstarch and water and mix until the cornstarch dissolves. Add the cornstarch mixture to the apple mixture and cook, stirring constantly, until the mixture has

continued

continued

Apple Pie with Easy Vanilla Mascarpone Ice Cream

thickened slightly, 1 to 2 minutes. Remove from the heat and stir in the cinnamon, pumpkin pie spice, orange zest, and vanilla. Set aside and let cool completely.

Preheat the oven to 400°F.

Assemble and bake: Once the dough is fully chilled, remove the pie dough from the fridge and let sit for 3 to 5 minutes, until a little softened to allow for easy rolling. Lightly flour a work surface and roll the larger dough disc into a 12- to 13-inch round, about ⅛-inch thick and around 3 inches bigger than your pie plate's diameter across the top. Line a 9-inch pie plate (see page 127) and trim the dough as close to the edge of your pie plate as you can. Cover with plastic wrap and place in the fridge for 15 to 25 minutes.

Using a rolling pin, roll the other dough disc into a 10-inch round. Cut the dough into 12 strips ¾ inch wide and chill in the fridge for 5 to 10 minutes before shaping. Remove the pie plate from the fridge and add the room temperature filling to the pie crust and spread evenly with an offset spatula. Remove the pie strips from the freezer and form the lattice for the top of the pie. First, lay 6 strips evenly spaced horizontally over the filling. Fold back every other strip and lay one strip vertically across the dish. Lay the horizontal strips back in place and fold back the other set of horizontal strips, using the pieces that were not folded back the first time. Lay a second vertical strip. Repeat this process until all

strips have been woven. Leaving ½ inch of dough hanging over the edge of the pie plate, cut the excess from the strips. Using your fingers, pinch the edges of the pie dough from the bottom to connect it with the top lattice. Brush the top of the pie with the egg wash. Sprinkle the top with the turbinado sugar.

Bake until golden brown, and the juices are bubbling, 45 to 55 minutes. If the top begins to brown too quickly, tent the top with aluminum foil.

Let the pie cool for at least 2 hours at room temperature. Serve with the ice cream.

Notes

♥ *If you serve the pie while warm, the pie will collapse a little, but it will still be delicious! Ideally, the pie should be baked far enough ahead that it can sit at room temperature for 5 to 6 hours to set fully before serving.*

♥ *The pie will be most delicious if eaten all in one day. If necessary, you can cover the pie with plastic wrap and store on the countertop or in the fridge for 1 to 2 days.*

♥ *You can also serve this apple pie with vanilla sauce (see page 89).*

Easy Vanilla Mascarpone Ice Cream

Serves 4 to 6

½ cup cold mascarpone cheese

4 ounces cream cheese, at room temperature

1 (14-ounce) can sweetened condensed milk

1 vanilla bean, split and scraped, 1 teaspoon vanilla bean paste, or 1½ teaspoons vanilla extract

2 cups cold heavy cream

Put a loaf pan or similar-size glass storage container in the freezer.

In a medium bowl, combine the mascarpone, cream cheese, condensed milk, and vanilla bean seeds. Mix, using a wooden spoon, until combined well.

In a large bowl with an electric mixer, whisk the heavy cream until soft peaks form. Fold the cream cheese mixture into the whipped cream until well combined.

Remove the loaf pan from the freezer and line with plastic wrap. Pour the mixture into the chilled loaf pan and freeze until solid, at least 3 to 4 hours or overnight. If frozen overnight, let sit at room temperature for 5 to 10 minutes before serving for easy scooping.

Notes

♥ *If you have an ice cream churn, you can use it for this recipe. Churn for 25 minutes or according to your machine's directions.*

♥ *You can use this ice cream for any dessert; we love to serve it as a replacement for the mascarpone cream in tiramisu.*

♥ *The ice cream will keep for up to 2 months in the freezer.*

Chocolate Tarts with Caramel or Raspberry Sauce

Makes two 6-inch tarts

I'm a savory person. If I were to choose dessert over a savory dish, it would have to be either chocolate or something creamy. But chocolate, particularly dark chocolate, is my first choice. I am enamored by the compatibility of chocolate with caramel, raspberry, and orange. My priority when creating desserts is to ensure they're not overly sweet, and my recipes reflect this. For this chocolate tart recipe, for example, I prepare the tart crust with less sugar than usual to balance the intense flavor of the caramel, creating perfect harmony. The raspberry version is ideal for those like me who prefer less sweetness. It's a versatile recipe that can be adjusted to anyone's taste at home by using two 6-inch tart pans and preparing two different versions.

DOUGH

1 cup (130g) all-purpose flour

¼ cup (30g) Dutch-process cocoa powder

¼ cup (25g) almond meal

⅓ cup (40g) powdered sugar

¼ teaspoon (2g) kosher salt

1 stick (4 oz/113g) cold unsalted butter

1 tablespoon (14g) cold water, plus more if needed

½ teaspoon (3g) vanilla extract

1 cold egg yolk

CHOCOLATE GANACHE

1½ cups heavy cream

2 cups semisweet chocolate chips

1½ teaspoons vanilla extract

CARAMEL TART

1 cup Caramel (recipe follows)

¼ cup chopped roasted hazelnuts (optional)

¼ cup white chocolate chips, melted (optional)

RASPBERRY TART

Raspberry Sauce (recipe follows)

4 ounces fresh raspberries, halved

¼ cup white chocolate chips, melted (optional)

Whole raspberries, for garnish

Make the dough: In a medium bowl, combine the flour, cocoa powder, almond meal, powdered sugar, and salt. Using a box grater, grate the cold butter into the dry ingredients. Caging your fingers, toss the butter into the flour mixture and pinch the butter pieces until they are the size of popcorn kernels. In a small bowl, whisk together the cold water, vanilla, and egg yolk. Pour the wet ingredients into the flour mixture and use your hands to fold and gently knead to combine until everything comes together. At this point, the tart dough should be about the consistency of Play-Doh—you can add 1 teaspoon additional cold water if needed to bring the mixture together. Use a bench scraper to divide the dough into 2 equal portions. Shape each into a rough ball. Place each ball on a piece of plastic wrap, flatten each into a 1-inch-thick disc, and wrap completely. Refrigerate for at least 30 minutes or up to 2 hours.

Place one disc of dough on a floured work surface. Using a rolling pin, roll the dough into an 8-inch round. Use a pastry brush to remove any excess flour from the crust. Gently roll the dough over the rolling pin and lift it over a 6 × 1-inch tart pan with a removable bottom. Unroll the dough into the shell and press the sides carefully into the tart pan without squishing the dough's thickness. Carefully

continued

continued

Chocolate Tarts with Caramel or Raspberry Sauce

press together any cracks that may appear. Cover the tart shell loosely with a 12-inch piece of aluminum foil and place in the fridge. Repeat with the second ball. Let rest for at least 30 minutes before baking.

Preheat the oven to 350°F.

Remove the tart shells from the fridge and use a sharp knife to trim any excess dough from the outside of the shell, pressing the flat of the knife against the top edge of the tart pan to cut perfectly around the rim. Using a fork, evenly pierce the bottom and sides of each shell, leaving ½ inch between the holes. Place the aluminum foil over the dough and fit it firmly to the sides and edges of the dough. Place the two covered tart shells on a baking sheet. Bake for 15 minutes and then remove the shells from the oven. Gently remove the foil and return the shells to the oven. Continue to bake for 9 to 10 additional minutes. Remove from the oven and let cool completely. Handle carefully, as they will still be fragile at this point. You will assemble and chill the tarts for serving while still in the pan.

Make the ganache: In a medium saucepan, heat the heavy cream over medium heat. Once it begins to foam and bubble, remove from the heat immediately—do not let it come to a boil. Add the chocolate, cover with a lid, and let sit for 2 to 3 minutes. Slowly begin to whisk the mixture until everything is well combined. Add the vanilla and continue to whisk until it is a smooth sauce, being careful to scrape the sides and bottom to fully incorporate all the chocolate. Let cool for at least 45 minutes to 1 hour until it's almost room temperature. (Alternatively, you can add the chocolate chips and heavy cream to a microwave-safe bowl and microwave in 30-second intervals,

stirring in between, until fully melted. Stir in the vanilla and let cool.)

To assemble the caramel tart: Spread ½ cup of caramel on the bottom of each tart shell. If desired, sprinkle each with 2 tablespoons of the chopped hazelnuts. Holding the saucepan of ganache close to the tart, divide the ganache between the tarts and use an offset spatula to spread it. Let cool in the fridge for at least 1 hour or overnight, making sure the ganache is set before serving. When serving, carefully remove the outside of the tart pan while keeping the bottom of the pan under the baked shell. Drizzle with the melted white chocolate, if desired, and slice before serving.

To assemble the raspberry tart: Spread ¼ cup of raspberry sauce on the bottom of each tart. Divide the raspberries between the tarts, setting them with the open edge of the raspberry facing down. Holding the saucepan of ganache close to the tart, divide the ganache between the tarts and use an offset spatula to spread it. Let cool in the fridge for at least 1 hour or overnight, making sure the ganache is set before serving. Drizzle with the melted white chocolate and garnish with additional fresh berries, if desired, and slice before serving.

Note

♥ *You can cover the leftovers with plastic wrap and keep in the fridge for up to 3 days—the tarts happen to get better every day!*

Caramel

Makes 1½ cups

1 cup granulated sugar

2 tablespoons unsalted butter

1 cup heavy cream

¼ teaspoon kosher salt

In a nonstick pan, heat the sugar over medium-low heat. Do not touch or stir the sugar, but keep an eye on it while it melts, 12 to 15 minutes. Once the sugar is completely melted and has browned to the color of caramel, add the butter, using a wooden spoon to incorporate. Once the butter is melted, remove from the heat and add the heavy cream. Stir for a few seconds. Return to the heat and cook until everything is well combined, 2 to 3 minutes. If the sugar is still not fully melted, reduce the heat to low and continue to cook until it is. Remove from the heat and stir in the salt. Transfer to a clean jar. Before using, allow to come to room temperature.

Notes

♥ *Store the caramel in a jar with a lid for 2 to 3 weeks in the fridge.*

♥ *If using this recipe for the caramel tart, you will have at least ½ cup left over. You can serve this with ice cream or any dessert of your choice.*

Raspberry Sauce

Makes ½ cup

6 ounces fresh raspberries

¼ cup granulated sugar

1 teaspoon fresh lemon juice

In a small saucepan, combine the raspberries, sugar, and lemon juice. Mash the raspberries with a wooden spoon and cook, stirring, over medium heat for 5 minutes. Reduce the heat to low and cook until thick and jammy, 5 to 7 additional minutes. Let cool before using.

Note

♥ *Store the raspberry sauce in a screw-top jar in the fridge for 4 to 7 days. Before using, allow to come to room temperature.*

Pumpkin Scones

Makes 8 scones

DOUGH

1 stick (4oz/113g) cold unsalted butter, unsliced

2¼ cups (293g) all-purpose flour, plus more for dusting

¼ cup (50g) packed light brown sugar

¼ cup (50g) granulated sugar

¼ teaspoon (1g) baking soda

2 teaspoons (8g) baking powder

¼ teaspoon (2g) kosher salt

1 teaspoon (3g) pumpkin pie spice

½ cup (113g) canned pumpkin puree

1 tablespoon (15g) buttermilk

1 large egg

½ tablespoon (8g) molasses

½ cup (90g) butterscotch chips

PUMPKIN ICING

1½ cups powdered sugar

2 tablespoons canned pumpkin puree

2 tablespoons unsalted butter, melted

¼ cup maple syrup

¼ teaspoon kosher salt

Throughout my culinary journey, baking scones and biscuits has been a joyous experience. They're simple to make and delightfully delicious. In fact, their flavor intensifies over time, making them the perfect pairing for autumn morning coffee.

Place the butter in the freezer to chill for 5 to 10 minutes before using.

Make the dough: In a large bowl, whisk together the flour, brown sugar, granulated sugar, baking soda, baking powder, salt, and pumpkin pie spice. In a medium bowl, whisk together the pumpkin puree, buttermilk, egg, and molasses. Coat the cold butter block with additional flour to allow for easy holding. Using the largest holes of a box grater, shred the cold butter into the flour mixture and stir with a fork just until combined. Add the pumpkin puree mixture to the flour mixture and add the butterscotch chips. Stir with a wooden spoon just to combine.

Set the dough on a lightly floured work surface. Use your hands to bring the dough together. Quickly press into a 6-inch round and then cut into quarters. Stack the quarters on top of one another and use your hands to press the dough into an 8-inch round. Cover with plastic wrap and let rest in the freezer for 5 to 10 minutes to chill. Preheat the oven to 400°F.

Line a baking sheet with parchment paper. Unwrap the dough and return to the work surface. Cut the dough round in half and then cut each half into 4 wedges, so you have 8 triangles. Transfer the scones to the baking sheet with at least 2 inches between them.

Bake until golden brown, 16 to 18 minutes.

Let cool completely on a cooling rack.

Make the pumpkin icing: In a small bowl, whisk together the powdered sugar, pumpkin puree, melted butter, maple syrup, and salt. Once the scones are fully cooled, cover the top of each with the icing. Let cool for 1 to 2 hours, until the icing is set.

Notes

♥ *The key to success here is making sure the butter is very cold and the dough is not overworked.*

♥ *If you want a fluffier, cakier texture, you can increase the buttermilk by 1 tablespoon.*

♥ *You can add 1 more tablespoon of pumpkin puree to the icing for a brighter color and more pumpkin flavor. This will make the icing just a little thinner as well.*

♥ *Store in an airtight storage bag at room temperature for 2 to 3 days or in the freezer for 1 to 3 months. To serve, place the scones in a cold oven and preheat to 350°F. Once it reaches temperature, the scones will be warm and ready. If frozen, let thaw at room temperature before warming.*

Vegan Lemon Blueberry Scones

Makes 6 scones

During the recipe testing period, these scones managed to secure straight A-pluses from everyone involved. The tantalizing glaze was the cherry on top, transforming these already moist and delectable treats into something truly special.

DOUGH

½ cup plus 1 tablespoon (135g) cold original soy milk, plus 2 tablespoons for brushing

2 teaspoons (10g) fresh lemon juice

2¼ cups (293g) all-purpose flour, plus more if needed

3½ tablespoons (45g) raw cane sugar

⅛ teaspoon (1g) kosher salt

1½ teaspoons (6g) baking powder

½ teaspoon (2g) baking soda

1½ teaspoons grated lemon zest

1 stick (4 oz/113g) cold vegan butter, cut into ½-inch cubes

1 cup (140g) fresh blueberries

1 tablespoon turbinado sugar, for sprinkling

BLUEBERRY GLAZE AND GARNISH

¼ cup fresh blueberries

1¼ cups powdered sugar

½ teaspoon lemon or vanilla extract

Melted white chocolate, for garnish

Make the dough: In a small bowl, whisk together ½ cup plus 1 tablespoon of the soy milk and the lemon juice and let rest for 7 to 10 minutes.

In a large bowl, mix together the flour, raw cane sugar, salt, baking powder, baking soda, and lemon zest. Add the vegan butter and use a pastry cutter to cut the ingredients together until you have chickpea-size pieces of butter. Add the soy milk mixture and use a wooden spoon to mix until well combined. Stir in the blueberries. If the dough is too wet, add 1 more tablespoon flour. Place the dough on a sheet of plastic wrap and use your hands and a bench scraper to press it into a 4 × 6-inch rectangle. Wrap up and refrigerate for 30 to 40 minutes.

Preheat the oven to 420°F. Line a work surface with parchment paper.

Place the dough on the parchment paper. Press the dough into a 5 × 8-inch rectangle. Use a knife to cut the dough in half lengthwise, then cut each half into 3 equal squares. Space the scones 2 inches apart. Place the parchment paper on a baking sheet. Brush the tops of the scones with the remaining 2 tablespoons soy milk and sprinkle with the turbinado sugar.

Bake until lightly golden brown, 17 to 22 minutes, and transfer to a rack to cool completely.

Meanwhile, make the blueberry glaze: Place the blueberries in a fine-mesh sieve set over a small bowl. Press hard with the back of a spoon until all the liquid has drained into the bowl. At this point, you should have 2 tablespoons of blueberry puree. Remove the sieve, add the powdered sugar and lemon extract to the blueberry puree, and mix well.

Once the scones are completely cool, spread the blueberry glaze over the top. Drizzle with melted white chocolate. Let rest for 20 to 30 minutes, until the glaze has solidified before serving.

Notes

♦ *If you do not plan on making the glaze, I recommend increasing the sugar in the dough by 1 tablespoon.*

♦ *Store the cooled scones before glazing in an airtight storage bag at room temperature for 3 days or in the freezer for up to 2 months. To serve, place the scones in a cold oven and preheat to 350°F. Once it reaches temperature, the scones will be warm and ready. If frozen, let thaw at room temperature before warming. Glaze before serving.*

Raspberry Key Lime Bars

Makes 9 bars

The combination of raspberry and lemon is as classic as the combination of chocolate and orange, as in my incredible Chocolate-Orange Rugelach (page 151). The flavors complement one another so beautifully, creating a taste sensation. In this recipe, a rich, buttery shortbread base underpins that harmony, resulting in a blend of flavors you must try. The shortbread is slightly thicker than usual, which perfectly balances the tartness of the lemon. And a special thanks to my amazing assistant, Beka, for this delightful recipe idea. Serve these with coffee or tea.

RASPBERRY SAUCE

12 ounces fresh raspberries

⅓ cup granulated sugar

1½ teaspoons fresh lemon juice

½ teaspoon raspberry extract (optional)

SHORTBREAD CRUST

10 tablespoons (5 oz/142g) unsalted butter, at room temperature, plus more for the pan

1¾ cups (227g) all-purpose flour

½ cup (60g) powdered sugar

1 teaspoon grated lime zest

Pinch of kosher salt

KEY LIME TOPPING

2¼ cups (450g) granulated sugar

1 tablespoon grated lemon zest

1½ teaspoons grated lime zest

⅓ cup (44g) all-purpose flour

1 tablespoon (9g) cornstarch

½ cup (110g) fresh lemon juice

¼ cup (55g) fresh key lime juice

½ teaspoon (3g) lemon extract, or more if desired

6 large eggs

Powdered sugar, for serving

Make the raspberry sauce: In a small saucepan, combine the raspberries, sugar, lemon juice, and raspberry extract (if using). Mash the raspberries with a wooden spoon or potato masher and cook over medium heat, stirring, for 4 to 5 minutes. Reduce the heat to medium-low and cook until it thickens enough to coat the back of a spoon, 6 to 9 minutes. Continue to check and stir periodically while cooking. The mixture will thicken further as it cools, so make sure to remove it from the heat once it reaches a jammy consistency. Remove from the heat and set aside to cool.

Make the shortbread crust: Preheat the oven to 350°F. Butter a 9-inch square baking dish and line with parchment paper, leaving an overhang on two sides of the dish.

In a stand mixer fitted with the paddle (or in a medium bowl), combine the flour, powdered sugar, lime zest, butter, and salt. Beat the mixture until combined well. Transfer the mixture to the prepared dish and evenly distribute and press down the dough with your hands. Then, using a flat-bottomed glass, firmly press the crust into the dish.

Bake until the crust is lightly golden brown, 14 to 16 minutes. Remove from the oven and let cool for 10 minutes. Leave the oven on.

Meanwhile, make the key lime topping: In a medium bowl, combine the granulated sugar, lemon zest, and lime zest. Using your fingers, rub the sugar into the zest to extract the oils. Add the flour and cornstarch and use your hand or a whisk

continued

continued

Raspberry Key Lime Bars

to mix everything together. Add the lemon juice, key lime juice, lemon extract, and eggs. Continue to whisk until the mixture is well combined. Once everything is mixed, there will be a foamy layer on top of the mixture. If you prefer, you can use a spoon to remove this layer to avoid a foamy appearance on top of the bars.

Spoon the raspberry sauce onto the cooled shortbread crust and use an offset spatula to spread the sauce evenly. To make sure the raspberry sauce is not disturbed, hold the bowl of key lime topping very close to the raspberry sauce and pour it slowly and gently over the top. You can also hold the back of a wooden spoon between the bowl and the raspberry sauce to slow the flow of key lime while pouring carefully.

Bake until the center of the key lime topping is almost set but still a touch wobbly, 32 to 37 minutes.

Let cool to room temperature, then move to the fridge and chill until the bars are fully set, at least 3 to 4 hours. Remove from the fridge and sprinkle with powdered sugar. Cut into 9 squares.

Notes

❦ *This shortbread crust can be used with any bar recipes. If you are not using it for a citrus bar, you can omit the lime zest and add 1 teaspoon vanilla extract.*

❦ *This is a thicker citrus bar with a high ratio of crust to filling—I love the thick shortbread crust; it adds a delicious texture and buttery flavor. If you want a thinner crust, you do not have to use all of the shortbread in the pan and can make cookies with the remaining dough (see Bonus Recipe! for shaping and baking directions).*

❦ *Store the leftovers in an airtight storage container or cover the baking dish with plastic wrap and keep in the fridge for 3 to 5 days.*

Bonus recipe!

SHORTBREAD COOKIES

To make shortbread cookies, make the dough for the shortbread crust but reduce the amount of flour to 1½ cups (195g). Pour the dough onto a piece of plastic wrap, shape it firmly into a 2-inch-diameter log, and wrap with the plastic wrap, twisting the ends well. Refrigerate for at least 3 to 4 hours or overnight. When ready to bake, preheat the oven to 350°F. Line a baking sheet with parchment paper. Remove the dough from the fridge. Beat 1 egg white in a small bowl. Brush all sides of the dough log with the egg white to coat evenly. Place ¼ cup finely crushed pistachios or cane sugar on a piece of plastic wrap or parchment paper. Roll the log in the pistachios or cane sugar and coat the outside evenly. Using a sharp knife, slice the log into ¼-inch-thick cookies. Place the cookies on the prepared baking sheet, leaving 1-inch between each. Bake for 10 to 12 minutes. Remove to a cooling rack to cool for 30 minutes before serving. You can also dip some of the shortbread in melted chocolate for a chocolate cookie version.

Chocolate-Orange Rugelach

Makes 24 large rugelach

Sometimes, the simplest gestures can be the most powerful expressions of love. Other times, you might present the most delicious, uniquely flavored cookies paired with a comforting cup of coffee. Just add a little note that says "I Love You" and let the sweetness of the moment express your sentiments. These chocolate-orange rugelach are a heartfelt way to show your loved ones how much they mean to you.

DOUGH

2 sticks (8 oz/226g) unsalted butter, cut into ½-inch cubes

8 ounces (226g) cream cheese, cut into ½-inch cubes

2¼ cups (293g) all-purpose flour, plus more for dusting

¼ cup (50g) granulated sugar

¼ teaspoon (2g) kosher salt

2 tablespoons (30g) cold full-fat sour cream

½ teaspoon (2g) cold apple cider vinegar

FILLING

⅔ cup semisweet chocolate chips

5 tablespoons unsalted butter

¼ cup Dutch-process cocoa powder

½ cup powdered sugar

½ teaspoon ground cinnamon

1 teaspoon grated orange zest

TO FINISH

Egg wash: 1 egg beaten with 1 teaspoon water

2 tablespoons turbinado sugar, for sprinkling

Make the dough: Place the cubes of butter and cream cheese in the freezer for 5 to 10 minutes. Fill a small bowl with water and ice cubes and set aside.

In a large food processor, pulse together the flour, granulated sugar, and salt. Add the cubes of cold butter, cream cheese, sour cream, and vinegar. Pulse 18 to 20 times, pausing for one second between each pulse, until the ingredients come together. It should still be crumbly at this time. Place the dough on a clean work surface. Dip your hands into the ice water and shake off excess liquid. Using your cold wet hands, bring the mixture together and squeeze and gather the dough repeatedly to shape into a ball. Rewet your hands once more if needed during this process if the dough continues to crumble and not come together. Using a sharp knife, divide the dough into 2 equal portions. Use your hands and a bench scraper to press each dough piece into an even 4 × 6-inch rectangle. Wrap each tightly with plastic wrap and refrigerate for at least 3 hours or overnight.

Make the filling: In a saucepan, combine the chocolate chips and butter and stir over medium-low heat until melted and fully combined. Remove from the heat and add the cocoa powder, powdered sugar, cinnamon, and orange zest. Using a silicone spatula or wooden spoon, stir the mixture until well combined. Set aside and let cool until spreadable, 15 to 20 minutes.

If the dough has been chilled overnight, remove from the fridge and let sit for 4 to 5 minutes before shaping. Flour a work surface. Using a rolling pin, roll one piece of dough into an 8 × 20-inch rectangle. If the edges crack, use your hands to press them together and continue to roll. Then use a sharp knife

continued

continued

Chocolate-Orange Rugelach

to trim ½ inch around the edges of the dough to make the rectangle perfectly straight. Using an offset spatula, spread half of the chocolate filling evenly over the top. If the filling is too thick to spread, microwave for 10 seconds to soften it slightly. With a long side of the rectangle facing you, use a pizza cutter or knife to slice the rectangle crosswise into 6 rectangles about 3 inches wide. Cut each small rectangle diagonally from corner to corner, so you have 2 equal triangles from each piece. Starting from the wide end of each triangle, roll tightly toward the point as you would a croissant. Repeat until each triangle is rolled. Repeat with the remaining dough and chocolate filling.

Preheat the oven to 350°F. Line two baking sheets with parchment paper.

Transfer the rugelach to the baking sheets with at least 2 inches between them, cover with plastic wrap, and keep in the fridge for at least 10 to 20 minutes while the oven preheats.

To finish: Brush the rugelach with the egg wash and sprinkle with the turbinado sugar.

Bake until golden brown and crispy, 23 to 27 minutes.

Let cool on the pans for at least 20 to 30 minutes before serving.

Traditional Rugelach

If you want traditional smaller rugelach, once the dough has come together, separate the dough ball into 4 equal portions. Roll each into a ball and then press into discs ½ inch thick. Wrap each well with plastic wrap and refrigerate for at least 3 hours or overnight. Once rested, roll each disc into a 9-inch round. Divide the chocolate filling among the 4 rounds. Cut each round into quarters and then each quarter into three triangles, so you have 12 equal triangles from each piece of dough, and a total of 48 rugelach. Tightly roll each triangle from the wide end to the point and place on a parchment paper–lined baking sheet. Let rest in the fridge for 15 to 20 minutes before baking at 350°F until lightly golden brown, 17 to 22 minutes. Let cool for 20 to 30 minutes before serving.

Notes

♥ *The rugelach may lose some filling and butter while baking, but don't worry! Much of this butter will soak up while resting and it will still remain delicious and crispy.*

♥ *Depending on your oven, the bottom of the rugelach may cook much more quickly than the top. I like to place a second baking sheet on the bottom rack to help balance the heat.*

♥ *Store leftovers on a plate, uncovered, at room temperature for the next 1 to 2 days. You can also store in an airtight storage bag in the freezer for 1 to 2 months. Let thaw before serving.*

Palmiers

Makes 18 to 20 cookies

The coffee shops in big cities have always been a great source of fascination for me. Even without purchasing anything, I find joy in perusing their cake displays, taking in the sweet sights. Palmiers have always been the dessert stars of these coffeehouses for me—the unique shape, the caramelized taste, the sheer simplicity makes them irresistibly delicious. These are among the simplest yet most gratifying cookies I've ever baked at home. And my secret? A touch of orange zest added to the sugar for an extra kick of flavor. As it bakes, the enticing aroma wafts through the house, tempting every heart. Once done, dipping them in chocolate transforms them into a treat that outshines even the fanciest coffee shop cookies.

½ teaspoon grated orange zest, plus more for garnish

½ cup granulated sugar, plus more for the sides

Rough Puff Pastry (page 132), refrigerated

½ cup semisweet chocolate chips

In a small bowl, combine the orange zest and sugar. Remove the puff pastry from the fridge. If it has been chilling for more than 3 hours, let sit for 3 to 5 minutes at room temperature before rolling.

Sprinkle 2 tablespoons of the sugar mixture over a clean work surface and place the folded puff pastry on top. Using a rolling pin, hit the top of the puff pastry evenly to flatten it slightly. Press to close any cracks that form. Sprinkle 2 tablespoons of the sugar mixture evenly over the top of the puff pastry. Roll the dough into a 10 × 14-inch rectangle. The dough will be hard, but use the rolling pin to firmly press and roll the dough, continuing to press together any cracks that may form. Roll the dough over the rolling pin to lift it and spread 2 tablespoons of the sugar mixture evenly on the work surface once again. Unroll the dough over the sugar and top the dough evenly with the remaining sugar. Use your hands and rolling pin to gently press the sugar into the dough.

With a short side of the rectangle facing you, use a bench scraper to gently mark the middle of the dough horizontally. From the bottom, fold the dough up two times to ¼ inch below the mark you made in the middle, pressing between each fold. Repeat the folding starting from the top so that both sides almost meet in the middle. Fold the dough in half at the middle "hinge" so the two sides meet. If desired, you can add 1 or 2 more tablespoons of sugar over the sides of the dough. Carefully cover the dough with plastic wrap and place on a plate.

continued

continued

Palmiers

Refrigerate for 15 to 30 minutes.

Preheat the oven to 390°F. Line two baking sheets with parchment paper.

Transfer the dough to a work surface. Using a sharp knife or bench scraper, cut the rough edges on the short sides of the dough so you have clean edges. Slice the dough into ½-inch-thick slices. Place the slices flat on the prepared pan, being sure to leave at least 2 inches between the cookies. Open the slices just slightly at the top so the cookies form a V shape.

Bake for 10 minutes. Remove from the oven and use a spatula to carefully flip each cookie. Return to the oven and bake until golden brown, 7 to 8 minutes.

Transfer to a rack to cool for at least 30 minutes.

Melt the chocolate chips in the microwave or over a pan of simmering water. Let the chocolate cool to room temperature.

Line a cooling rack with parchment paper. Dip one of the top corners of a palmier into the chocolate and place on the rack. Sprinkle with some orange zest and repeat with each cookie. Let cool completely before serving.

Notes

♦ *The sugar called for is perfect for my sweet tooth, but you can add 1 to 2 tablespoons more for rolling if you like a sweeter cookie.*

♦ *Store the palmiers in an airtight container at room temperature for 4 to 5 days.*

Biscotti

Makes 24 biscotti

These delightful Italian cookies have become an indispensable part of my holiday gift boxes. I'm a firm believer in the magic of handmade gifts, and there's nothing I enjoy more than curating homemade gift boxes. I carefully tuck cookies, dried fruits, and sometimes even my homemade jams into vintage boxes, adding a personal note and tying it all up with velvet ribbons. The process takes an entire day, but seeing the twinkle in my loved ones' eyes makes it all worthwhile.

The main reasons biscotti are a staple in my gift boxes are that they remain fresh for a long time and are so versatile you can customize the cookies for your giftee (see Notes). A little tip: Tuck in an unexpected candid photo of you with the recipient. I assure you, it will make the gift all the more memorable!

3½ cups (455g) all-purpose flour, plus more for dusting

¼ teaspoon (2g) kosher salt

1 tablespoon (12g) baking powder

1 stick (4 oz/113g) unsalted butter, at room temperature

¼ cup (55g) peanut oil or other neutral oil

1¼ cups (250g) granulated sugar

3 large eggs

1 teaspoon (5g) vanilla extract

½ teaspoon (2g) almond extract

¼ cup (40g) mini semisweet chocolate chips

¼ cup (35g) chopped roasted hazelnuts

1 cup (100g) sliced almonds

Egg wash: 1 egg beaten with 1 teaspoon water

2 tablespoons turbinado sugar

TO FINISH

1 cup semisweet chocolate chips

Preheat the oven to 350°F. Line two baking sheets with parchment paper.

In a medium bowl, stir together the flour, salt, and baking powder and set aside.

In another medium bowl, with an electric mixer, beat the butter, peanut oil, and granulated sugar on medium-low speed until creamed together, 1 to 2 minutes. Add the eggs one at a time, beating well after each addition. Add the vanilla and almond extracts and mix to combine well.

Slowly add the flour mixture, stirring just until incorporated, 30 to 60 seconds. Add the chocolate chips, chopped hazelnuts, and sliced almonds. Using your hands or a silicone spatula, stir the dough just until everything is incorporated.

Using a silicone spatula, scoop the dough out onto a lightly floured work surface and make sure to scrape all dough from the sides of the bowl and beaters. Using a sharp knife or bench scraper, divide the dough into 2 equal portions. Roll each piece into a small rough log. Place a log of dough on each baking sheet and use your hands to gently press and shape the logs into 12 × 3-inch rectangles.

Brush the top of each dough log with the egg wash and sprinkle with 1 tablespoon of the turbinado sugar.

Bake until lightly golden brown and almost set, 25 to 30 minutes.

Remove from the oven and let cool on the baking sheets for 15 to 20 minutes. Leave the oven on but reduce the oven temperature to 325°F.

The baked dough logs will be fragile at this point. Very carefully slide one of the parchment papers onto a work surface and use a sharp bread knife to cut the log into 1-inch slices. Gently turn each slice onto its side. Repeat with the other log.

Slide the parchment paper and biscotti back onto the baking sheets and return to the oven. Bake for 7 to 10 minutes. Flip the biscotti onto the other cut side and bake until both sides are lightly golden brown and the biscotti are crispy, an additional 7 to 10 minutes.

Remove the biscotti from the baking sheets and place on a rack to cool completely.

To finish: Line two cooling racks with parchment paper. In a shallow bowl, melt the chocolate chips in the microwave in 30-second bursts, stirring between each, or over a pan of simmering water. Let cool to room temperature. Dip the bottom of each biscotti into the chocolate. Place chocolate side up on the racks, making sure the pieces do not touch, and let the chocolate set.

Notes

❧ *I like to load my biscotti up with an assortment of nuts for that extra crunch and to keep me satiated for longer. But you can add a mix of ingredients that appeal to you or your loved ones. Cranberries, pistachios, pecans, white chocolate, or even fruit zest could be exciting additions.*

❧ *Keep the biscotti in a glass storage jar on the counter as a snack for 1 to 2 weeks. Or store in an airtight storage bag in the freezer for up to 3 months. Remove from the freezer and let thaw at room temperature before serving.*

Ginger Cookie Sandwiches with Cookie Butter Ice Cream

Makes 9 ice cream sandwiches

The recipes in this cookbook have been tried, tested, and loved by many, from my husband and his students to my neighbors, my lovely taste tester, and even her actor friends. But these ginger cookie sandwiches got the ultimate seal of approval from the toughest critics—my son and his friends. The group polished them off within seconds during a photo shoot! I recommend preparing these sandwiches the night before, so the moisture of the ice cream gives the cookies the perfect softness. And don't worry, kids are brutally honest—if these cookies weren't absolutely delicious, I'd have heard about it!

COOKIE BUTTER ICE CREAM

42 ounces vanilla ice cream

⅓ cup cookie butter

SOFT GINGER COOKIES

2 cups (260g) all-purpose flour

1½ teaspoons (6g) baking soda

½ teaspoon (2g) baking powder

1 teaspoon (3g) ground ginger

1½ teaspoons (5g) ground cinnamon

¼ teaspoon (1g) ground allspice

¼ teaspoon (1g) ground cloves

¼ teaspoon (2g) kosher salt

1 stick (4 oz/113g) unsalted butter, at room temperature

¼ cup plus 2 teaspoons (54g) shortening, at room temperature

¾ cup (150g) packed dark brown sugar

1 large egg

¼ cup (80g) molasses

¼ cup (100g) turbinado sugar or granulated sugar

Make the cookie butter ice cream: Remove the vanilla ice cream from the fridge and let sit at room temperature for 7 to 10 minutes until just softened. Transfer the ice cream to a medium bowl and add the cookie butter. Using a wooden spoon or spatula, gently stir the cookie butter into the ice cream to create swirls.

Line an 8-inch square pan with plastic wrap. Transfer the ice cream to the pan and smooth with an offset spatula. Place in the freezer for 1 to 2 hours, until fully frozen.

Make the soft ginger cookies: Preheat the oven to 350°F. Line a baking sheet with parchment paper and set aside.

In a medium bowl, mix together the flour, baking soda, baking powder, ginger, cinnamon, allspice, cloves, and salt. In a separate medium bowl, with an electric mixer, cream the butter, shortening, and brown sugar on medium speed until smooth and creamy. Add the egg and molasses and continue to mix for 1 to 2 minutes until well combined. Add the dry ingredients to the wet ingredients and mix until just combined.

Spread the turbinado sugar in a shallow dish. Using a 1-tablespoon ice cream scoop, scoop a ball of dough into your hands and roll gently to smooth the shape. Place in the sugar dish and coat well before placing on the prepared baking sheet, leaving 1½ inches between the balls.

Bake until just cooked through, 10 to 12 minutes; do not overbake or your soft ginger cookie will be hard and crispy!

Let cool for 5 to 10 minutes on the pan before transferring to a rack to cool completely.

To build the sandwiches, take the 18 cookies that are closest in size (save the remaining cookies for snacking). Remove the ice cream from the freezer and cut into 9 rounds with a 2¼-inch round cookie cutter (or a size that matches your ginger cookies). Place one round of ice cream on a ginger cookie and top with another cookie to make a sandwich. Serve immediately.

Notes

♥ *This ice cream recipe yields enough for very thick ice cream sandwiches, which is my favorite. You can decrease the ice cream ingredients to 28 ounces of ice cream and ¼ cup cookie butter for a thinner sandwich.*

♥ *You can also assemble the sandwiches and leave them in the freezer overnight. The ice cream will make the cookies a little softer. Let sit at room temperature for 3 to 5 minutes before serving.*

♥ *This recipe makes a smaller/thinner cookie for sandwiches. If you are eating the cookies on their own, you can refrigerate the dough for 45 minutes to 3 hours before using and then use a 2 tablespoon scoop of dough for an extra soft and delicious ginger cookie. Bake for an additional 2 to 3 minutes.*

Zucchini Cream Cheese Biscuits

Makes 8 biscuits

As an imaginative child, one of my many dreams was to own a bakery—a space where my love for the kitchen could run wild. While that bakery may not yet exist, its spirit lives on in these zucchini biscuits. Their special flavor comes from a healthy sprinkling of smoked salt before baking.

4 tablespoons (2 oz/56g) unsalted butter, cubed

¼ cup (56g) cream cheese, cubed

1 cup (160g) grated zucchini

2½ cups (325g) all-purpose flour, plus more for dusting

1 teaspoon (6g) kosher salt

¾ teaspoon (3g) granulated sugar

1 tablespoon plus ¼ teaspoon (13g) baking powder

¾ teaspoon (3g) baking soda

1 cup (240g) cold buttermilk

⅓ cup (40g) crumbled feta cheese

⅓ cup (35g) shredded sharp cheddar cheese

3 tablespoons (1.5g) chopped fresh dill

Egg wash: 1 egg beaten with 1 teaspoon water and a pinch of sugar

Smoked salt, for sprinkling

FOR SERVING

3 tablespoons unsalted butter, at room temperature

Smoked salt

Fresh dill

Place the butter and cream cheese on a plate in the freezer for 5 to 10 minutes.

Line a small bowl with cheesecloth. Grate the zucchini into the cheesecloth. Squeeze the cheesecloth to remove any excess liquid from the zucchini. Transfer to a plate and set aside.

In a large bowl, whisk together the flour, salt, sugar, baking powder, and baking soda. Add the butter and cream cheese. Using a pastry cutter, cut the cubes into the flour mixture until they are chickpea-size pieces. Add the buttermilk, feta, and cheddar. Using a spatula, fold together until fully incorporated. Add the dill and zucchini and continue to fold until just combined.

Turn the dough out on a piece of plastic wrap. Use your hands to bring the dough together and squeeze it into a firm ball. Press into a 6-inch round. Slice the dough in 4 equal wedges and stack the quarters. Firmly press the pieces together into a 2-inch-thick rectangle. Cover with plastic wrap and let rest in the fridge for 15 to 30 minutes.

Preheat the oven to 420°F. Line a baking sheet with parchment paper.

Place the dough on a lightly floured work surface. Using a rolling pin, roll the dough into a 1-inch-thick rectangle. Using a 2½-inch round cookie cutter or glass, cut out 6 biscuits and set on the baking sheet. Gather the scraps and press firmly together to cut out 2 more biscuits. Brush the tops of the biscuits with egg wash and sprinkle with smoked salt.

Bake until golden brown, 14 to 17 minutes. Remove from the oven and let cool until just warm.

To serve: In a small bowl, whisk the butter until smooth and creamy. Serve the biscuits topped with whipped butter, smoked salt, and fresh dill.

Notes

♥ *This makes a really delicious base for a smoked salmon sandwich.*

♥ *Store the leftover biscuits in an airtight storage bag at room temperature for 2 to 4 days or in the freezer for up to 2 months. If frozen, let thaw for 10 to 15 minutes at room temperature before heating. Before serving, put biscuits in a cold oven and preheat it to 350°F. Once the oven reaches temperature, the biscuits will be ready to eat.*

Cheddar-Jalapeño Biscuits

Makes 6 to 8 biscuits

I absolutely love making biscuits. The total preparation time is roughly 10 minutes, and they can be ready for Sunday breakfast before your household is downstairs. I like to split them open by hand and slather some honey inside. As the biscuits cool slightly, you can turn them into breakfast sandwiches or even eggs Benedict—assuming they're not gobbled up as soon as they're out of the oven.

1 stick (4 oz/113g) cold unsalted butter, cut into ½-inch cubes

2½ cups (325g) all-purpose flour, plus more for dusting

1 teaspoon (6g) kosher salt

1 teaspoon (4g) granulated sugar

½ teaspoon (2g) baking soda

1 tablespoon (12g) baking powder

¾ cup (180g) cold buttermilk, plus more if needed

¼ cup (60g) cold heavy cream

1 cup (110 g) shredded yellow cheddar cheese

1 medium jalapeño, diced

TO FINISH

Egg wash: 1 egg beaten with 1 teaspoon honey and 1 teaspoon extra-virgin olive oil

1 tablespoon butter, melted, for the top

1 tablespoon honey (optional), for the top

Place the cubed butter in the freezer for 5 to 10 minutes before use. In a large bowl, whisk together the flour, salt, sugar, baking soda, and baking powder. Add the cubes of cold butter and, using a pastry cutter, cut the butter into the dry ingredients and toss until the flour coats the butter and the mixture forms chickpea-size pieces. Using your hands, make a well in the center of the mixture. Add the cold buttermilk and heavy cream to the well and toss with your hands until just combined. Fold in the cheddar and jalapeño until just incorporated, taking care not to overmix.

Set the dough on a lightly floured work surface. Use your hands to gather the dough into a rough ball. If the dough is too dry, add up to 1 tablespoon additional buttermilk. Using your hands, press the dough into a 1-inch-thick rectangle. Using a sharp knife, cut the dough into quarters. Stack the pieces of dough on top of one another. Press the dough into a 4 × 6-inch rectangle. Wrap with plastic wrap and let sit in the freezer for 10 minutes.

Preheat the oven to 420°F. Line a baking sheet with parchment paper.

To finish: Set the dough on the work surface and roll it out to a 6 × 9-inch rectangle. Using a 2½- to 3-inch round cookie cutter or upside-down glass, cut out 6 biscuits. Gather the scraps and press together to cut 2 more biscuits. (If preferred, you can use a sharp knife to cut the dough into 6 rectangular pieces.) Transfer the biscuits to the baking sheet. Brush the biscuits with the egg wash.

Bake until golden brown, 14 to 17 minutes. Transfer to a cooling rack. Brush the top of the biscuits with butter and honey (if using). Serve warm.

Notes

♦ *The keys to successful biscuits is to keep your ingredients, particularly the butter and buttermilk, extremely cold and avoid overhandling the dough.*

♦ *Once at room temperature, store the biscuits in an airtight storage bag for 1 to 2 days or in the freezer for up to 2 months. Before serving, place the biscuits in a cold oven. Preheat the oven to 350°F, and once it reaches temperature, the biscuits will be warm and ready to serve. If frozen, let thaw for 10 to 15 minutes at room temperature before heating.*

Four-Cheese Tomato Galette

Serves 4

Growing up in a big city apartment, trapped among towering buildings, I thought of summer as a dull time. But my husband gradually influenced me to relish the bounty of summer evenings. This recipe is a tribute to our shared summer tables—the perfect blend of a delightful dough, a quartet of cheeses, and luscious, sun-ripened tomatoes.

DOUGH

1½ cups (195g) all-purpose flour, plus more for dusting

¼ cup (30g) ground walnuts

¼ cup (25g) freshly grated Parmesan cheese

1 teaspoon (6g) kosher salt

1 teaspoon (4g) granulated sugar

4 tablespoons (2 oz/56g) cold unsalted butter, cut into ½-inch cubes

2 tablespoons (28g) extra-virgin olive oil

1 tablespoon (15g) sour cream

¼ teaspoon (2g) distilled white vinegar

2 tablespoons (28g) ice water, plus more if needed

FILLING

½ cup whole-milk ricotta cheese

½ cup shredded mozzarella cheese

¼ cup crumbled feta cheese or goat cheese

¼ cup freshly grated Parmesan cheese

1 teaspoon grated lemon zest (optional)

ASSEMBLY

3 to 4 heirloom tomatoes, cut into ¼-inch slices

Kosher salt

¼ cup Basil Pesto (page 35)

3 to 4 cherry tomatoes, halved

Egg wash: 1 egg beaten with 1 teaspoon extra-virgin olive oil

1 tablespoon sesame seeds (optional)

Make the dough: In a food processor, combine the flour, walnuts, Parmesan, salt, and sugar. Pulse a few times to mix. Add the butter, olive oil, sour cream, and vinegar and pulse until the mixture forms chickpea-size pieces. Drizzle the ice water over the dough and pulse until the water is incorporated and the texture is crumbly.

Transfer the dough to a work surface. Using your hands, squeeze the dough so everything comes together. Press the dough into a 1-inch-thick disc and wrap with plastic wrap. Place in the fridge for at least 30 to 40 minutes.

Make the filling: In a medium bowl, mix together the ricotta, mozzarella, feta, Parmesan, and lemon zest (if using). Set aside.

To assemble: Line a plate with paper towels and place the heirloom tomatoes on it. Sprinkle the slices with salt and let them sit for 5 to 10 minutes. Pat dry before using.

Preheat the oven to 400°F.

Line a work surface with parchment paper and lightly flour the top. Place the dough in the center of the paper and set another large piece of parchment on the top. Press down and use a rolling pin to roll the dough into a 11- to 13-inch round about ⅛ inch thick. Peel the parchment paper from the top. Spread the cheese filling over the dough, leaving a 2-inch border around the edge. Spread the pesto over the cheese and arrange the tomato slices and cherry tomato halves on the top. Fold the edges of the dough 1½ inches over the tomatoes.

Brush the edges with egg wash and sprinkle with sesame seeds (if using).

Bake until the crust is golden brown, 40 to 50 minutes. Let cool for 15 to 20 minutes. Serve warm.

Notes

♥ *You can prepare the galette dough in advance, wrap with plastic wrap, and store in an airtight storage bag. It will keep in the fridge for up to 2 days or in the freezer for 1 month. If frozen, let thaw in the fridge before using.*

♥ *This is a great recipe for using up scraps of leftover cheese from your fridge.*

Spinach-Mushroom Deep-Dish Quiche

Serves 8 to 10

Having battled the fear of a cracked quiche crust and resulting seepage for the longest time, I perfected this foolproof recipe that stands up to the challenge. No breaks, no cracks, just perfect quiche every time. I whip it up in my food processor in mere minutes. Trust me when I say this will become your new favorite quiche recipe. Feel free to experiment with any filling of your choice.

DOUGH

1¾ cups (227g) all-purpose flour, plus more for dusting

1 teaspoon (6g) kosher salt

½ teaspoon (2g) granulated sugar

1 tablespoon pistachios (optional)

1 stick (4 oz/113g) cold unsalted butter, cut into ½-inch cubes

1 cold medium egg

2 tablespoons (28g) cold water, plus more if needed

FILLING

4 tablespoons extra-virgin olive oil

10 to 12 medium white mushrooms, cut into ¼-inch slices

1 teaspoon kosher salt

1 medium onion, diced

1 garlic clove, minced

6 ounces baby spinach

½ teaspoon garlic powder

½ teaspoon freshly ground black pepper

½ teaspoon red pepper flakes

CUSTARD

4 medium eggs

1½ cups heavy cream

½ cup sour cream

1 cup (about 3½ ounces) shredded Gruyère cheese

¼ cup shredded Parmesan cheese

½ teaspoon garlic salt

½ teaspoon kosher salt

½ teaspoon freshly ground black pepper

2 tablespoons chopped fennel fronds or fresh dill

TO FINISH

Egg wash: 1 egg, lightly beaten

2 green onions, chopped

Fresh dill, for garnish

Spring mix salad, for serving

Make the dough: In a food processor, combine the flour, salt, sugar, and pistachios (if using). Pulse until combined. Add the butter and egg and pulse several times until the butter is just larger than chickpea-size. Drizzle in the cold water and pulse a few times until just incorporated. Transfer the dough mixture to a large piece of plastic wrap and use your hands to bring everything together, squeezing and pressing the dough into a ball. It will be just a little wetter than regular pie dough, not too floury in texture. Flatten the dough into a 6-inch round. Wrap with the plastic wrap and let rest in the fridge for 30 to 45 minutes.

Make the filling: Heat a large skillet or nonstick pan over medium heat. Add 2 tablespoons of the olive oil, the mushrooms, and ¼ teaspoon of the salt and cook, stirring occasionally, until lightly browned, 3 to 4 minutes. Transfer the mushrooms to a plate.

Add the remaining 2 tablespoons olive oil and the onions to the pan and sauté, continuing to stir occasionally, until golden brown, 4 to 5 minutes. Add the garlic and cook for 1 minute. Stir in the spinach and cover with a lid for 2 minutes. Uncover and add the remaining ¾ teaspoon salt, the garlic powder, black pepper, and red pepper flakes. Sauté until the spinach is wilted and all the liquid has evaporated, 5 to 7 minutes. Remove from the heat and stir in two-thirds of the cooked mushrooms. Taste and season to your preference. Let cool to room temperature.

Make the custard: In a medium bowl, whisk together the eggs, heavy cream, and sour cream until smooth and creamy. Stir in ¾ cup of the Gruyère, the Parmesan, garlic salt, salt, black pepper, and fennel fronds until well combined. Set aside at room temperature until ready to use.

continued

Spinach-Mushroom Deep-Dish Quiche

Place the dough on a lightly floured work surface. Using a rolling pin, roll the dough into a 13-inch round. Roll the dough over the rolling pin and lift to center over an 8-inch springform pan. Use your fingers to press the dough firmly into the bottom and sides of the pan. Use the tines of a fork to press the top ¼ inch of the dough into the sides of the pan to create an impression. Pierce the bottom and sides of the dough several times with the fork. Cover with plastic wrap and let rest in the fridge for 15 to 20 minutes.

Preheat the oven to 375°F.

To finish: Line the dough with parchment paper or aluminum foil, leaving at least 2 inches of paper overhanging. Fill the crust with pie weights or dried beans. Place the springform pan on a baking sheet. Bake the crust for 15 to 17 minutes. Remove from the oven, very carefully remove the paper and the pie weights, and continue to bake for an additional 4 to 7 minutes, until just lightly golden. Remove from the oven.

Reduce the oven temperature to 350°F. Brush the bottom of the crust lightly with the egg wash. Return to the oven and bake for 2 to 4 minutes to set the egg wash. Remove from the oven and let cool for 15 to 20 minutes.

Reduce the oven temperature to 325°F.

Once the crust is cool, spread the remaining Gruyère cheese and the green onions evenly over the bottom of the crust. Spread the spinach-mushroom filling evenly on top. Carefully pour in the custard and finish with the reserved cooked mushrooms.

Bake for 50 to 55 minutes.

Increase the oven temperature to 350°F and bake until the top is golden brown and the filling is set, an additional 8 to 12 minutes.

Let cool to room temperature for at least 3 hours to fully set. I prefer to leave the quiche in the fridge for an additional 30 minutes to 1 hour until I am confident it is fully set before slicing and warming lightly. Don't be fooled if the sides of the pan are cool—the middle will take a long time to set entirely. Serve topped with fresh dill and spring mix salad on the side.

Note

❦ *Place any leftover slices of quiche in a storage container or on a plate covered with plastic wrap. Store in the fridge for up to 3 to 4 days. Reheat in the microwave, if desired, before serving.*

Tahini Cookies

Makes 16 to 18 cookies

Tahini isn't just for savory dishes; it's a star player in some of Türkiye's sweetest recipes, including these melt-in-your-mouth cookies. You may find their halva-like texture a bit different at first, but a sip of coffee or tea between bites will let their flavor unfold and soon have you craving more. These cookies are the epitome of a unique taste experience, and despite any initial texture surprises, I am confident you'll love them as much as I do. The key to this recipe is the high-quality tahini—the right tahini will be very finely ground with a consistency similar to honey.

1 cup (250g) high-quality tahini

½ cup (60g) powdered sugar

¼ cup (55g) peanut oil or other neutral oil

1½ teaspoons (7g) vanilla extract

2 cups (260g) all-purpose flour

Crushed roasted hazelnuts or walnuts

Preheat the oven to 350°F. Line a baking sheet with parchment paper.

In a medium bowl, combine the tahini, powdered sugar, peanut oil, and vanilla. Mix well using a wooden spoon. Add the flour and knead the dough with your hands for 4 to 5 minutes, until everything is well combined and a dough forms.

Place the nuts in a small bowl. Scoop out 1½ tablespoons of dough and roll it into a ball on the palm of your hand. Coat the top with the crushed nuts and place on the prepared baking sheet with 1 inch between each cookie. Repeat with the remaining dough.

Bake until lightly golden brown, 13 to 15 minutes.

Let cool fully on the pan before serving.

Notes

♥ *You can make a chocolate version by reducing the flour by 1½ tablespoons and replacing it with 1 tablespoon cocoa powder.*

♥ *If your tahini is very thick, decrease the flour by ¼ cup.*

♥ *Store the cookies on a plate at room temperature for 2 to 3 days.*

UNLEAVENED DOUGHS

In the world of unleavened dough, simplicity reigns supreme. These doughs, unburdened by the need for rising agents, stand testament to the beauty of minimalism. Watch as flour, water, and fat come together to create flatbreads, pastas, and tortillas that are anything but flat in flavor. And let's not forget the magic of steam-leavened wonders like choux pastry, giving rise to airy cream puffs and éclairs. Easy and unpretentious, these doughs promise success with a whisper rather than a shout. These diverse creations prove a profound truth: In the world of baking, the simplest ingredients often yield the richest flavors.

KEY TECHNIQUES

SPECIAL EQUIPMENT

❀ **Pasta Roller and Cutters:** I'm willing to say that an electric pasta roller might be your new favorite kitchen tool. I used to use my hand-cranked roller but recently invested in a KitchenAid attachment—it is incredible and I use it for many recipes that aren't even pasta. This will make your life much easier for any recipe that requires thin doughs or lots of rolling, everything from börek to wonton wrappers. If you have a KitchenAid stand mixer, I highly recommend buying this. I included the KitchenAid settings for each relevant recipe in the cookbook. I find that hand rollers tend to roll more thinly than the motorized attachment, so you may need to do some research about which levels are comparable to your pasta roller. Depending on your pasta preferences, it might also be helpful for you to purchase pasta cutters. I recommend having a thin spaghetti option and thicker fettuccine option, as well as a gnocchi board.

❀ **Pasta Stand:** A practical product for drying strands of homemade pasta. If you don't have one, the back of a clean chair can substitute.

Water Drop Test

In order to test if a surface is properly heated before cooking, such as with a baking steel or griddle pan, you can perform a water drop test. Complete this by drizzling a few drops of water onto the heated surface. If it immediately sizzles away, it's hot enough! If not, allow to heat for a few more minutes before retesting.

Working with Pasta and Noodle Dough

Kneading hard doughs, such as for pasta and noodles, can be a challenge. They often require 10 to 15 minutes of kneading, particularly when dealing with egg dough, which is stiffer. However, I've developed my own technique, which involves breaks in between kneading sessions to make this process a little easier. Here's how it works:

1. Mix the dough ingredients and prepare the dough as indicated in the recipe.

2. Once the dough comes together, turn it out onto a counter. Using the basic kneading technique (see page 22), grasp the part of the dough farthest from you with the inner surface of your fingers and pull it toward you, folding it over itself. Press the dough away from you with the palm of your hand.

3. Fold the slightly stretched dough onto itself and rotate the dough 45 degrees periodically. Avoid adding excess flour to your counter during this process.

4. Continue this process for 5 to 6 minutes, until the dough holds its shape and is no longer sticky. The dough may still look rough at this stage, but don't worry. Wrap it in plastic wrap and let rest at room temperature for 20 to 25 minutes.

5. Unwrap the dough and knead for another 5 to 6 minutes using the same method. By this point, your dough should look shiny and smooth, with a velvety texture.

6. Allow the dough to rest for an additional 20 to 30 minutes. Once your dough is ready, you can let it rest for the time specified in the recipe, then shape and prepare it.

TROUBLESHOOTING PASTA AND NOODLE DOUGH

While preparing pasta and noodle dough, you may encounter several challenges. Here are some common issues and ways to solve them:

Hard or Gummy Cooked Pasta

Overly stiff dough: If your pasta or noodles turn out hard or gum-like, this could be due to overly stiff dough. If you're using a kitchen scale to measure your ingredients, this shouldn't happen. Since eggs (common in pasta dough) vary in size and weight, the consistency of your dough may be affected if you're not using a scale. Smaller eggs might result in harder dough. If you notice that your dough is too hard during kneading, dampen it slightly with a clean, damp cloth or a little water spritz. Then wrap it in plastic wrap and let rest for 15 to 20 minutes. After resting, knead the dough again until it reaches the desired texture.

Dough rolled too thick: Another reason for hard or gummy pasta could be that you've rolled or cut the dough too thickly. A pasta roller can help ensure the right thickness.

Dough Sticking During Rolling

If your dough is too sticky after resting, or if it sticks too much to your pasta machine during rolling, your dough may be too soft. When initially kneading pasta dough, it might seem hard but it will soften after resting. If this happens, add a little flour and knead until it reaches the desired consistency, then let it rest.

Pasty or Tasteless Cooked Pasta

Not enough water: If your pasta or noodles have a pasty consistency after cooking, it could be that you're not boiling them in enough water. You should boil pasta and noodles in a large amount of water to prevent them from sticking together. For each pound of fresh pasta or noodles, use about 4 to 4½ quarts of water. Make sure to use a large pot.

Not enough salt: If your pasta or noodles are tasteless and soft, you may not have added enough salt to the cooking water. Typically, I recommend adding 1½ to 2 teaspoons of kosher salt per quart when boiling pasta or noodles.

Slurry at the Bottom of the Pasta Pot

If you add too much flour or semolina to your pasta or noodles before cooking, the excess flour may form a slurry at the bottom of your pot. To prevent this, shake off the excess flour before adding the pasta to the water. If you notice that a slurry formed during cooking, when the pasta is done use a slotted spoon to transfer the pasta or noodles to serving plates instead of draining the pot.

Working with Choux Dough

Many find preparing choux dough daunting, but it is actually one of the simplest doughs to make. It doesn't require kneading or resting, making it relatively quick to prepare. The key to perfecting choux dough lies in paying attention to a few critical points, so let's discuss them and the methods I prefer.

I. When making choux dough, precise measurements are important. Therefore,

---

Notes

♦ When processing my pasta and noodle dough I like to hang the pasta/noodle sheets to dry for 15 to 20 minutes before cutting them. This helps prevent the pasta from sticking together during the cutting process. Make sure to check the pasta after the first 10 minutes to prevent it from drying out too much.

I recommend using a kitchen scale to prepare all the ingredients.

2. Use a nonstick saucepan to make the dough, mixing with a wooden spoon or a rubber or silicone spatula.

3. Always opt for unsalted butter, and make sure the butter, salt, and sugar are completely dissolved in the water before adding the flour.

4. To prevent the flour from cooking too quickly and forming lumps, remove the pan from the heat before adding the flour. Add the flour all at once and stir it into the mixture quickly using a wooden spoon or a flexible spatula.

5. Once the flour is fully incorporated, immediately return the pot to the heat. If there are any lumps of flour in the dough, use the back of your spoon to break them down and incorporate them into the mixture. Stir the dough constantly for just 2 to 2½ minutes so that the flour can cook. The dough should have a smooth texture similar to very soft Play-Doh.

6. Before adding the eggs, allow the dough to cool to slightly warmer than room temperature—it should never be hot as this could cause the eggs to cook prematurely or your dough to develop an eggy smell.

7. When the dough is ready, transfer it to a deep bowl (or the bowl of a stand mixer if you have one) to prevent it from splattering when you beat it. Add the eggs one at a time, making sure each one is fully incorporated before adding the next. It's essential that your eggs be the right size according to the recipe, so measure them before adding.

V-Test

To determine if your dough has reached the ideal consistency, pull your mixer back from the dough. If it stretches out like a paste and forms a V shape, your dough is ready. Transfer the dough to a piping bag using a spatula and proceed with the recipe of your choice.

TROUBLESHOOTING CHOUX DOUGH

Now, let's discuss some common issues you might face while preparing choux dough and how to solve them.

Dough Doesn't Rise or Collapses

The primary reason choux pastries collapse or flatten is that they come into contact with air before they are fully cooked. To prevent this, make sure your dough is baked at the correct temperature. A properly heated oven is crucial for achieving well-risen pastries. Never bake your dough at temperatures lower than 350°F, and avoid opening the oven door during the first 15 minutes of baking. The sudden drop in oven temperature when the door is opened can cause your pastries to collapse. Use the oven light to observe your choux dough through the oven glass. If your oven doesn't have a light, rest assured that your dough won't overcook in the first 15 minutes. Once the dough is cooked, turn off the oven and prop open the oven door with a wooden spoon, allowing your pastry to cool a bit in the oven for about 15 minutes. After removing your pastry from the oven, use a sharp knife to make very small holes at their base to let the steam escape. Trapped steam can sometimes cause the pastries to collapse.

Flat Choux Dough

Another reason for flat choux pastries may be that the dough is too soft. If your dough is more like a batter, fails to hold shape, and spreads when piped onto the baking sheet, this indicates that the dough is too soft, which will prevent it from rising and cause it to flatten. To avoid this, I recommend using a kitchen scale for accurate measurements. You can also perform the V-test to check the consistency of your dough before you put it in the piping bag. Lastly, remember to add the eggs one at a time, making sure each one is thoroughly mixed before adding the next—otherwise, the mixture can become too wet.

Basic Pasta Dough

*Makes 18 ounces
(serves 4 to 6)*

At first glance, the thought of making pasta from scratch might send shivers down your spine. But trust me, the process is more therapeutic than intimidating. In fact, with a bit of patience and attention to resting times, you can whip up a batch of homemade pasta in about two hours.

The other day, I shared on Instagram my longing for an Italian vacation and how making homemade pasta was my consolation. One of my followers humorously commented on the irony—too busy for a vacation but able to make homemade pasta. The comment, spotted and pointed out to me by my husband, had me chuckling. Though it may seem paradoxical, I truly believe that making homemade pasta can be a soothing ritual on busy days. It's a way to show yourself some love and offer an escape when a vacation is just a dream. Kneading the dough and feeling its silky texture is enough to cast aside the stress of the day.

A little heads-up: My recipe veers from the traditional a tad. Purists might raise an eyebrow at the addition of lemon and olive oil, but it's a technique I've borrowed from my grandmother. These two ingredients lend an incredible texture and flavor to the dough that's simply irresistible.

2½ cups (325g) Type "oo" or all-purpose flour

1 teaspoon (6g) kosher salt, plus more for pasta water

¼ teaspoon (1g) granulated sugar

3 large eggs plus 2 egg yolks

½ teaspoon (3g) fresh lemon juice

1 teaspoon (5g) extra-virgin olive oil, plus more for cooking the pasta

Semolina flour, for rolling

Place the flour on a work surface and mix in the salt and sugar with a fork. Using your hands or the bottom of a bowl, make a well in the center of the flour. Add the whole eggs, egg yolks, and lemon juice to the well. Using a fork, pierce the egg yolks and whisk. Slowly incorporate flour from the bottom and sides to the well with your fork until the egg mixture has thickened. Be careful not to incorporate flour from the top of the well first or you will end up with eggs all over your table. Drizzle the oil on the surface of the dough and use a bench scraper to continue to fold the flour into the mixture until everything is combined well. Using your hands, perform the basic kneading technique (see page 172) and knead for 5 to 7 minutes, until it is elastic and no longer sticky. At this point, the dough will still not be perfectly smooth and that's okay. Wrap the dough with plastic wrap and let rest for 20 to 25 minutes at room temperature.

continued

continued

Basic Pasta Dough

Unwrap the dough and continue to knead for 4 to 5 minutes, making sure the dough is now perfectly smooth and the top has a velvety texture. Wrap the dough in plastic wrap and let rest for 30 minutes.

Uncover the dough and use a bench scraper or sharp knife to divide it into 4 equal portions. One at a time, use your fingers to gather the edges of a portion of dough to form a ball. Place on a plate and cover with plastic wrap. Using a rolling pin, roll the first piece of dough into a 4 × 6-inch oval. Starting at the thickest setting of a pasta roller (1 on a KitchenAid), roll the piece of dough once at each setting, decreasing the size until you reach setting 3. Place the sheet on the work surface and fold the short ends of the dough into the middle so you have three layers and about a 4- to 5-inch rectangle. Lightly flour the sheets, if necessary. With the short edge first, roll the dough through the pasta roller at setting 1 once again. Continue rolling once at settings 4, 5, or 6 to your preferred thinness. If the pasta sheet is too long to handle, you can cut it in half for easier rolling. Place the dough sheet on a pasta drying rack or over the back of a clean chair. Repeat for all the dough.

Once the dough sheets have dried for at least 10 to 15 minutes, begin with your first rolled sheet. Cut the sheets horizontally so each piece is 10 to 12 inches long. Lightly sprinkle the sheet with semolina flour and use a pasta cutter attachment to cut the sheets to your ideal width. Sprinkle the cut pasta with a bit of extra semolina flour and place it on a pasta drying rack or over the back of a clean chair once again for 10 to 15 minutes to dry out slightly. (Alternatively, you can flour and portion the pasta into approximate servings and roll each portion into a loose nest with your hands to dry.)

To cook, bring a large pot of salted water to boil. Add 1 tablespoon olive oil to the water to prevent boiling over. Add the pasta and cook until al dente, stirring periodically, checking for doneness at about 3 minutes. Serve with your favorite sauce!

Notes

❦ *Placing the flour on a surface and making a well is the traditional method of mixing your pasta dough. If you prefer, you can place your flour in a bowl instead and make a well before adding the eggs. This will ensure that the eggs do not leak from the center of the flour. Follow the remaining instructions as written.*

❦ *Folding the pasta dough in the middle of rolling laminates the dough and makes for a chewier texture. You can skip this step if desired.*

❦ *I change the thickness of the pasta dough based on how I am going to cut it. For example, I prefer to roll spaghetti and fettuccine to setting 5 or 6 on the KitchenAid.*

❦ *If you are going to use a hand pasta rolling machine, the highest numbers correspond to the thickest settings. So in that case I roll through each thickness until I reach setting 3 or 4.*

❦ *To make decorative pasta, follow the steps as written until rolling to the size 3 setting on the pasta roller. At this point, you can cut the sheet into two sections and scatter edible flowers or herb leaves on top of one sheet. Carefully top with the second sheet and press the edges to close it well. Roll once again at setting 3 and then continue to roll to your preferred thickness.*

Roasted Cherry Tomato Pasta

Serves 4 to 6

This recipe holds a multitude of sentimental memories for me. The video of this pasta, made with homemade dough, quickly became my highest viewed online, reaching an audience of approximately 45 million in no time. I was overwhelmed by the numerous shares and the thousands who made homemade pasta for the first time with this recipe. The stories of families cooking together, of parents and children trying their hands at pasta-making, were touching. It was as if they had welcomed me into their families, sharing their precious moments with me. Some even moved me to tears. Each time I revisited their stories, it rekindled my love for what I do.

Basic Pasta Dough (page 177), with sheets cut into spaghetti

2 to 4 medium garlic cloves, peeled

3 mini red sweet peppers

18 ounces cherry tomatoes

2 tablespoons fresh basil leaves

¼ cup extra-virgin olive oil

1 teaspoon kosher salt, plus more for the pasta water

½ teaspoon freshly ground black pepper

1 tablespoon double-concentrated tomato paste (optional; see Note)

FOR SERVING

Burrata, torn, or Stracciatella cheese

Extra-virgin olive oil, for drizzling

Grated Parmesan cheese

Fresh basil leaves, for garnish

Preheat the oven to 450°F.

On a baking sheet or in a baking dish, mix the garlic cloves, red peppers, tomatoes, and basil with the olive oil, salt, and black pepper until well combined. Roast until the tomatoes are collapsed and lightly charred, 30 to 40 minutes. Remove from the oven and set aside to cool for 5 to 10 minutes.

Bring a large pot of salted water to a boil. Add the spaghetti and cook until al dente, 4 to 6 minutes, checking after 3 minutes for your preferred doneness. Reserving 1½ cups of the cooking water, drain the pasta.

In a blender or food processor, puree the roasted vegetables and tomato paste, if using. Transfer the sauce to a large saucepan and set over medium heat. Add the drained pasta and about 1 cup of the reserved pasta water. Toss gently to combine and cook for 1 to 2 minutes. At this point, add more pasta water if you prefer the sauce to be a little thinner.

Transfer to pasta bowls and serve with torn burrata, a drizzle of olive oil, Parmesan, and fresh basil. Serve immediately.

Bon appétit!

Note

❦ *If your cherry tomatoes are very ripe and sweet, you may not need to use tomato paste. Taste and adjust to your preference.*

Vegan Semolina Pasta Dough

*Makes 29 ounces
(serves 6 to 8)*

This pasta dough is made from just semolina flour, water, salt, and sugar without eggs. Thanks to the semolina flour, the dough is robust and perfect for preparing pasta in multiple shapes and sizes. All you need are your hands and a few everyday kitchen tools. The resulting pasta is firmer and sturdier than the typical wheat flour and egg variety, making it an excellent choice for dishes like ragu.

3¼ cups (540g) fine semolina flour

1½ teaspoons (9g) kosher salt

½ teaspoon (2g) granulated sugar

I cup plus 3 tablespoons (265g) hot but not boiling water (120°F), plus I to 2 tablespoons more, depending on your flour

In a medium bowl, whisk together the semolina flour, salt, and sugar. Add the hot water and mix with your hands or a dough whisk until the ingredients begin to come together into a crumbly dough. Transfer to a work surface and, using your hands, perform the basic kneading technique (see page 22) and knead for 5 to 7 minutes. The dough will be a little bit dry and a little hard, but it's okay! If it really isn't coming together, you can add I to 2 tablespoons more hot water. Cover the dough with plastic wrap and let rest for 30 to 40 minutes at room temperature.

Once rested, continue to knead for 5 to 7 minutes, until smooth. Cover with plastic wrap once again and let rest for 1½ to 2 hours at room temperature.

Place the dough on a work surface and roll into a log. Use a sharp knife or bench scraper to divide the dough into 8 equal portions. Cover the pieces with plastic wrap to prevent drying. At this point, you can shape the dough into your preferred pasta shape. Due to the texture of the semolina pasta, I prefer to make cavatelli. Roll the first piece into a rope ¾ inch thick and then cut the rope into ½-inch slices. With a gnocchi board or a fork, use your thumb to press each piece onto the textured surface and roll it slightly to create a small ridged shape resembling gnocchi. Repeat with each piece of dough.

Bring a large pot of salted water to a boil. Add the pasta and cook for 5 to 7 minutes, checking for your preferred doneness beginning at 4 minutes. Serve with your favorite pasta sauce.

Notes

♥ *This dough will be one of the more difficult to knead. Depending on your brand of semolina flour, you may need to add a little more water, but be careful not to add too much.*

♥ *You can shape this dough into any of your preferred shapes! It makes beautiful orecchiette, busiate, lorighittas, or any other you like.*

♥ *This is a naturally chewy pasta by nature, so it takes a long time to cook beyond al dente. Semolina makes a delicious alternative to other pasta doughs!*

Veggie Pasta Dough

Makes 29 ounces
(serves 6 to 8)

Homemade vegetable pasta has played a pivotal role in my baking journey. Many of my kneading experiences revolve around this colorful pasta, which my sister and I dubbed *makarnama* in our childhood. Every month, we'd prepare batches of this pasta, let it air-dry on a kitchen towel, then cut it into short fettuccine strips with a sharp knife. They'd last us a month, just in time for a fresh batch. Sometimes, I'd fall asleep waiting for them to harden, wake up in the dead of night to cut the pasta, and drift back to sleep. Nowadays, I make it frequently just for the joy of it—the vibrancy is truly delightful.

RED PASTA

1½ ounces (45g) cooked red beets

1½ teaspoons (7g) whole milk

1 teaspoon (5g) extra-virgin olive oil

1 large egg

1¼ cups (162g) all-purpose flour, plus more for dusting

¾ teaspoon (5g) kosher salt

¼ teaspoon (1g) granulated sugar

ORANGE PASTA

1½ ounces (45g) cooked carrot

1½ teaspoons (7g) whole milk

1 teaspoon (5g) extra-virgin olive oil

1 large egg

1¼ cups (162g) all-purpose flour, plus more for dusting

¾ teaspoon (5g) kosher salt

¼ teaspoon (1g) granulated sugar

GREEN PASTA

2 ounces (60g) raw baby spinach

2 teaspoons (10g) whole milk

1 teaspoon (5g) extra-virgin olive oil

1 large egg

1¼ cups (162g) all-purpose flour, plus more for dusting

¾ teaspoon (5g) kosher salt

¼ teaspoon (1g) granulated sugar

FOR COOKING

Salt

1 tablespoon extra-virgin olive oil

Make the red pasta: In a food processor, combine the beets, milk, olive oil, and egg. Process until everything is a smooth puree. Place the flour on a clean work surface and sprinkle with the salt and sugar. Using the bottom of a bowl, press a well into the middle of the flour. Add the puree to the middle of the well. Using a fork, slowly incorporate the flour into the puree. When the mixture comes together, use your hands to perform the basic kneading technique (see page 172) and knead for 4 to 5 minutes, until almost smooth. Cover with a large bowl or plastic wrap and let rest for 30 to 40 minutes.

Meanwhile, make the orange pasta: Rinse and dry the food processor and combine the carrots, milk, olive oil, and egg. Continue the process as described for making the red pasta. Cover with a large bowl or plastic wrap and let rest for 30 to 40 minutes.

Make the green pasta: In a medium saucepan, bring 4 cups water to a boil over medium-high heat. Prepare a medium bowl of ice water and set aside. Add the spinach to the boiling water and cook for 2 to 3 minutes. Using a straining spoon, transfer the cooked spinach to the ice water. Let rest in the cold water for 5 to 10 seconds. Remove the spinach and squeeze with your hands until all excess water is removed. You should have 30g to 35g of cooked spinach at this time.

Rinse and dry the food processor and combine the spinach, milk, olive oil, and egg. Continue the process as for the red pasta. Cover with a large bowl or plastic wrap and let rest for 30 to 40 minutes.

continued

continued

Veggie Pasta Dough

Place the red pasta dough on a work surface and repeat the basic kneading technique until the dough is perfectly smooth, 4 to 5 minutes. Cover once again and let rest for 10 to 15 minutes. Repeat the kneading for the orange and green doughs.

Divide the red dough into 2 equal portions. Use your fingers to pinch the edges together to form a ball. Flour the balls and, using a rolling pin, roll each into a 4 × 6-inch oval. Flour the dough once again. Starting at the thickest setting of a pasta roller (1 on a KitchenAid), roll the pasta dough one time through each setting, decreasing the thickness until you reach setting 3. Place the sheet on the work surface and fold the short ends of the dough over the middle so you have three layers and about a 4-to-5-inch rectangle. Lightly flour the sheets, if necessary. With the short edge first, roll the dough through the pasta roller at setting 1 once again. Continue rolling the pasta at decreasing thickness, rolling once at each setting, until you reach setting 4, 5, or 6 (or your preferred thinness). If the pasta sheet is too long to handle, you can cut it in half for easier rolling. Place the rolled sheets on a drying rack or the back of a clean chair, allowing them to dry slightly (about 10 to 15 minutes) before cutting, making sure they do not touch. Repeat this process with the other half of the dough.

Repeat this entire rolling and drying process with the orange and green doughs.

Beginning with the sheets of red pasta, cut each sheet to the length of fettuccine, around 10 to 12 inches. Use a fettuccine pasta cutter to cut the dough and place the cut pasta on the drying rack or back of the chair once again. Make sure the strands are not touching each other so they will dry properly, about 10 to 15 minutes. Repeat for each sheet of all the doughs.

To cook: Bring a large pot of salted water to a boil. Add the olive oil to avoid boiling over. Add the pasta and let return to a boil. Cook the pasta until al dente, 4 to 6 minutes or to your preferred doneness. You can toss this pasta with olive oil or your preferred sauce. It is so delicious on its own that I always pair it with a very simple sauce.

Note

❦ *You can double or triple this recipe and store it for later! Once the sheets are mostly dried, you can stack the sheets with a dusting of flour between and cut 2-inch strips. Let them dry completely on a parchment paper–lined surface. At this point, you can store the pasta in airtight storage bags in the fridge for 7 to 10 days or the freezer for up to 2 months. To cook, add to the boiling water straight from the cold (fridge or freezer) and cook to al dente, 6 to 8 minutes.*

Potato Gnocchi

*Makes 21 ounces
(serves 4)*

May I confess? I've never once cooked store-bought gnocchi. I've no clue how it tastes or feels. But homemade gnocchi? Now, that's a treat I've savored many a time. For a potato enthusiast, gnocchi is a delicacy that stands toe-to-toe with homemade pasta. To cope with my hectic work routine, I often prepare recipes for the freezer as a quick fix for busy days or surprise dinner guests. Gnocchi is a freezer-friendly favorite, easy to make, and absolutely delicious—a taste guaranteed to impress.

1 pound russet potatoes (about 4 medium)

1 teaspoon (6g) kosher salt, plus more for the pasta water

Pinch of granulated sugar

1 egg yolk

½ teaspoon (1g) dried basil

1 cup plus 2 tablespoons (146g) all-purpose flour or Type "oo" flour, plus more as needed

1 tablespoon (14g) extra-virgin olive oil

Preheat the oven to 500°F.

Wrap the potatoes individually in foil and place them on the middle rack of the oven. Bake until very tender, 50 to 60 minutes.

Let the potatoes cool enough to handle. Using a sharp knife, halve the potatoes lengthwise and use a spoon to scoop the flesh out of the skin and onto a plate. Place the flesh into a potato ricer and press onto a work surface. Let cool for 12 to 15 minutes, until close to room temperature.

Sprinkle the salt and sugar evenly over the top of the potatoes. In a small bowl, give the egg yolk a quick stir to break it up. Pour the egg yolk over the top of the potatoes and sprinkle on the dried basil. Place the flour in a sifter and use it to sprinkle the flour evenly on top of the potatoes. Use a bench scraper in a cutting motion to combine the ingredients, periodically lifting the ingredients from the bottom over the top, until the dough comes together. Using your hands, press the dough into a ball, turning and pressing again until the dough is well combined. It is important to avoid kneading the dough to keep the gnocchi light and fluffy. At this point, if the dough is too sticky, you can add 1 to 2 tablespoons additional flour and continue to press the dough together. The dough may have some visible egg yolk at this point but do not worry. It's important not to overwork the dough but ensure the flour is well combined.

Once the dough is ready, wash and dry your hands well. Lightly flour a work surface and place the dough in the middle. Use a sharp knife or bench scraper to divide the dough into 8 equal portions. Use your hands to roll each piece into a rope 14 to 16 inches long and about ½ inch in diameter. Cut each rope into ½- to ¾-inch pieces as you prefer. Lightly flour the top of the dough pieces and the pad of your thumb. Next, using a fork or a gnocchi board (mucca rigagnocchi), place a piece of dough against the textured surface and press lightly with your thumb, rolling the piece along the surface to create a small ridged oval. Lightly flour a baking sheet and place the gnocchi on it, leaving space between them so they don't stick together.

In a 4-quart or larger pot, bring 12 to 13 cups of well-salted water to a boil over high heat. Add the olive oil to the water to keep it from boiling over. Add the gnocchi and return to a boil. Once the water is boiling again and the gnocchi have risen to the surface, reduce the heat to medium and check for doneness after 2 to 3 minutes. Cook to your preferred texture. Remove from the heat and use a strainer spoon to remove the gnocchi. Reserve some of the gnocchi water, if necessary, for your sauce. Serve immediately with your favorite sauce.

Notes

♥ You can cook the potatoes by boiling them in a large pot of water. I prefer to bake them because I find boiling makes the texture of the dough too soft.

♥ If you wait too long between steps, the dough will become sticky and difficult to work with. You'll then need to add more flour, which will make for chewier gnocchi. Avoid this by beginning the gnocchi only once you are ready to cook or freeze immediately.

♥ You do not have to roll the gnocchi for the classic shape. You can also cook the gnocchi immediately after cutting the dough into ½- to ¾-inch pieces for a more rustic look.

♥ Gnocchi require a lot of water to cook properly. If your large pot cannot comfortably fit all of the gnocchi at one time, boil only 2 servings at a time. If you try to boil all the prepared gnocchi at the same time, they will lose their shape.

♥ Store the uncooked gnocchi by freezing on the baking sheet for at least 2 hours, until it sets. Transfer the gnocchi to an airtight storage bag and store in the freezer for 1 to 2 months. To serve, boil a large pot of salted water and cook the gnocchi straight from the freezer for 3 to 5 additional minutes.

Brown Butter and Sage Gnocchi

Serves 4

I'd be hard-pressed to think of a recipe brown butter doesn't make better. This magical ingredient adds something special to both sweet and savory dishes. If I had to choose, I'd say the best partners for brown butter have to be gnocchi and pasta. From the moment the aroma hits your nose to each flavorful bite you take, this dish is truly impressive.

4 tablespoons salted butter (see Notes)

1 garlic clove, minced

6 to 8 fresh sage leaves

Potato Gnocchi (page 186), uncooked

Kosher salt

1 tablespoon extra-virgin olive oil

¼ cup freshly shredded Parmesan cheese, plus more for serving

Red pepper flakes, for garnish

Freshly ground black pepper, for garnish

Fill a large bowl with ice water and set aside. Slice the butter into 4 to 6 pieces. In a small light-colored saucepan, melt the butter pieces over medium heat. Stir the butter and use a spoon to observe the color. It should begin to foam and then quickly begin to brown and smell nutty. Keep watching to make sure that it does not burn. Once the butter has reached your preferred color, add the garlic and sage leaves and quickly remove from the heat. Set the saucepan in the ice water bowl, being careful not to let any water into the butter. Once cool, remove from the water and set aside.

Make the gnocchi as directed. In a 4-quart or larger pot, bring at least 12 to 13 cups of salted water to a boil over high heat. Add the olive oil to the water to keep it from boiling over. Add the gnocchi and return to a boil. Once the water is boiling again and the gnocchi have risen to the surface, reduce the heat to medium and check for doneness after 2 to 3 minutes cooking for up to 4 to 6 minutes, until they reach your preferred texture. Remove from the heat and use a strainer spoon to remove the gnocchi. Reserve 1½ cups of the gnocchi water. Add ½ cup of the gnocchi water, along with the strained gnocchi, back into the pot (hold on to the rest of the water).

Remove the sage leaves from the brown butter and set them aside. Pour the brown butter over the cooked gnocchi and add more to taste. Add the Parmesan and add more pasta water as needed to reach your preferred sauce texture. Use a wooden spoon to stir gently and cook over medium heat for 30 to 60 seconds until creamy.

Divide among four serving bowls or plates. Top with more Parmesan, red pepper flakes, black pepper, and the reserved sage leaves. Serve immediately.

Notes

♥ *The amount of butter for the sauce is based on my testers' and family's preferences, but you can add 2 additional tablespoons of butter if you would like a richer sauce. You can also add 1 to 2 tablespoons heavy cream with the pasta water for a creamier sauce.*

♥ *Using a light-colored pan, such as stainless steel, for the browned butter will make it far easier to observe the color and avoid burning. If you only have dark-colored pans, be extra careful to use a spoon to check the color often while cooking.*

♥ *Store any remaining brown butter in a small jar in the fridge for up to 1 week and then use it for any other recipe, including scrambled eggs or pasta.*

Egg Noodles

Serves 4

After a stressful day, we often turn to quick meals like instant noodles. But what if you could make homemade noodles over the weekend? Trust me, as you slurp up a bowl of hand-cut noodles that you made from scratch, you'll realize it was well worth the effort. Whether it's a chicken noodle soup or a ramen-style dish, the choice is yours. Just remember, you deserve it.

1 medium egg

¾ cup (165g) water, plus more if needed

3 cups plus 2 tablespoons (406g) Type "00" or all-purpose flour, plus more for dusting

1½ teaspoons (9g) kosher salt

¼ teaspoon (1g) granulated sugar

FOR COOKING

Kosher salt

1 tablespoon extra-virgin olive oil

In a small bowl, whisk together the egg and water. In a medium bowl, mound the flour and make a well. Sprinkle the salt and sugar over the flour. Add the egg mixture to the well. Using your hand shaped like a claw or a dough hook, stir and squeeze the dough until the ingredients come together. Turn out onto a work surface. Using your hands, perform the basic kneading technique (see page 172) and knead for 4 to 5 minutes. It is going to be a little dry and tough initially, but don't worry! Continue to knead and the dough will stick together after a while. Transfer the dough to a bowl and cover with plastic wrap. Let rest at room temperature for 1 hour.

Return the dough to the work surface and knead for an additional 5 to 7 minutes, until smooth. Cover it with plastic wrap again and let rest for an additional 30 minutes. If the dough is still dry at this point, wet your hands and repeat the process one more time until it is smooth.

Transfer the dough to a work surface. Using a sharp knife or bench scraper, divide the dough into 4 equal portions. Using a rolling pin, roll the first piece of dough into a 4 × 6-inch oval. Starting at the thickest setting of a pasta roller (1 on a KitchenAid), roll the piece of dough once at each setting, decreasing the size until you reach setting 3. Place the sheet on the work surface and fold the short ends of the dough into the middle (letter fold) so you have three layers and about a 4- to 5-inch rectangle. Lightly flour the sheet, if necessary. With the short end first, roll the dough through the pasta roller at setting 1 once again. Continue rolling the pasta once at each decreasing setting, until you reach 4 or 5. The dough should be just thicker than a millimeter. Hang the dough sheet on a drying rack or the back of a clean chair and let dry for around 15 minutes. Repeat with each piece of dough.

Beginning with the first dough sheet, slice the sheet in half to make it easier to handle. Use a spaghetti cutter attachment or an attachment for your preferred shape to cut the sheets into noodles. Sprinkle with a bit of extra flour and hang once again. Repeat with each dough sheet. Dry the noodles for 7 to 10 minutes before cooking.

To cook: Bring a large pot of salted water to a boil. Add the olive oil to prevent boiling over. Add the noodles and cook until al dente, 2 to 3 minutes or to your preferred doneness. Drain and rinse the noodles with cold water.

Serve with your preferred sauce or topping.

Notes

❦ *You can use this dough for delicious American-style chicken noodle soup.*

❦ *These noodles are best prepared and cooked immediately; otherwise, they may stick together.*

Chicken Ramen with Soy Eggs

Serves 4

Ramen noodles are a comfort food for many of us. As someone who could happily eat ramen every day for lunch during a nine-day winter vacation, I never tire of it. However, I can't say my husband and son share my enthusiasm for ramen. Hence, we have a single family-approved ramen recipe: very mild and simple. It's a triumph to have convinced them to love ramen this much! I make the ramen broth especially mild to suit everyone's tastes, but you can adjust it to your liking before serving by adding more soy sauce, vinegar, or oil. For the chicken broth, I usually prefer homemade, as it's healthier and tastier. If you're making homemade chicken broth, I like to keep the ingredients simple with just green onions, garlic, and black peppercorns rather than adding lots of vegetables. Don't forget to make the soy eggs ahead—with those on hand, you're all set for a fantastic lunch.

Egg Noodles (page 190)

CHICKEN

2 garlic cloves, minced

2 tablespoons soy sauce

2 tablespoons extra-virgin olive oil

1 tablespoon sesame oil

1½ teaspoons light brown sugar

½ teaspoon rice vinegar

4 medium boneless, skinless chicken thighs

1 cup chicken broth

RAMEN BROTH

1 teaspoon black peppercorns

2 star anise pods

3 to 4 whole cloves

⅓ of a small cinnamon stick

8 cups chicken broth

2 teaspoons mushroom powder

1½ teaspoons minced fresh ginger

2 garlic cloves, minced

2 teaspoons sesame oil

1 tablespoon chili oil

2 teaspoons rice vinegar

4 to 5 tablespoons soy sauce

½ teaspoon kosher salt, or more to taste

4 to 6 fresh shiitake mushrooms, halved or quartered

ASSEMBLY

Kosher salt

1 tablespoon extra-virgin olive oil

4 Soy Eggs (recipe follows)

2 scallions, chopped, for garnish

1 tablespoon sesame seeds, for garnish

¼ cup chopped fresh cilantro, for garnish

Chili oil, for drizzling

Make the egg noodles as directed, but don't cook them yet.

Prepare the chicken: In a medium shallow bowl, combine the garlic, soy sauce, olive oil, sesame oil, brown sugar, and vinegar and mix well. Taste and adjust the seasoning to your preference. Add the chicken thighs and coat well. Cover with plastic wrap and transfer the bowl to the fridge. Let marinate for at least 30 minutes and preferably up to 3 hours.

Heat a skillet over medium-high heat and place the chicken in the skillet. Sear each side until the chicken is golden brown, 60 to 70 seconds. Add the chicken broth, reduce the heat to medium-low, and simmer until cooked through but still tender, 8 to 12 minutes. Remove from the heat and let rest for 10 to 15 minutes before slicing.

Make the ramen broth: In a square of cheesecloth or a spice bag, combine the peppercorns, star anise, cloves, and cinnamon stick and tie off.

In a medium pot, stir together the chicken broth, spice bundle, mushroom powder, ginger, garlic, sesame oil, chili oil, rice vinegar, soy sauce, salt, and shiitake mushrooms. Bring to a boil over medium heat, then reduce the heat to medium-low and simmer until the mushrooms are tender but not too soft, 6 to 8 minutes. Scoop out the mushrooms and set aside. Taste the broth and adjust the seasoning as desired.

continued

continued

Chicken Ramen with Soy Eggs

Assemble the bowls: Bring a large pot of salted water to a boil. Add the olive oil to prevent boiling over. Add the noodles and cook until al dente, 2 to 3 minutes or to your preferred doneness. Drain and rinse the noodles with cold water.

Divide the noodles among four serving bowls and pour the very hot broth evenly over each. Remove the soy eggs from the marinade and slice in half. Dress each bowl of ramen with sliced chicken, shiitake mushrooms, soy egg, scallions, sesame seeds, and cilantro. Drizzle with chili oil for extra spice.

Note

♦ *Don't forget the mushroom powder—it is a small ingredient that goes a long way in making a delicious broth! If you don't have it, you should increase the salt and spices to step up the flavor.*

Soy Eggs

Makes 4 eggs

6 tablespoons soy sauce

6 tablespoons water

3 tablespoons rice vinegar

1 teaspoon chili oil

1 teaspoon light brown sugar, or more to taste

1 tablespoon chopped fresh cilantro

1½ tablespoons chopped scallions

4 Soft-Boiled Eggs (recipe follows), peeled

In a small screw-top jar with a lid or a sandwich-size airtight storage bag, combine the soy sauce, water, rice vinegar, chili oil, brown sugar, cilantro, and scallions. Stir to combine well. Place the soft-boiled eggs in the liquid. Add more water, if necessary, to make sure the eggs are fully covered. Taste the marinade and add soy sauce, brown sugar, and salt to your preference. Cover the jar and keep in the fridge for a minimum of 3 hours or overnight.

Soft-Boiled Eggs

Makes 4 eggs

4 large eggs, cold

½ teaspoon lemon juice

Fill a medium saucepan three-quarters full of water and bring to a boil over high heat. Once boiling, use a wooden spoon to carefully place the eggs in the water and add the lemon juice. Reduce the heat to medium and cook for 6 to 7 minutes for a runny egg and 7 to 8 minutes for a soft-boiled egg. Meanwhile, fill a medium bowl with ice water. Using a straining spoon, transfer the eggs to the ice bath. Let sit for 10 to 15 minutes. Once cooled completely, crack the shell and peel carefully.

Dumpling Wrappers

Makes 35 to 40 wrappers

Recently, a social media follower asked if I ever get tired of cooking from scratch. The answer? Absolutely not! Making your own dumpling wrappers might seem daunting, but with a pasta roller at hand, you're set to make any dumplings your heart desires.

1 teaspoon (6g) kosher salt

¼ teaspoon (1g) granulated sugar

¾ cup plus 2 tablespoons (195g) hot water, plus more if needed

3 cups (390g) all-purpose flour, plus more for dusting

Cornstarch, for dusting

In a small bowl, mix together the salt, sugar, and water until dissolved. In a medium bowl, combine the flour and the sugar/salt mixture. Using your hand shaped as a claw, bring the dough together, stirring and squeezing the dough periodically for 2 to 3 minutes. Transfer the dough to a work surface. Using your hands, perform the basic kneading technique (see page 172) for 4 to 5 minutes. The dough will be a little dry and won't look perfectly smooth at the end of this process, but don't worry. Cover with plastic wrap and let rest at room temperature for 30 to 40 minutes.

After resting, knead for 4 to 5 minutes, until smooth and elastic. Cover with plastic wrap and let rest at room temperature for 1 hour or up to 4 hours.

Set the dough on a work surface and knead for 1 to 2 minutes until smooth. Roll the dough into a log and use a sharp knife to divide into 4 equal portions. Round each piece of dough into a smooth ball (see page 22). Place the balls on a floured plate and cover the plate loosely with plastic wrap.

Place a ball of dough on the work surface. Using a rolling pin, roll into a 3 × 6-inch oval. Starting at the thickest setting of a pasta roller (1 on a KitchenAid), roll the dough, decreasing the thickness each time, until you reach setting 6 on a KitchenAid. (If the dough sticks while rolling, lightly dust the sheets with cornstarch.) Lightly dust a work surface and the top of the dough sheet with cornstarch, spreading it evenly. Using a 3½- to 4-inch round cookie cutter, cut the dumpling wrappers, stacking them on a plate loosely covered with plastic wrap to keep them from drying out. Repeat with all the dough. Gather all the scraps into a ball and repeat the rolling and cutting process one more time. Your wrappers are now ready to be used in your favorite dumpling recipe.

Notes

♥ *If you do not have a pasta roller or prefer to roll wrappers by hand, you can roll the dough into an 18-inch rope and divide it into 15g pieces. On a lightly floured or cornstarched surface, use a rolling pin to roll each piece into a 3½-inch round. Follow the rest of the recipe as written.*

♥ *If not making dumplings immediately, you can place the four balls of dough into an airtight container or storage bags rather than on a plate. Keep dough in the fridge for up to 2 days and then let sit until almost room temperature, about 30 to 45 minutes, before shaping.*

♥ *You can also use this dough as a vegan noodle dough! Follow the shaping instructions for Egg Noodles (page 190) for a delicious vegan ramen option.*

Chicken Dumplings

Serves 4 to 6

Have you tried fried chicken dumplings made with homemade wrappers? If not, these dumplings should absolutely be your project this weekend. These scrumptious treats are one of those recipes that can be turned into a delightful family activity, with each step enjoyable in its own way. With their juicy and flavorful filling and crispy outer layer, these dumplings are worth every bit of effort. At our house, there's usually no chance of having leftovers to store in the freezer—they're all devoured within the same day. But if you're someone who takes comfort in having ready meals in the freezer for emergencies, you can easily make a batch over the weekend and store them for later.

Dumpling Wrappers
(page 197)

CHICKEN FILLING

1 pound ground chicken thighs

¼ medium head napa cabbage, shredded

1 small onion, finely diced

2 garlic cloves, minced

1 carrot, grated

1½ teaspoons minced fresh ginger

2 to 3 green onions, chopped

½ cup chopped fresh cilantro

1 tablespoon plus ½ teaspoon sesame oil

3 tablespoons peanut oil

1 teaspoon kosher salt

1 teaspoon freshly ground black pepper

1 tablespoon soy sauce

DUMPLINGS

Egg white (optional)

Sesame seeds (optional)

Extra-virgin olive oil, for cooking

Warm water, for cooking

DIPPING SAUCE

½ cup soy sauce

¼ cup water

1 tablespoon chili oil

2 teaspoons sesame oil

2 teaspoons rice vinegar

2 teaspoons honey

2 small garlic cloves, minced

2 tablespoons sesame seeds, toasted

4 scallions, chopped, for garnish

Make the dumpling wrappers as directed.

Prepare the chicken filling: Spread the chicken in a large bowl. Sprinkle the napa cabbage, onion, garlic, carrot, ginger, green onions, and cilantro on top of the chicken but do not mix.

In a small saucepan, heat the sesame and peanut oils together over medium heat. Once the oil is very hot, remove from the heat and pour directly over the vegetables. Add the salt, pepper, and soy sauce. Using a wooden spoon or your hands, stir thoroughly until the mixture is well combined and has an almost paste-like consistency.

Prepare the dumplings: Set the dumpling wrappers on a clean work surface. Place 2 tablespoons of the chicken filling in the middle of a dumpling wrapper. Dip your finger in water and moisten the outer edge of the wrapper. Fold the wrapper in half and press the edge to seal. Starting from the left corner, pinch together the edge with the forefingers and thumbs of both hands. Moving right across the top of the dumpling, pinch the outer edge with your left hand while lightly folding the dough over it with the fingers of the right. This will create the traditional wave pattern. Pinch tightly as you go to ensure a tight seal. Once completely sealed, lightly flatten the bottom of the dumpling so it can sit upright. Place on a baking a sheet and cover loosely with plastic wrap. Repeat this process with each wrapper.

continued

continued

Chicken Dumplings

Once finished, if extra crunch is desired, use your finger to lightly moisten the bottom of the dumplings with water or egg white and dip in sesame seeds.

In a large nonstick skillet, heat 2 tablespoons of olive oil over medium heat. Working in batches of 10 to 12 dumplings (so they do not touch), sear the bottoms for 2 to 3 minutes while watching. Add ¼ cup of warm water and immediately cover with a lid. Reduce the heat to medium-low and cook until the dumplings are tender and the water has evaporated, 8 to 10 minutes. Remove from the heat and place on a plate. Repeat with the remaining dumplings, using 2 tablespoons of oil and ¼ cup of warm water per batch.

Make the dipping sauce: In a small bowl, mix the soy sauce, water, chili oil, sesame oil, vinegar, honey, garlic, and sesame seeds.

Serve the hot dumplings with dipping sauce on the side and garnish with scallions.

Note

♦ *If not cooking immediately, you can place the filled dumplings on a baking sheet lined with parchment paper, cover with plastic wrap, and freeze for 2 hours. Once frozen, place them in an airtight storage bag and keep in the freezer for up to 3 months. To cook, follow the instructions but add 1 to 2 additional minutes to ensure they cook through.*

Wonton Wrappers

Makes 16 to 18 large (6-inch) square wrappers or 64 to 70 small (3-inch) square wrappers

You might be wondering why you should make these wrappers at home when you can conveniently pick them up from the supermarket. While it's okay to take shortcuts occasionally, nothing compares to the flavor and satisfaction of homemade wrappers. If you have a pasta roller, preparing them is a breeze and their taste and healthfulness far outshine any ready-made wrappers.

2 cups (260g) all-purpose flour

1 teaspoon (6g) kosher salt

½ teaspoon (2g) granulated sugar

½ cup plus 1 tablespoon (125g) water, at room temperature (75° to 80°F), plus more if needed

¼ teaspoon (1g) distilled white vinegar

Cornstarch, for dusting

In a medium bowl, mound the flour and make a well in the middle. Add the salt and sugar evenly over the flour, then add the water and vinegar to the well and mix together. Using your hands or a dough whisk, mix the dough until the ingredients come together. Transfer the dough to a work surface. Using your hands, perform the basic kneading technique (see page 172) and knead for 4 to 5 minutes. The dough may seem dry at first, but continue to knead well. After 2 to 3 minutes of kneading, if it still isn't coming together, you can add ½ to 1 tablespoon additional water. The dough should be almost fully together, but do not worry if it's a little dry. Cover with plastic wrap or a kitchen towel and let rest for 30 to 40 minutes at room temperature.

After resting, use the same technique to knead the dough for an additional 4 to 5 minutes. At this point, if it is still not smooth, cover and repeat the resting and kneading process one more time.

Place the dough on a work surface and roll into a log. Use a sharp knife or bench scraper to divide the dough into 4 equal portions. Place the pieces on a plate and cover with plastic wrap to avoid drying out. Take a piece of dough and use a rolling pin to roll it into a 4 × 5-inch oval. Starting at the thickest setting of a pasta roller (1 on a KitchenAid), roll the wonton sheet once at each setting, reducing the thickness each time until it reaches setting 8, the thinnest setting. If the pieces become too long to handle, cut them in half and continue to roll them through. Place the dough sheets on a clean work surface and lightly dust them with cornstarch on both sides as they are finished. Use a sharp knife or pizza cutter to cut the finished sheets to size according to your recipe. For large rolls, cut 6-inch

continued

continued

Wonton Wrappers

squares. For small wontons, cut 6-inch squares into four 3-inch squares. Stack the wrappers on top of one another on a baking sheet and cover with a clean kitchen towel or loosely with plastic wrap. Repeat this process until all the wrappers have been cut.

Use the wrappers within an hour of preparation to avoid sticking. Fill them with your favorite filling, such as buffalo chicken (see Buffalo Chicken Rangoons, page 203).

Note

❦ *You can store the wonton dough before shaping by splitting it into 2 equal logs and placing them in an airtight container or storage bag. Keep them in the fridge for up to 2 days, then let sit at room temperature for 30 minutes before shaping according to the recipe.*

Buffalo Chicken Rangoons

Makes 64 to 70 rangoons

Some recipes are inspired by the amazing dishes I've tried during my travels. On a trip to St. Petersburg, I stumbled upon delicious rangoons in a quaint little restaurant we found by chance, and I absolutely loved them. The dish stuck with me, so as soon as I got home, I gave this recipe a go. It was an instant hit: crispy on the outside, cheesy and dreamy on the inside. I usually serve these rolls as a starter, but rangoons are so delightful that they can be enjoyed any time of the day, even as a snack. Just a word of advice: If you're watching your intake, make sure to count how many you put on your plate or you might end up eating more than you realize!

BUFFALO CHICKEN FILLING

1½ cups shredded cooked chicken breast

1 medium garlic clove, minced

4 ounces cream cheese, at room temperature

2 to 3 tablespoons sour cream, at room temperature

2½ tablespoons minced scallion

2 tablespoons minced fresh parsley

¼ cup Buffalo Sauce (recipe follows)

Kosher salt

RANGOONS

Wonton Wrappers (page 201), cut into 3-inch squares

1 cup finely shredded mozzarella or white cheddar cheese

Neutral oil, for deep-frying

Ranch dressing, for serving

Buffalo Sauce (recipe follows), for serving

Make the Buffalo chicken filling: In a large bowl, combine the chicken, garlic, cream cheese, 2 tablespoons of the sour cream, the scallion, parsley, and Buffalo sauce. Mix well with a wooden spoon and add an additional tablespoon of sour cream for a thinner consistency if preferred. Taste and add more salt or Buffalo sauce, if desired. Set aside.

Shape the rangoons: On a clean kitchen counter, set a wonton wrapper with a corner facing you. Add ½ tablespoon of the cheese and ½ tablespoon of the Buffalo chicken filling to the center. Fill a small bowl with water and dip your finger into it. Use it to lightly wet all edges of the wrapper. Connect the bottom and top corners of the wrapper so it is a triangle shape, but do not pinch the corners together. Then lift the wrapper so the top of the triangle points upward and the middle of the wrapper is sitting on the counter. Bring the left and right corners together into the middle so all four corners meet evenly. Lightly wet your finger again and seal the corners and edges tightly. Place the completed rangoons on a large plate and cover loosely with plastic wrap or a clean kitchen towel to avoid drying out while you shape the remaining pieces. The rangoons can touch but do not squish them.

Line a large plate with paper towels and set near the stove. Pour 2½ inches neutral oil into a medium pot and heat over medium heat to 350°F.

Working in batches of 6 to 8 pieces, carefully place the rangoons in the hot oil and fry, turning periodically

continued

continued

Buffalo Chicken Rangoons

and watching constantly, until nicely golden brown, 2 to 4 minutes. Using a strainer spoon, remove them from the oil and place on the paper towels. Repeat the process with the remaining rangoons.

Serve immediately with Buffalo sauce and ranch on the side.

Buffalo Chicken Rolls

Make the wonton wrappers as directed and cut into 6-inch squares. Make the chicken filling as directed. Set a wonton wrapper with a corner facing you. Add 2 tablespoons shredded cheese in a line just below the middle of the wrapper. Add 1½ tablespoons of the chicken filling over the cheese. Fill a small bowl with water and set aside. Fold the right and left corners over the top of the filling to meet in the middle. Fold the bottom corner into the middle, so the roll resembles an envelope with the top open. Then, roll up from the bottom edge. Once the roll nears the top corner, lightly wet the tip of your finger with the water and wet the corner of the dough. Continue rolling upward to seal the roll. Place the completed rolls on a large plate and cover loosely with plastic wrap or a clean kitchen towel to avoid drying out while you shape the remaining pieces. The rolls can touch but do not squish them.

Follow the directions for deep-frying rangoons, working in batches of 3 to 5, turning periodically until golden brown, 3 to 5 minutes. Drain on paper towels and serve as directed.

Notes

♦ *To easily shred the cooked chicken, place it in a large bowl and use the whisk attachment of an electric mixer to shred the chicken until it is in small pieces.*

♦ *You can bake the rangoons in the oven. Preheat the oven to 350°F. Arrange them on a lined baking sheet with ½ inch between them and drizzle the tops with olive oil. Bake 12 to 14 minutes.*

Buffalo Sauce

Makes 1½ cups

1 stick unsalted butter

¾ cup hot sauce

1 tablespoon white vinegar

1 teaspoon honey

½ teaspoon garlic powder

½ teaspoon hot paprika or cayenne

Salt

In a small saucepan, melt the butter over medium heat. Add the hot sauce, vinegar, honey, garlic powder, and paprika and use a wooden spoon to stir well. Taste and add salt if needed. Remove from the heat and let cool. Transfer to a clean jar and keep in the fridge for up to 2 weeks. Bring to room temperature and mix well before serving.

Flour Tortillas

Makes twelve 6-inch tortillas

A delicious flour tortilla can be the start of hundreds of dishes—tacos, burritos, enchiladas, quesadillas, tostadas, wraps, chips, and more. It's a staple in my kitchen. Drop by my house unexpectedly in the morning, and you'll likely be greeted with a breakfast burrito or a gooey, cheese-filled quesadilla. With this easy and delightful recipe, you can make a dozen small tortillas or seven larger ones.

2 cups (260g)
all-purpose flour

1½ teaspoons (9g)
kosher salt

¼ teaspoon (1g)
granulated sugar

1½ teaspoons (6g)
baking powder

¼ cup plus 1 teaspoon
(50g) vegetable shortening,
at room temperature

¾ cup (165g) hot water
(120°F), plus more
if needed

In a medium bowl, whisk together the flour, salt, sugar, and baking powder. Add the vegetable shortening and using your hands, toss the shortening into the ingredients, smushing large pieces between your thumbs and forefingers to make sure they are evenly incorporated into the dough and no pieces are larger than a popcorn kernel. Add the hot water. Using a dough whisk or wooden spoon, stir to incorporate everything together.

Transfer the mixture to a work surface. Using your hands, perform the basic kneading technique (see page 22) and knead for 4 to 5 minutes, until the dough is elastic and no longer sticky. Place the dough back in the bowl and cover with plastic wrap. Let rest for 20 minutes.

Uncover the dough and use the same technique to knead for an additional 3 to 5 minutes, until perfectly smooth and shiny. Cover with plastic wrap and let rest at room temperature for at least another 30 minutes and up to 2 hours.

Transfer the dough to a clean work surface and roll into a log. Divide into 12 portions (see Notes). Round each piece of dough into a smooth ball (see page 22). Cover with plastic wrap as you work to make sure the balls do not dry out.

Heat a nonstick griddle over medium-high heat. Test the pan by drizzling it with water. If it is hot enough, the water should immediately evaporate. Ensure the pan is dry before placing a tortilla on it. Roll one ball of dough with a rolling pin into a 6- to 7-inch round and immediately place on the hot griddle. Cook the first side for 7 to 10 seconds and then flip. Continue to cook each side for 7 to 10 seconds, flipping two more times, cooking for a total of 40 to 60 seconds. Each piece should be just barely cooked; if overcooked the tortilla will be dry and difficult to bend. Remove from the griddle and place in a tortilla warmer or on a plate or basket covered with a kitchen towel to avoid drying out. Repeat this process until each piece is cooked.

Serve with your favorite taco fillings.

Notes

❧ *If you are looking for larger tortillas, you can cut the dough into 6 or 7 equal portions and roll them to 10- to 12-inch rounds. Follow cooking instructions, but for 50 to 70 seconds in total.*

❧ *These tortillas will keep at room temperature in an airtight storage bag for 1 day or for 2 to 3 days in the fridge. Warm lightly before using. Store them in the freezer for up to 2 months with pieces of parchment paper between them.*

❧ *You can use butter or lard for this recipe instead of shortening. Lard is the traditional fat used, but as a Muslim I don't use lard, so I prefer shortening as a substitute.*

Fish Tacos with Red Cabbage Slaw, Jalapeño Sour Cream Sauce, and Pico de Gallo

Makes 9 tacos (serves 3)

If you're as big a fan of fish tacos as my family is, this will soon become your absolute favorite recipe. Its addictive flavor will keep you coming back for more. While the deep-fried version is an unparalleled treat, the oven version is a great choice for fewer dishes and a healthier meal. It's a frequently cooked recipe in our house, a celebrated highlight of our Taco Thursdays (yes, I mean Taco Thursdays). It's easy to whip up, and depending on how you feel, you can opt for the decadent fried version or the simpler oven version.

FRIED FISH

3 tilapia or other white fish fillets (1 pound)

½ cup plus 1 tablespoon all-purpose flour

1 teaspoon garlic powder

½ teaspoon onion powder

1 teaspoon chili powder

1 teaspoon kosher salt, plus more to taste

Pinch of granulated sugar

½ teaspoon baking powder

1 cup sparkling water

3 cups cornflakes, for coating

Neutral oil, for deep-frying

TACOS

9 Flour Tortillas (page 206)

Jalapeño Sour Cream Sauce (recipe follows)

Red Cabbage Slaw (recipe follows)

Pico de Gallo (recipe follows)

Pickled jalapeños, for serving

Lime wedges, for squeezing

Prepare the fried fish: Using a sharp knife, cut each tilapia fillet into 6 equal pieces. I prefer to cut the wide sections in half lengthwise and then in half again. Finally, cut the smaller tail into two pieces.

In a large bowl, combine the flour, garlic powder, onion powder, chili powder, salt, sugar, and baking powder. Whisk together the dry ingredients and then whisk in the sparkling water until combined well. The batter should be about the thickness of buttermilk. Add the tilapia pieces to the batter, cover with plastic wrap, and let rest in the fridge for 3 to 4 hours.

When ready to cook, use a blender to crush the cornflakes into crumbs. Place the crumbs in a medium shallow bowl.

Line a cooling rack with paper towels and set near the stove. Pour 2½ inches oil into a large saucepan and heat over medium heat to 350°F (test by dropping in a crumb, and if it immediately sizzles, the oil is ready).

Meanwhile, set another cooling rack over a baking sheet. Use tongs to remove a piece of fish from the batter and coat it well with the cornflake crumbs, making sure it is fully covered. Place on the cooling rack and repeat to coat all the fish pieces.

When the oil reaches temperature, use tongs to carefully place a piece of fish in the hot oil and cook for 2 to 3 minutes on each side, until golden brown

continued

continued

Fish Tacos with Red Cabbage Slaw, Jalapeño Sour Cream Sauce, and Pico de Gallo

and crispy, 4 to 6 minutes total. Remove from the oil with a strainer spoon and place on the paper towels to drain. Fry the fish pieces either one at a time or in batches, depending on the size of your pan, to make sure you do not overcrowd the oil.

Assemble the tacos: In a large skillet over medium heat, warm two tortillas at a time for 10 seconds on each side. You can also warm both sides of the tortilla over a gas stove with tongs.

Place a tortilla on a plate and add 1½ tablespoons of the jalapeño sour cream sauce and cabbage slaw. Top with two pieces of the hot fried fish and pico de gallo and pickled jalapeños. Serve immediately with lime wedges and extra jalapeño sauce.

Oven-Baked Fish Tacos

Baking the fish in the oven is a little quicker and simpler than frying. Preheat the oven to 400°F and line a baking sheet with parchment paper. In a small bowl, mix the garlic powder, onion powder, chili powder, salt, and sugar and sprinkle over the fish. Toss to coat well. Beat 2 eggs with a dash of salt and pepper in a shallow dish and spread the cornflake crumbs in another shallow bowl. Dip the fish in the egg mixture and then the cornflakes and arrange on the lined baking sheet. Drizzle some olive oil lightly all over the fish. Bake until golden brown and crispy, 13 to 15 minutes. Assemble the tacos according to the recipe.

Red Cabbage Slaw

Makes 1½ cups

½ small head red cabbage (or ¼ medium)

1 tablespoon apple cider vinegar

1 tablespoon fresh lemon juice

½ teaspoon kosher salt

¼ teaspoon granulated sugar

2 tablespoons extra-virgin olive oil

Using a mandoline, shave the red cabbage into thin slices. In a medium bowl, combine the cabbage, vinegar, lemon juice, salt, sugar, and olive oil. Using your hands, massage the mixture into the cabbage. Transfer the slaw to a clear jar or container with a lid and let marinate at room temperature for at least 30 minutes before using. The slaw can be stored in the fridge for 7 to 10 days. You can use this with salads or in sandwich recipes.

Jalapeño Sour Cream Sauce

Makes 1½ cups

½ cup sour cream

3 tablespoons buttermilk

3 tablespoons mayonnaise

3 to 4 tablespoons minced
pickled jalapeño, to taste

2 tablespoons chopped
fresh cilantro

2 tablespoons brine from
the pickled jalapeños

2 teaspoons fresh
lemon juice

2 to 4 canned chipotle
peppers in adobo sauce,
chopped

Kosher salt

¼ teaspoon freshly
ground black pepper

In a medium bowl, combine the sour cream, buttermilk, mayo, pickled jalapeños, chopped cilantro, pickle brine, lemon juice, and chipotle peppers to taste and mix well. Add salt to taste and the black pepper. Refrigerate until ready to use. You can add this to any burrito or wrap or use as a salad or sandwich dressing. Store in a clean jar in the fridge for up to 4 days.

Pico de Gallo

Makes 1½ cups

2 medium tomatoes, diced

1 small red onion, diced

¼ cup chopped fresh
cilantro

1 medium jalapeño, diced
(optional)

1 teaspoon fresh lime juice

Kosher salt

In a small bowl, mix together the tomatoes, red onion, cilantro, jalapeño (if using), and lime juice. Add salt to taste and stir. Prepare just before use. If not serving immediately, wait to add the lime juice and salt until the last minute to preserve the texture of the vegetables.

Beef Empanadas with Salsa Roja and Salsa Verde

Makes 18 empanadas (serves 6)

Sometimes, the kitchen feels like a magical place where experimentation leads to delightful surprises. That's exactly what happened when I developed this recipe exclusively for this cookbook and the outcome surpassed even my own high expectations—wow!

I'm thrilled to share one of the most exciting and mouthwatering recipes in the book. Once you've tried it, you'll be plotting your next kitchen date just to make it again. The combination of crispy fried dough and cheesy filling is irresistible—it's a dish that will haunt your taste buds in the best possible way. Pair the warm empanadas with fresh salsas and let your palate revel in the flavors.

You can bake these empanadas for a lighter option, but I must emphasize that frying them truly brings out their deliciousness.

EMPANADA DOUGH

2¾ cups plus 2 tablespoons (375g) all-purpose flour, plus more if needed

1 stick (4 oz/113g) cold butter

1¼ teaspoons (8g) kosher salt

1 teaspoon (4g) granulated sugar

1 cup (220g) cold water

BEEF FILLING

2 tablespoons extra-virgin olive oil

1 large onion, diced

1 pound ground beef (85/15)

2 tablespoons double-concentrated tomato paste

2 large garlic cloves, minced

½ red bell pepper, diced

½ yellow bell pepper, diced

1 jalapeño, diced

¾ cup water

1 teaspoon dried thyme

½ teaspoon dried oregano

1 teaspoon garlic powder

2 teaspoons dried parsley

1 teaspoon chili powder

1 teaspoon kosher salt, or more to taste

1 teaspoon freshly ground black pepper

½ teaspoon ancho chile powder

EMPANADAS

1½ cups shredded Oaxaca cheese, for filling

Neutral oil, for frying

Salsa Roja (recipe follows), for serving

Salsa Verde (recipe follows), for serving

Make the empanada dough: In a large bowl, mound the flour and grate the cold butter into it. Using your fingers, toss the butter to coat with the flour. Add the salt, sugar, and cold water and use your hands to bring the mixture from the bottom and toss it over the top, pressing with the base of your hand and repeating this motion for 2 to 3 minutes to combine the mixture well.

Turn the dough out onto a lightly floured work surface and, using the basic kneading technique (see page 22), knead for 3 to 5 minutes, until smooth. Form the dough into a ball, wrap well with plastic wrap, and refrigerate for at least 1 hour and preferably up to 3 hours.

Meanwhile, make the filling: In a large skillet, heat the olive oil over medium-high heat. Add the onion and cook for 3 to 4 minutes. Add the ground beef and cook until browned, stirring occasionally, about 7 to 10 minutes. Stir in the tomato paste and garlic and cook for 2 to 3 minutes. Add the bell peppers and jalapeño and cook for 2 minutes.

continued

Beef Empanadas with Salsa Roja and Salsa Verde

Add the water, reduce the heat to medium-low, and add the thyme, oregano, garlic powder, dried parsley, chili powder, salt, pepper, and ancho chile powder and cover with a lid. Cook, stirring occasionally, until the ground beef is done and the water cooked out, about 10 minutes. Remove from the heat and let cool to room temperature.

Make the empanadas: Place the dough on a work surface. Lightly flour a baking sheet and set aside. Repeating the kneading technique, knead for an additional minute. Roll the dough into a log and use a sharp knife or bench scraper to cut it into 18 portions of 40g each. Round each piece of dough into a smooth ball (see page 22). Place on a plate and cover with plastic wrap.

Use a rolling pin to roll the first ball into a 5-inch round. Place 2 tablespoons of the filling mixture and 1½ tablespoons of shredded cheese in the middle. Fold the dough in half, pulling the bottom over the top edge. Use your fingers to pinch in a wave pattern to seal the edge. Place on the prepared baking sheet and cover loosely with plastic wrap. Repeat to make all the empanadas.

Line a plate with paper towels. Pour 2½ inches of oil into a large pot and heat to 350°F over medium heat.

Working in batches of 2 or 3 empanadas, add them to the hot oil, and cook for 1 to 2 minutes on one side, then flip them to the other side. Repeat this process one or two more times, cooking for 5 to 6 minutes total, to make sure they are golden brown and flaky on both sides. Remove from the oil and place on the paper towels to drain.

Serve hot with salsa roja and salsa verde on the side.

Notes

♦ You can prepare the dough and filling 1 to 2 days in advance and store them separately in the fridge. If you don't plan to eat all the empanadas in one go, cook half and store the rest of the dough and filling separately and fill and cook fresh the next day.

♦ If you do not want to roll out the dough rounds one by one, you can use a pasta roller. After you remove the dough from the fridge, cut it into 6 equal portions. Roll one portion into a ball and place on a plate and cover with plastic wrap. Then with the first piece of dough, use a rolling pin to roll it into a 5 × 7-inch oval. Lightly flour the dough. Starting at the thickest setting of a pasta roller (1 on a KitchenAid), roll the oval through the pasta roller twice, flouring the dough sheet in between if needed. Then roll the dough twice at setting 2. Transfer the dough sheet to a lightly floured work surface and use a 5-inch round cookie cutter to cut the dough. Follow the filling instructions from the recipe and cover with plastic wrap as described. Repeat with the remaining dough. Follow the rest of the recipe as written. You can reroll any excess dough for more empanadas, or you can fry the extra pieces as little chips!

♦ It probably won't happen, but just in case you have leftover empanadas, let cool to room temperature and then store them in an airtight storage bag in the fridge for up to 4 days. Reheat in a 400°F oven for 4 to 5 minutes before serving.

♦ I also love to eat these empanadas with pico de gallo (see page 211) and a squeeze of lime juice. I cut them in half and then squeeze the lime juice in the middle.

Salsa Roja

Makes 1½ cups

1 tablespoon extra-virgin olive oil

3 Roma tomatoes, quartered

1 tomatillo, quartered

2 large garlic cloves, peeled

½ small onion

1 small dried guajillo chile, stemmed

12 to 13 dried chiles de árbol, stemmed

½ cup water

2 canned chipotle peppers in adobo sauce

¼ cup chopped fresh cilantro

½ teaspoon grated lime zest

1½ teaspoons fresh lime juice, plus more as needed

¼ teaspoon granulated sugar

½ teaspoon kosher salt, plus more as needed

½ teaspoon freshly ground black pepper, plus more as needed

Heat a medium nonstick skillet over medium heat. Add the olive oil, tomatoes, and tomatillo, searing the vegetables for 2 to 3 minutes on each side. Add the garlic and onion, peeling apart the onion's layers. Cook until the vegetables begin to brown, 1 to 2 minutes. Add the dried chiles and cook until just fragrant, 25 to 30 seconds. Add the water, reduce the heat to medium-low, and cook until the chiles are lightly softened and the water has evaporated, 2 to 4 minutes.

Transfer the vegetables to a food processor. Add the chipotles, cilantro, lime zest, lime juice, sugar, salt, and black pepper and process until the sauce is smooth. Add additional lime juice, salt, and pepper to taste. Transfer to a medium jar and store in the fridge for 5 to 7 days.

Salsa Verde

Makes 1½ cups

1 tablespoon extra-virgin olive oil

5 tomatillos, quartered

2 large garlic cloves, peeled

½ small onion

1 medium jalapeño, halved and seeded

2 serrano chiles

¼ cup chopped fresh cilantro

2 dried chiles de árbol

1 tablespoon fresh lime juice, plus more as needed

½ teaspoon kosher salt, plus more as needed

½ teaspoon freshly ground black pepper, plus more as needed

Heat a medium nonstick skillet over medium heat. Add the olive oil and tomatillos, roasting the tomatillos for 2 to 3 minutes on each side. Transfer the tomatillos to a food processor.

To the same skillet, add the garlic, onion (peeling apart the onion), jalapeño, and serranos. Sear until the vegetables begin to brown, 2 to 3 minutes per side.

Transfer the vegetables to the food processor. Add the cilantro, chiles de árbol, and lime juice and process until well combined. Add the salt and black pepper. Add more salt, pepper, and lime juice to taste. Transfer to a jar and keep in the fridge for 5 to 7 days.

Choux

Picture me, little Betül, just fourteen and so excited to try my hand at making choux dough for the first time. It was a big day—and I was following a chef's recipe from TV. I made a mess at first, but I stuck to my mom's rule, Never give up. After wrestling with the dough and eggs for what felt like ages, I finally managed to pipe some oddly shaped eclairs onto the baking sheet. The result? Absolutely perfect.

½ cup (110g) water

½ cup (110g) whole milk

2 teaspoons (8g) granulated sugar

Pinch of kosher salt

6 tablespoons (3 oz/86g) unsalted butter, cubed

1 cup (130g) all-purpose flour

4 large eggs, at room temperature

½ teaspoon (3g) vanilla extract

In a medium saucepan, combine the water, milk, sugar, salt, and butter. Bring just to a boil over medium-low heat. Remove from the heat and add all the flour at once. Using a spatula, stir for a few seconds, until well combined, using the back of the spatula to press the mixture against the bottom of the pan and scrape to stir.

Immediately return the pan to medium heat and cook, stirring, until the texture is smooth and resembles Play-Doh with no visible pockets of flour, 2 to 2½ minutes. Remove from the heat and turn the dough out onto a cold work surface. Let cool for 5 to 7 minutes, flattening with your hands periodically to prevent drying and to aid in the cooling process.

Transfer the dough to a medium bowl. Using an electric mixer on medium speed, add the eggs one at a time and mix until almost fully incorporated before adding the next egg. Add the vanilla with the last egg. Continue to mix until smooth, then use a spatula to scrape the sides of the bowl and make sure there are no visible differences in texture. Perform a V-test (page 174) to ensure proper thickness. Fit a large piping bag with a ½-inch round tip (or French star tip for Paris-Brest). Roll the edges of the bag down and hang it inside a 1-quart bowl or container. Use a spatula to transfer the dough into the piping bag. Pull up the edges of the bag and lay it flat on a work surface. Use a plastic bench scraper on the outside of the bag to push all the dough toward the tip, making sure there are no air pockets in the dough. Then squeeze from the top, pushing the dough just into the tip. You can now pipe the dough for any of the following recipes or your preferred choux recipe.

Notes

❧ It is very important that you do not open the door for the first 20 minutes that the choux is baking. This will cause the choux to collapse. Keeping the temperature in the oven consistent is essential to maintaining the puffy choux. This is also why placing a spoon in the door while they cool is very important after the choux is baked.

❧ If you have leftover prepared pastries, cover them with plastic wrap and store in the fridge for 2 to 3 days. However, it is better to store the empty shells and pastry cream separately. Stored the shells in an airtight storage bag in the freezer for up to 1 month. To serve, let come to room temperature and then place on a baking sheet in a 350°F oven for 4 to 5 minutes until fresh and crispy.

Mini Paris-Brests

Makes 8 to 10 pastries

Preheat the oven to 375°F. Line two baking sheets with silicone baking mats or parchment paper.

Dip a 3-inch round cookie cutter or mold into cocoa powder and press it onto the baking sheets as a guide, then pipe the dough into a thick circle. Lightly brush the surface of the dough with egg white and sprinkle sliced almonds over the top.

Just before baking, reduce the oven to 355°F. Bake until deeply golden brown, 33 to 35 minutes. Turn off the oven and prop the door open with a wooden spoon. Leave the choux rings in the oven for 10 to 15 minutes until they dry out well.

Let the rings cool completely before slicing in half horizontally. Add ¼ cup of almond butter or blended almond praline to Pastry Cream (page 222) and mix well. Pipe evenly over the bottom of the choux rings. Cover with the top halves of the choux shell. Refrigerate for 20 to 30 minutes. Sprinkle with powdered sugar and sliced almonds before serving.

Profiteroles

Makes 38 to 40 puffs

Preheat the oven to 375°F. Line two baking sheets with silicone baking mats or parchment paper.

Pipe the dough into 1¼-inch mounds with at least 1 inch of space between.

Just before baking, reduce the oven to 355°F. Bake until golden brown, 24 to 26 minutes. Turn off the oven and prop the door open with a wooden spoon. Leave the puffs in the oven for 5 to 10 minutes to dry out well.

Remove from the oven and poke a small hole in the bottoms with the handle of a wooden spoon. When completely cool, fill with Pastry Cream (page 222) or whipped cream. Drizzle with chocolate sauce just before serving.

Karpatka

Serves 10 to 12

I stumbled upon this mouthwatering Polish karpatka recipe years ago while web surfing, and it was love at first bite. Named for the Carpathian Mountains, it's a delectable pastry that's like a giant éclair cake but with an ice cream–like twist owing to a generous dollop of butter in the cream. It's easier to prepare than regular éclairs as you make the choux dough in a mold rather than piping them out one by one, using a spoon to make the cake top's signature wave pattern that mimics the mountain range it's named for. My personal favorite way to devour karpatka? Drizzled with a bit of chocolate sauce. My husband, on the other hand, likes a plateful of fruit alongside. Whatever your preference, be it fruity or chocolaty, this dessert delivers.

CARPATHIAN PASTRY CREAM

8 egg yolks

1½ cups (300g) granulated sugar

½ cup plus 2 tablespoons (90g) cornstarch

3½ cups (770g) whole milk

1 cup (240g) heavy cream

1 whole vanilla bean, 1 teaspoon vanilla paste, split, or 1½ teaspoons vanilla extract

14 tablespoons (200g) unsalted butter, at room temperature

ASSEMBLY

Choux (page 216)

½ cup heavy cream

½ cup semisweet chocolate chips

Pinch of kosher salt

Powdered sugar, for serving

Fresh berries, for serving

Make the Carpathian pastry cream: In a medium bowl, whisk together the egg yolks and sugar until fluffy and lightened in color, 1 to 2 minutes. Add the cornstarch and continue to whisk, until well combined.

In a medium saucepan, combine the milk, heavy cream, and vanilla bean, if using, and bring almost to a boil over medium heat. Remove from the heat and remove the vanilla bean, squeezing out any liquid or seeds. Whisking constantly, very slowly drizzle ¼ cup of the hot milk mixture into the egg mixture to warm it up slowly. Once fully incorporated, repeat with another ½ cup of the milk mixture. Transfer the warmed egg mixture into the saucepan with the remaining milk while whisking.

Return the mixture to medium heat, stirring constantly. Once the mixture just comes to a boil, cook for an additional 40 to 60 seconds while continuing to stir. If it has not thickened, continue to cook for 30 to 40 seconds longer. Remove from the heat and add the vanilla paste or extract, if using, and let rest for 3 to 5 minutes.

Pour the custard into a medium glass bowl and cover with plastic wrap, pressing the wrap onto the top of the pastry cream to prevent a skin forming. Let cool for 15 to 20 minutes at room temperature and then refrigerate for 3 to 4 hours, until well chilled.

continued

continued

Karpatka

Remove the custard from the fridge and use an electric mixer to whisk until creamy. Add the soft butter and continue to whisk until perfectly smooth. Cover with plastic wrap as before and let rest in the fridge until ready to use.

Assemble the dessert: Preheat the oven to 375°F. Place a piece of parchment paper in the bottoms of two 9-inch springform pans (see Notes) before closing the sides.

Make the choux dough and transfer to a piping bag as directed. Pipe half of the dough along the bottom of one of the pans and use a wooden spoon to make sure it is evenly spread. Use the handle of the spoon to gently make a wave pattern over the top of the choux, creating uneven peaks that puff beautifully during baking. Repeat with the second springform pan and remaining choux.

Just before baking, reduce the oven to 355°F. Bake until golden brown, 35 to 40 minutes. Turn off the oven and prop the door open with a wooden spoon. Allow the choux to cool for 10 to 15 minutes, until the pastry is dried out well.

Place the choux on a cooling rack, carefully removing the sides and bottoms of the springform pans (hold on to one of the sides). Let cool completely.

With an electric mixer, whisk the chilled pastry cream quickly to make sure it is smooth. Place one of the choux layers on a serving plate. Wrap an acetate collar or parchment paper around the circumference of the choux, taping to hold it in place. Close the sides of a springform pan around the collar. Pour the pastry cream over the choux

base and spread evenly. Top with the second choux round and press lightly to adhere to the pastry cream. Cover with plastic wrap and refrigerate for at least 5 hours or overnight, until well chilled.

When ready to serve, in a microwave-safe bowl or medium saucepan, heat the cream until bubbling, just short of a boil. Remove from the heat and add the chocolate chips and salt. Let stand for 4 to 5 minutes, then stir well until smooth. Let cool to room temperature before using.

Before serving, dust the karpatka with powdered sugar. Slice and serve with a drizzle of chocolate sauce and fresh berries.

Notes

♥ *If you do not have two springform pans, you can bake one choux round and then the other.*

♥ *You can bake the choux in two 8-inch springform pans for a thicker karpatka.*

♥ *Take care to whisk the pastry cream well before adding the butter. Make sure the butter is very soft before combining, or you will have little bits of hardened butter in your cream.*

♥ *To store, cover the cake with plastic wrap and refrigerate for 3 to 4 days. Slice and serve with berries and powdered sugar.*

Choux au Craquelin (Craquelin Cream Puffs)

Makes 24 to 28 cream puffs

This cream puff recipe captures the essence of a good dessert—a crunchy exterior, soft choux dough, and a dreamy pastry cream filling. The beauty of this dessert is its versatility—swap out the filling with whipped cream, chocolate ganache, or even ice cream!

Pastry Cream
(recipe follows)

CRAQUELIN
1 stick (4 oz/113g) unsalted butter, at room temperature

½ cup (100g) packed light brown sugar

¾ cup plus 2 tablespoons (113g) all-purpose flour, plus more for dusting

Choux (page 216)

Fresh berries, finely chopped, for serving

Make the pastry cream as directed and refrigerate until ready to use.

To make the craquelin: In a medium bowl, mix the butter and brown sugar with a spatula until smooth and creamy. Add the flour and fold until fully combined. Place a piece of parchment paper on a work surface. Lightly flour it and place half of the dough in the middle. Lightly flour the dough and cover with a second sheet of parchment paper. Roll until the dough is ⅛ inch thick and place on a baking sheet. Repeat with the second half of the dough. Place both baking sheets in the fridge and chill for at least 30 minutes.

Make the choux and transfer to a piping bag as directed in the recipe.

Preheat the oven to 375°F. Line two baking sheets with silicone baking mats or parchment paper.

Pipe the dough into 1¾-inch rounds with at least 1½ inches of space between them. Remove the craquelin from the fridge and cut 2-inch rounds with a cookie cutter. Carefully scrape the craquelin off the parchment paper with a pastry spatula. Immediately place one round of craquelin on top of each dough round.

Just before baking, reduce the oven to 355°F. Bake until golden brown, 27 to 30 minutes. Turn off the oven and prop the door open with a wooden spoon. Leave the puffs in the oven for 5 to 10 minutes to dry out well.

Use a sharp knife to poke a small hole in the bottom of each puff to release steam and let cool to room temperature.

Transfer the pastry cream to a piping bag with a ½-inch star tip. Slice off the top of each puff and add some fresh berries to the bottoms, then overfill the puffs with pastry cream and replace the tops. Let cool in the fridge at least 30 minutes before serving.

Notes

♥ *If you prefer to leave the cream puffs whole, you can make a hole in the bottom with a wooden spoon and fill from the bottom. If you use this method, fold ½ cup whipped cream into the pastry cream to make it easier to pipe. This makes for a light but creamy texture.*

♥ *Store leftovers on a plate covered with plastic wrap and in the fridge for 2 to 3 days.*

♥ *You can pipe a little caramel or chocolate ganache into the bottom of the cream puff before adding the pastry cream.*

♥ *For an even richer filling, use the Carpathian Pastry Cream (page 219), folding ½ cup of whipped cream into the mixture to make it easier to fill.*

continued

continued

Choux au Craquelin (Craquelin Cream Puffs)

Pastry Cream

Makes 3 cups

6 egg yolks

½ cup (100g) sugar

¼ cup (36g) cornstarch

2 teaspoons (6g)
all-purpose flour

2 cups (440g) whole milk

2 teaspoons vanilla bean
paste or 1 small vanilla
bean

1 stick (4 oz/113g) butter,
at room temperature

½ teaspoon (3g) lemon
extract (optional)

In a medium bowl, whisk together the egg yolks and sugar. Add the cornstarch and flour and whisk for 2 minutes, until lightened in color.

In a medium saucepan, combine the milk and whole vanilla bean, if using. Bring to a simmer over medium heat and then remove from the heat. Remove the vanilla pod, squeezing out any excess liquid or beans. Whisking constantly, very slowly drizzle ¼ cup of the hot milk into the egg mixture to slowly warm it. Once fully incorporated, repeat with another ¼ cup of the milk mixture, then repeat one more time. Return the milk to medium heat, and while whisking constantly, pour the warmed egg mixture into the saucepan. Slowly bring to a boil while continuing to stir constantly. Once the mixture just comes to a boil, cook for about 1 minute, until slightly thickened, while continuing to stir. If it is still very thin, cook for an additional 30 to 60 seconds.

Remove from the heat and add 4 tablespoons of the butter, vanilla bean paste (if using), and lemon extract, if desired. Mix until fully melted and incorporated well. Let rest for 3 to 5 minutes.

Pour into a medium glass bowl and cover with plastic wrap, pressing the wrap onto the top of the pastry cream to prevent a skin from forming. Let cool at room temperature for 15 to 20 minutes, then refrigerate for 3 to 4 hours, until completely cooled.

Remove from the fridge and, with an electric mixer, whip the pastry cream on high speed until smooth and creamy. Add the remaining 4 tablespoons butter. Continue to mix until the cream is perfectly smooth. Cover carefully with plastic wrap as before and let rest in the fridge until ready to use.

Notes

♥ *Just before using/piping, whip with an electric mixer to ensure it's perfectly smooth.*

Churros with Chocolate Sauce

Serves 4 to 6

Churros are a delightful treat, originally from Spain but loved worldwide. Traditional Spanish churros are made with just flour, water, a little oil, and salt, and they're usually enjoyed with hot chocolate. But Mexican-style churros are made using choux dough—just how I like to make mine! I add fewer eggs, though, because I've found that too many can make the dough go soft and lose its shape. My secret touch? A bit of semolina flour for an irresistible crunch.

DOUGH

1½ cups (330g) water

1½ tablespoons (18g) granulated sugar

¼ teaspoon (2g) kosher salt

1 teaspoon (5g) vanilla extract

4 tablespoons (2 oz/56g) unsalted butter

1¾ cups (227g) all-purpose flour

1 tablespoon (11g) semolina flour

2 large eggs (100g total), at room temperature

CHURROS

Neutral oil, for deep-frying

¾ cup granulated sugar

1 teaspoon ground cinnamon

Chocolate Sauce (recipe follows) or Caramel (page 141), for dipping

Make the dough: In a medium saucepan, combine the water, sugar, salt, vanilla, and butter and bring just to a boil over medium heat. Remove from the heat and add the all-purpose flour all at once. Using a spatula, stir, for a few seconds, until well combined. Use the back of your spatula to press the mixture against the bottom of the pan and scrape up from the bottom to stir. Return to medium heat and cook, stirring, for 1 to 2 minutes, until there are no visible pockets of flour. Remove from the heat and add the semolina flour. Continue to stir using the wooden spoon until fully incorporated.

Turn the dough out onto a cold work surface and let cool for 5 to 7 minutes, pressing with your hands periodically to aid in the cooling process. Transfer the dough to a medium bowl. Add the eggs one at a time, whisking with a hand or electric mixer until smooth. This will be a fairly thick dough compared to other choux doughs, so be sure the eggs are fully incorporated. Transfer the dough to a piping bag fitted with a large closed star tip.

Make the churros: Line a plate with paper towels. Pour 2½ inches oil into a medium saucepan and heat the oil over medium heat to 330°F.

In a shallow bowl, mix together the sugar and cinnamon and keep near the frying station. Place a large piece of parchment paper on a work surface and pipe 5-inch ropes of dough onto the paper, leaving 1 inch between each rope. Use your fingers or tongs to carefully place 4 to 6 churros in the hot oil at a time. Fry until golden brown and crispy, 5 to 8 minutes, flipping periodically with a strainer

Notes

✦ *I recommend the Ateco #846 or #847 or Wilton 1M star tips for this recipe. You can also use a French star tip, but avoid tips that are larger than ½ inch, as the churros won't shape or cook properly.*

✦ *Churros are best eaten fresh, so share any leftovers with your loved ones or neighbors.*

spoon. Reduce the heat as necessary to maintain the oil temperature between 330° and 350°F; this temperature ensures the outside of the churros is crispy and the inside is fully cooked. Set on the paper towels to drain. Repeat with remaining batches of dough.

Once the churros have cooled for 1 to 2 minutes, toss them in the cinnamon-sugar. Serve with chocolate sauce or caramel for dipping.

Chocolate Sauce

Makes 1 cup

½ cup heavy cream

½ cup semisweet chocolate chips

¼ teaspoon ground cinnamon

In a microwave-safe bowl or a medium saucepan, heat the cream until bubbling but not quite boiling. Remove from the heat and add the chocolate chips. Let stand for 4 to 5 minutes, then add the cinnamon and stir well until smooth. Let cool to room temperature before serving.

DOUGHS FROM TÜRKİYE

This section is my culinary love letter to Türkiye, filled with handpicked recipes that I have cradled in my heart since childhood. Here, I'm not just sharing ingredients or methods; I'm inviting you into the warm, aromatic kitchens of my past, where every dish is a memory, every scent a story. From my heritage to your kitchen, these recipes span all types of dough, each carrying a piece of my history, my culture, and most important, my heart. Welcome to my world!

Simit

Makes 7 simit

Simit, Türkiye's universal street food, holds a special place in the country's vibrant, bustling food scene. Imagine walking down the enchanting alleys of Istanbul, the rich, historic city unfurling around you as you savor each bite of this scrumptious street pastry. Or picture yourself aboard a ferry with the calming rhythm of the waves beneath and a flock of seagulls circling above, eagerly awaiting a piece of your simit.

These delicately twisted sesame-encrusted rings are not just a food item; they are symbolic of Turkish culture, representing communal harmony, shared meals, and simple, everyday joys. Simit vendors are a common sight on the streets, their carts full of these freshly baked golden rings which instantly attract passersby. The aroma floating from these carts is a part of the Turkish memory, reminding locals and visitors alike of home and heritage.

The beauty of simit lies not just in its simplicity but also in its versatility. While it's really satisfying on its own, pairing it with feta cheese and the fresh crunch of tomatoes and cucumbers transforms it into a wholesome breakfast. It's a taste so cherished, so deeply ingrained in my palate, that every time I visit Türkiye, my father greets me with fresh, warm simits. Throughout my visit, our breakfast table is never without a pile of freshly baked simits. They form a part of our shared meals, our bonding over food and family.

As I share this recipe with you, I hope to bring a slice of the Turkish streets into your kitchen. May every bite of the simit evoke a sense of exploration and inspire you to discover more about the rich culinary tapestry that is Turkish cuisine. Serve the simit with Turkish tea.

1¼ cups (275g) warm water (110°F)

1½ teaspoons (5g) instant (quick-rise) yeast

2 tablespoons (25g) granulated sugar

3¾ cups (490g) bread flour

2 tablespoons (28g) extra-virgin olive oil, plus more for the work surface

1½ teaspoons (9g) kosher salt

MOLASSES SYRUP

¼ cup molasses

⅓ cup water

1 cup sesame seeds, toasted (see Notes, page 230), for dipping

In a large bowl (or the bowl of a stand mixer), whisk together the water, yeast, and 1 teaspoon of the sugar. Let rest for 5 to 7 minutes, until foamy. Add the flour, the remaining sugar, the oil, and salt. Knead the dough using your hands (or a dough hook on medium speed) for 2 minutes. If using your hands, shape your hand like a claw and bring the ingredients together, mixing and periodically squeezing the dough together. Continue this process for 2 to 4 minutes, until everything is fully incorporated. Cover the bowl with plastic wrap and allow it to rest for 15 minutes.

continued

Simit

Either continue to knead the dough in the stand mixer on medium speed for 2 to 4 minutes or turn the dough out onto a lightly floured work surface. Using your hands, perform the basic kneading technique (see page 22) and knead for 3 to 5 minutes, until elastic and smooth. Round the dough (see page 22). Lightly grease a large bowl with olive oil and place the dough in the middle with the open edge down. Cover with plastic wrap and let rest for 15 to 20 minutes.

Meanwhile, make the molasses syrup: In a shallow dish, whisk together the molasses and water until fully combined. In another shallow dish, spread out the sesame seeds. Set both aside.

Turn the dough out onto the work surface. Roll the dough into a log and use a sharp knife or bench scraper to divide it into 7 equal portions. Roll each piece into a rope about 5 inches long. Grease the work surface very lightly with olive oil and place the pieces on the oiled surface. Brush the dough very lightly with olive oil and cover with plastic wrap. Let rest for 10 to 12 minutes.

Line two baking sheets with parchment paper. Take one piece of dough and use your hands to roll it into a rope about 18 inches long. Hold each end of the dough and twist it in opposite directions to shape it. Seal the two ends together to form a 5-inch loop/ring. For more defined twists, halve each piece of dough into two and roll both parts into 18-inch ropes. Twist the two pieces around each other and seal with your hands. Coat the ring with the molasses mixture and then place in the sesame seeds to coat thoroughly. Slightly stretching the simit as you lift it, place it on a prepared baking sheet. Repeat with the remaining dough pieces. Cover with parchment paper and let rest for 10 to 15 minutes.

Place a small cast-iron pan in the bottom of the oven and preheat to 390°F.

Place the baking sheets in the oven and gently throw 7 to 8 ice cubes into the cast-iron pan. Bake the simit for 20 minutes, then increase the oven temperature to 400°F. Bake until golden brown, an additional 4 to 5 minutes.

Place the simit on a rack to cool for 15 to 20 minutes. Serve warm.

Notes

♦ *Traditional simit recipes usually use grape or mulberry molasses, but you can use regular molasses.*

♦ *To toast sesame seeds: In a dry medium skillet over medium heat, stir the sesame seeds occasionally until lightly golden brown, 3 to 4 minutes. Be careful not to burn them. Transfer to a large plate to stop the cooking. Cool completely before using.*

♦ *You can also cook the simit on a baking steel for a crispier texture. Use a water drop test (see page 172) to make sure the steel is properly heated first and follow the rest of the recipe as written.*

♦ *Once cooled, store in an airtight storage bag at room temperature for 2 to 3 days or in the freezer for 2 to 3 months. Before serving, let come to room temperature and warm for 4 to 5 minutes in a 350°F oven.*

Mantı

Serves 6 to 8

Mantı was the favorite dish of my late brother-in-law, Zeki, and every weekend we cooked and enjoyed it together as a family. Even though it's been years since his passing, every time I make this recipe it brings me back to those important family moments. Mantı is a time-intensive endeavor, perfect for family gatherings or friendly get-togethers. The traditional method of rolling and shaping requires an *oklava* to roll the whole dough in a large circle at once. This can be a little tricky, so this recipe includes my preferred technique to make it easier. There's something delightful about chatting while shaping tiny ravioli with family, and it's also an excellent way to keep kids busy during holidays!

DOUGH

4 cups (520g) all-purpose flour, plus more for dusting

2 teaspoons (12g) kosher salt

¼ teaspoon (1g) granulated sugar

2 large eggs

¾ cup (165g) water

1 teaspoon (5g) fresh lemon juice

1½ teaspoons (7g) extra-virgin olive oil

BEEF FILLING

1 medium onion, quartered

2 medium garlic cloves, peeled

10 ounces ground beef (80/20)

2 scallions, chopped

1½ tablespoons double-concentrated tomato paste

1 tablespoon mild Turkish red pepper paste

1½ teaspoons kosher salt

1 teaspoon paprika

1 teaspoon red pepper flakes

1 teaspoon freshly ground black pepper

½ cup chopped fresh parsley

TOMATO SAUCE

2 tablespoons extra-virgin olive oil

¼ cup tomato paste

2 tablespoons mild Turkish red pepper paste

1 small garlic clove, minced

1 cup water

1 teaspoon kosher salt

1 teaspoon red pepper flakes

½ teaspoon freshly ground black pepper

ASSEMBLY

Kosher salt, for pasta water

1½ cups whole-milk yogurt

½ cup full-fat sour cream

1 teaspoon kosher salt, more to taste

1 stick butter

Fresh mint, for serving

Make the dough: In a medium bowl, combine the flour, salt, and sugar. Mix together and make a well in the center of the flour mixture. Add the eggs, water, and lemon juice to the well. Using a fork, whisk the liquid in the center without incorporating the flour. Once the liquid is mixed, slowly begin incorporating the flour until everything is combined. Drizzle the olive oil over the top of the dough.

With the dough in the bowl, perform the basic kneading technique (see page 22) and knead for 3 to 4 minutes. Turn the dough out onto a lightly floured work surface and continue kneading for 3 to 4 additional minutes. The dough may look a little dry but will come together as it rests—don't worry, this is the correct texture! Return the dough to the bowl. (Alternatively, you can put the ingredients in the bowl of a stand mixer and knead with a dough hook on medium speed for 4 to 7 minutes, until the dough has come together.) Cover the dough and let rest for 1 to 3 hours at room temperature.

Meanwhile, make the beef filling: In a food processor, pulse the onion and garlic until minced. If there is a lot of liquid, press with the back of a spoon and drain lightly after mincing. Transfer the onion mixture to a medium bowl and add the beef, scallions, tomato paste, red pepper paste, salt, paprika, red pepper flakes, black pepper, and parsley. Using your hands or a wooden spoon, mix the ingredients until fully incorporated. Cover with plastic wrap and set aside at room temperature.

continued

continued

Mantı

Transfer the dough to a work surface and knead again using the basic technique for 5 to 7 minutes, until nice and smooth. Using a sharp knife or bench scraper, divide the dough into 6 equal portions. Round each piece of dough into a smooth ball (see page 22). Lightly flour a plate and place the dough balls on it, leaving ½ inch between them. Cover with plastic wrap.

Take a piece of dough and use a rolling pin to roll it into a 4 × 6-inch oval. Using a pasta roller, run the dough through starting at the thickest setting (1 on a KitchenAid). Roll through once at each setting until you reach the second thinnest (7 on a KitchenAid). Transfer the pasta sheet to a lightly floured work surface and, using a ravioli or pizza cutter, cut the dough into 1- or 1¼-inch squares.

Line a baking sheet with parchment paper. Place ¼ teaspoon of the ground beef filling, about the size of a chickpea or slightly more, in the center of each dough square. Using your fingers, pinch the four corners of the dough together and press to seal. Lightly flour the mantı and transfer to the prepared baking sheet with space between them so they are not touching. Repeat with the remaining portions of dough and filling, using another baking sheet.

Make the tomato sauce: In a medium saucepan, heat the olive oil over medium heat. Once hot, add the tomato paste, red pepper paste, and garlic and cook for 1 to 2 minutes while stirring. Add the water and mix to combine. Add the salt, red pepper flakes, and black pepper and continue to cook for 1 to 2 minutes, until thickened to a sauce.

To assemble: Bring an extra-large pot (see Notes) of salted water to a boil.

Meanwhile, in a medium bowl, whisk together the yogurt, sour cream, and 1 teaspoon salt.

In a small saucepan, melt the butter over medium heat. Once melted, continue to cook, stirring occasionally. Once lightly browned and foamy with a nutty smell, remove from the heat and set aside.

Add the mantı to the boiling water. Once the water returns to a boil, cook for 3 to 5 minutes, stirring occasionally to make sure it doesn't boil over. Reserving ½ cup of the cooking liquid, drain the mantı and return to the pot. Stir in the brown butter until combined, adding the ½ cup of cooking liquid if you would like a thinner sauce.

Divide the mantı among serving plates and top with the yogurt sauce, tomato sauce, and fresh mint.

Notes

❧ *If you don't have a large enough pot, you can cook half of the mantı at a time. Be careful not to overcrowd the pot.*

❧ *If you aren't cooking the mantı immediately, place half on a baking sheet in the freezer for 30 minutes, then place in an airtight storage bag. Repeat with the remaining mantı to preserve their shape and freshness in storage. Mantı keep in the freezer for 3 to 6 months. To cook, bring salted water to a boil and add the frozen mantı as directed in the recipe. When the water returns to a boil, cook for 4 to 6 minutes, according to your preferred doneness.*

Lahmacun with Onion Salad

Serves 6

My father was a dedicated small business owner who spent long hours working during the week. His only day off, Sunday, was devoted solely to family time, and he took charge of everything, including meals. A nostalgic summer Sunday ritual involved lahmacuns and Adana kebabs from my uncle's restaurant, followed by a trip to the city's summer fair. We'd feast together, enjoying these delicious meals and creating lasting memories. Now, every time I cook lahmacun, the rich aroma transports me back to those innocent days, making me feel like a gleeful five-year-old pretending to fall asleep in her father's lap.

Lahmacun is a flatbread with a ground lamb topping filled with an abundance of vegetables. The thin dough is baked for a few minutes in a hot stone oven, then served fresh with onion salad on top, accompanied by Ayran (page 255), a Turkish yogurt drink, or turnip juice.

DOUGH

3¾ cups (490g) all-purpose flour, plus more for dusting

1¼ cups (275g) water, at room temperature

2 tablespoons (28g) extra-virgin olive oil

½ teaspoon (2g) granulated sugar

1½ teaspoons (9g) kosher salt

LAMB FILLING

1 medium yellow onion, quartered

2 medium tomatoes, quartered

1 small red bell pepper, quartered

2 small green Anaheim peppers, quartered

2 garlic cloves, peeled

1 pound ground lamb

½ cup chopped fresh parsley

1 tablespoon kosher salt, plus more to taste

1 teaspoon red pepper flakes

1 teaspoon hot paprika

½ teaspoon freshly ground black pepper

2 tablespoons double-concentrated tomato paste

1 tablespoon mild Turkish red pepper paste

1 tablespoon extra-virgin olive oil

2 tablespoons water, at room temperature

ONION SALAD

1 medium red onion, julienned

½ cup chopped fresh parsley

1 tablespoon isot (urfa biber) pepper

2 to 3 tablespoons extra-virgin olive oil

¼ teaspoon kosher salt

FOR SERVING

1½ lemons, cut into wedges for squeezing

3 Roma tomatoes, halved and sliced, for serving

Make the dough: In a medium bowl, mound the flour and make a well. Add the water, olive oil, sugar, and salt to the well and knead for 2 to 3 minutes, until combined, shaping your hand like a claw to bring the ingredients together, mixing and periodically squeezing the dough. At this point, the dough will not be perfectly smooth. Cover with plastic wrap and let rest for 15 to 20 minutes. Transfer the dough to a lightly floured work surface and perform the basic kneading technique (page 22) for an additional 4 to 5 minutes, until nice and smooth. Place back in the bowl and cover with plastic wrap again. Let rest at room temperature for 30 minutes to 1 hour.

Transfer the dough to a lightly floured work surface and roll the dough into a log. Using a sharp knife or bench scraper, divide it into 12 equal portions. Round each piece of dough into a smooth ball (see page 22). Toss the balls lightly in flour and place on a plate or baking sheet. Cover loosely with plastic wrap and let rest for 30 minutes to 1 hour.

Meanwhile, make the lamb filling: In a food processor, combine the onion, tomatoes, red bell peppers, Anaheim peppers, and garlic. Pulse until finely minced. (If your food processor is small, you can divide the ingredients in half and repeat the process.)

continued

Lahmacun with Onion Salad

Transfer the minced vegetables to a medium bowl. Add the lamb, parsley, salt, red pepper flakes, hot paprika, black pepper, tomato paste, red pepper paste, olive oil, and water. Using your hands or a wooden spoon, mix the ingredients until combined very well. Cover with plastic wrap and keep in the fridge until ready to use.

Make the onion salad: In a small bowl, combine the red onion, parsley, isot pepper, olive oil, and salt. Mix to combine and set aside.

Preheat the oven to 500°F, with a baking steel on the middle rack, for at least 15 to 20 minutes.

Make the lahmacun: Transfer a ball of dough to a lightly floured work surface. Using a rolling pin, roll the dough into a 12-inch-long oval or 10-inch round. Place about ½ cup of the lamb filling in the middle of the dough. Using your hands or a spatula, spread and press the filling evenly over the top of the dough, leaving a ½-inch border around the edges.

Perform a water drop test (see page 172) to ensure the baking steel is properly heated. Using a pizza paddle, transfer the first lahmacun onto the baking steel. Turn the oven to a low broil and cook for 4 to 5 minutes while keeping an eye on it, turning once halfway through to cook evenly. Remove from the oven and place onto a cooling rack in a warm place. Repeat with each piece of dough. If after a few pieces, the bottom of the lahmacun begin to brown less quickly, reheat your baking steel and perform the water drop test to make sure it's hot enough. Serve immediately and see first and second notes.

To serve: Squeeze lemon juice over the lahmacuns. Add the onion salad and tomato slices in the middle. Roll the lahmacun into a wrap.

Notes

♦ *This is a two-person operation—having someone roll the lahmacun while someone else cooks, then trading off, ensures you'll both get to eat lahmacun at peak deliciousness.*

♦ *You can cook all the lahmacun at once and store stacked in a warm place until serving, but I much prefer to eat them fresh as soon as they are cooked so the wrap is nice and crunchy. If you are stacking the lahmacun, place them meat-side together and dough sides together so the meat does not make the dough soggy.*

♦ *If you do not have a baking steel, you can heat a cast-iron skillet on the stovetop over high heat, then do the water drop test (see page 172) to make sure it's hot enough. Using a pizza paddle, transfer the lahmacun into the hot skillet. Cook for 1 to 2 minutes over medium heat until the dough is nice and golden. Transfer to a baking sheet and broil on low for 2 to 3 minutes.*

♦ *Store cooked, cooled lahmacun in an airtight storage bag and keep in the fridge for 1 to 2 days. Before serving, heat on a hot skillet.*

♦ *You can serve lahmacun with Acılı Ezme (page 255), a spicy Turkish relish, as a side.*

Turkish Pistachio Baklava

Serves 14 to 18

Let me bring you the culinary secrets of my family's baklava master, my eldest sister. Prior to starting the baklava recipe trials for this book, I phoned her for a novice-friendly recipe since I hadn't ventured into this territory which involves cornstarch, because I cannot stand how it feels. With gloved hands, I bravely started my baklava journey, and the result is an easy-to-make masterpiece that you'll roll out with nothing more than a simple roller.

Baklava is a world-renowned Turkish dessert, with two traditional preparation methods. The bakery version involves thin sheets of dough rolled out by master bakers, a challenging process for many home cooks. However, there's a homestyle baklava that involves a more forgiving dough, softened by ingredients such as oil, milk, and occasionally yogurt. Today, I present to you the finest version of this homestyle baklava, loaded with delicious Turkish pistachios. Personally, I relish the deeply aromatic tones that Turkish pistachios bring to baklava, but feel free to substitute walnuts or regular pistachios. Serve with Turkish coffee or tea.

DOUGH

¾ cup (165g) milk, at room temperature

1 large egg

2 tablespoons (1 oz/28g) unsalted butter, melted

¼ cup (55g) neutral oil

1 tablespoon (14g) apple cider vinegar

3 cups (390g) all-purpose flour

½ teaspoon (3g) kosher salt

SYRUP

2½ cups granulated sugar

2½ cups water

⅛ teaspoon kosher salt

¼ of a lemon

TO FINISH

2 sticks unsalted butter

¼ cup neutral oil

1⅓ cups cornstarch, for rolling

1½ cups coarsely ground Turkish Antep pistachios

Make the dough: In a medium bowl, whisk together the milk, egg, melted butter, oil, and vinegar. Add the flour and salt. Using your hand shaped like a claw, stir and squeeze the ingredients together for 2 to 3 minutes until everything begins to come together. Turn the dough out onto a work surface. Using your hands, perform the basic kneading technique (see page 22) and knead for 6 to 8 minutes, until smooth. Return to the bowl and cover with plastic wrap. Let rest for 1½ hours at room temperature.

Return the dough to the work surface and continue to knead for 3 to 5 minutes. Return to the bowl, cover, and let rest for an additional 1½ to 2 hours.

Make the syrup: In a saucepan, stir to combine the sugar, water, and salt. Bring to a boil over medium-high heat. Squeeze the lemon into the syrup and throw in the spent lemon rind. Reduce the heat to medium-low and simmer for 11 to 13 minutes. Test for doneness by dipping a teaspoon into the syrup. Shake off the excess syrup and then hold the teaspoon above the saucepan. If the remaining syrup slowly drips off the spoon, the syrup is ready. If it falls quickly,

continued

Turkish Pistachio Baklava

continue to simmer for 2 to 3 minutes. Remove the syrup from the heat, remove the lemon, and let cool to room temperature.

Turn the dough out on a lightly floured work surface. Roll the dough into a log and use a sharp knife or bench scraper to cut it into 20 equal portions. Round each piece of dough into a smooth ball (see page 22). Place each ball on a plate as you work and cover with plastic wrap to avoid drying out.

To finish: In a small saucepan, melt the butter and add the oil, mixing to combine. Set aside.

Lightly cover the work surface with cornstarch and place a ball of dough on the surface. Using a rolling pin, roll into a 6- to 7-inch round. Add 1 tablespoon of the cornstarch on top of the dough round and use your hands to cover the dough evenly. Repeat this process with each ball of dough, stacking the rounds in groups of two and making sure each is covered with cornstarch. As you go, continue stacking dough rounds in twos, so you have 10 stacks by the end.

Beginning with the first stack of 2 dough rounds, use a long rolling pin or Turkish oklava to roll the stacked dough into an 18- to 20-inch round. Sprinkle with additional cornstarch as necessary for easy rolling. Place a 9 × 13-inch baking dish on top of the large round. Using a sharp knife, trace the bottom of the baking dish into the dough and cut. Place the dough rectangle in the base of the dish. Piece together the dough scraps on top of the bottom rectangle as a second layer of dough. Drizzle 2 tablespoons of the butter mixture over the dough layers. Repeat this process until you have added four of the dough stacks. At this point, spread ½ cup of the Turkish pistachios evenly over the dough. Roll out two more dough stacks and repeat the shaping and drizzling process. Add another ½ cup of the Turkish pistachios and continue to roll and add dough layers until all the dough has been used.

Preheat the oven to 350°F.

Using a sharp knife, cut the baklava into 1½-inch squares. Pour the remaining butter evenly over the top, being careful to retain the milk solids on the bottom of the pan.

Bake the baklava until golden brown, 45 to 50 minutes.

Let rest on the counter for 2 to 3 minutes before evenly pouring the cooled syrup over the hot baklava. Set aside at room temperature to allow the syrup to fully soak in, 4 to 5 hours or overnight.

Serve with the remaining pistachios beneath and on top of the baklava pieces.

Notes

♥ *Turkish Antep pistachios make the most delicious baklava—once you try them you will really see the difference. You can purchase them online, but if you cannot find them, use regular pistachios or walnuts.*

♥ *Baklava requires lots of very, very thin layers. In the second rolling step, roll the dough as thin and as wide as you can.*

♥ *Baklava is best the first day, when the layers are crisp and crunchy. To store, cover with plastic wrap and keep at room temperature for 2 to 3 days.*

Grandma's Lavash

Makes 10 pieces

This recipe holds a special place in my heart. Although I never got to meet my grandma, this lavash recipe keeps her spirit alive in our family. My mom would prepare lavash often for breakfast. Fresh from the oven, we'd slather it with clarified butter or dress it up with a soft-boiled egg, chopped scallions, fresh herbs, and a good sprinkle of black pepper and red pepper flakes. This all-purpose lavash has served as a breakfast staple, a base for siron (a traditional Turkish dish), and even as bread for a kebab. No matter where I eat breakfast, this special dish takes me right back to those cherished family moments.

1½ teaspoons (5g) instant (quick-rise) yeast

½ teaspoon (2g) granulated sugar

¾ cup (165g) warm water (110°F)

¼ cup (55g) extra-virgin olive oil

½ cup (110g) milk, at room temperature

3¼ cups (423g) all-purpose flour, plus more for dusting

1¼ teaspoons (8g) kosher salt

Clarified butter for serving

In a medium bowl, combine the yeast, sugar, and warm water and let rest for 3 to 5 minutes. Add the olive oil and milk and stir to incorporate. Add the flour and salt and use your hands to mix the dough until incorporated. With the dough still in the bowl, use your hands to perform the basic kneading technique (see page 22) and knead for 3 to 5 minutes, until almost smooth. Cover with plastic wrap and let rest for 20 minutes.

Transfer the dough to a lightly floured work surface and continue using the basic kneading technique for an additional 4 to 5 minutes, until smooth. Roll the dough into a log and use a sharp knife or bench scraper to cut it into 10 equal portions (70g to 75g each). Round each piece of dough into a smooth ball (see page 22). Dip the balls into flour and place on a plate. Cover the plate loosely with plastic wrap and let rest for 15 to 20 minutes.

Heat a nonstick griddle pan or other nonstick skillet over medium-high heat. Lightly flour the work surface and place the balls on it. Using a rolling pin, roll a piece of dough into an 8 × 12-inch oval. Before cooking, test to make sure the pan is hot enough by drizzling water onto it. The water should immediately sizzle away.

Transfer the rolled out dough to the hot griddle pan and cook for 7 to 10 seconds on one side. Flip the dough and cook the other side for 6 to 10 seconds. Repeat this process one more time so each side

continued

continued

Grandma's Lavash

cooks twice, cooking for 40 to 60 seconds total. Remove from the heat and immediately roll up the cooked lavash. Store in a tortilla warmer or wrap in a clean kitchen towel and store in a basket. Repeat with each piece of dough.

You can serve the warm lavash on its own, brushed with clarified butter, or with your favorite kebabs.

Notes

❧ *This is easiest as a two-person project. Having someone cook while someone else rolls ensures all the lavash are freshly cooked when served.*

❧ *The short cooking time is very important to make sure the dough does not dry out or overcook, so make sure the lavash are rolled thin and flip constantly. This is the secret to having perfectly cooked tortillas or lavash!*

❧ *Lavash is best enjoyed freshly cooked, but if you do have leftovers, let them cool to room temperature before storing in an airtight storage bag at room temperature for 1 to 2 days. Before using, remove from the bag and quickly warm in a microwave or in a hot skillet.*

❧ *Some people fold the cooked lavash into quarters or store them in a manner similar to tortillas. My mom always rolled it, so that's what I do.*

Poğaça

Makes 14 buns

Türkiye is celebrated for its remarkable bakery culture. Every neighborhood proudly hosts a local fırın, a Turkish bakery, dispensing fresh bread and pastries each day. Along with various types of bread, Simit (page 228) and poğaça are irreplaceable favorites. The early bird in the family usually makes a morning run to the local fırın, returning with warm, freshly baked goods for breakfast. Poğaça, akin to a savory bun, is a divine blend of soft buttery dough filled with your choice of stuffing. Though cheese or olive paste are popular choices, my father's favorite mincemeat version is truly delightful. A sure hit for a brunch or lunch alternative. Serve with Turkish tea.

DOUGH

2¼ teaspoons (7g) instant (quick-rise) yeast

⅓ cup (74g) warm water (110°F)

1 tablespoon (12g) granulated sugar

2 sticks (8 oz/226g) unsalted butter, at room temperature

3 tablespoons (47g) whole-milk yogurt

1 large egg

1 egg white

3½ cups (455g) all-purpose flour, plus more for dusting

1¼ teaspoons (8g) kosher salt

BEEF FILLING

½ pound ground beef (80/20)

1 large yellow onion, finely diced

¼ cup warm water

½ teaspoon kosher salt

½ teaspoon freshly ground black pepper

½ teaspoon red pepper flakes

½ cup chopped fresh parsley

2 scallions, chopped (optional)

ASSEMBLY

1 cup shredded mozzarella cheese

Egg wash: 1 egg yolk beaten with 1 teaspoon extra-virgin olive oil

White and black sesame seeds (optional)

Make the dough: In a medium bowl, combine the yeast, warm water, and ½ teaspoon of the sugar. Stir and let rest for 5 to 7 minutes, until foamy. Add the butter, yogurt, whole egg, and egg white. Use a dough whisk or wooden spoon to mix until combined. Add the flour, the remaining sugar, and the salt. Using your hand, bring the dough together for 2 to 3 minutes.

Transfer the dough to a work surface. Using your hands, perform the basic kneading technique (see page 22) and knead for 4 to 5 minutes, until it is elastic and no longer sticky. The dough will look buttery at this point, but don't worry. Cover with plastic wrap and let rest at room temperature until doubled in size, 1 hour to 1 hour and 10 minutes.

Meanwhile, make the beef filling: Heat a medium saucepan over medium heat. Add the beef and yellow onion and use a potato masher or wooden spoon to mash the ground beef very well and cook until browned, stirring periodically. Add the water, reduce the heat to low, and cook, continuing to stir, until the water is dissolved and onions are very tender, 15 to 20 minutes. If necessary, add a little more water while cooking. Stir in the salt, black pepper, and red pepper flakes and cook for 1 to 2 minutes. Let cool completely to room temperature. Once cool, add the parsley and scallions.

continued

continued

Poğaça

Assemble the Poğaça: Line two baking sheets with parchment paper and keep them near you. Transfer the dough to a lightly floured surface. Roll the dough into a log and use a sharp knife or bench scraper to cut it into 14 equal portions (about 65g each). Round each piece of dough into a smooth ball (see page 22). Take a ball of dough and press it into a 3-inch round in the palm of your hand or on a work surface. Add 1 tablespoon of the mozzarella and 1 heaping tablespoon of the beef filling to the middle of the dough round. Using your fingers, pull the edges together and pinch to seal. With the open edge down, lightly roll to shape back into a ball, being careful not to squish out any filling, and place the ball with the open edge down on one of the baking sheets. Repeat with all the dough, leaving 2 to 3 inches between the buns. Using your hand, gently press the top of each bun to flatten slightly. Cover loosely with plastic wrap and let rest at room temperature for 15 to 20 minutes.

Preheat the oven to 375°F.

Brush the buns with the egg wash. Using a fork, make perpendicular lines in a cross on the middle of the bun. Top with sesame seeds, if desired.

Bake until golden brown, 20 to 25 minutes.

Let cool for 15 minutes and serve while warm.

Notes

♦ *If your baking steel is not large enough to bake both pide at once, shape and bake one piece of dough before repeating with the second piece.*

♦ *You can prepare this recipe without the filling for a regular savory bun or use a feta cheese filling (see page 268) for another traditional Turkish approach. You can also use any savory filling of your choice—it would be very delicious with the filling from Spinach-Artichoke Stuffed Garlic Knots (page 39).*

♦ *Store the buns in an airtight storage bag in the fridge for up to 1 week or in the freezer for up to 3 months. To serve, let sit at room temperature for 10 minutes before placing in a cold oven. Preheat the oven to 350°F. Once the oven reaches temperature, the buns will be warm and ready to serve.*

Ramadan Pidesi

Makes two 10-inch pide

The enchanting aroma of this freshly baked Ramadan flatbread is one of my earliest and dearest childhood memories. My father would return home every evening, just before iftar, carrying warm, crispy, fragrant bread from the neighborhood bakery. The anticipation of breaking the fast with the bread would make the waiting unbearable. The warmth of the freshly baked bread, wrapped in newspaper, against my small arms is a feeling I still cherish. Each time I bake Ramadan pita, I time it just right, serving it hot on the dinner table with olives and cheese, a tradition that stirs the same old happiness in me.

2¼ teaspoons (7g) instant (quick-rise) yeast

1 teaspoon (4g) granulated sugar

1¼ cups (275g) warm water (110°F)

2 tablespoons (30g) heavy cream

3 cups (390g) bread flour

1¼ teaspoons (8g) kosher salt

1½ teaspoons (7g) extra-virgin olive oil

Semolina flour, for rolling

2 egg yolks

White and black sesame seeds (see Notes), for garnish

In a medium bowl, combine the yeast, ½ teaspoon of the sugar, and ½ cup (110g) of the warm water. Stir and let rest for 3 to 5 minutes. Add the remaining ¾ cup (165g) water, remaining ½ teaspoon sugar, the heavy cream, flour, and salt. Using your hand as a claw, mix and knead the dough for 3 to 4 minutes, until well combined. Drizzle the olive oil over the top of the dough and continue to knead for 1 to 2 minutes, until the dough is almost smooth but still a little sticky. Cover with plastic wrap and let rest for 10 to 15 minutes.

Turn the dough out on a lightly floured work surface and flour your hands. Slap and fold (see page 21) the dough several times until smooth. At this point, the dough will still be a little soft. Divide the dough into 2 equal portions. Flour your hands, gather the edges of one piece of dough together, and pinch the edges so you have a ball. Place your hands on either side of the dough and lightly round the edges, being careful not to squeeze out the air. Repeat with the second piece of dough.

Cut two pieces of parchment paper into 14- to 16-inch squares. Generously spread semolina flour over each piece of parchment paper. Place each ball on the semolina flour with the open edge down and lightly flatten the top. Cover loosely with plastic wrap or with a large bowl. If using plastic wrap, be sure to flour the top of the dough with bread flour. Rest at room temperature until doubled in size, 30 to 45 minutes.

continued

continued

Ramadan Pidesi

Preheat the oven to 420°F with a baking steel on the middle rack and a cast-iron pan on the bottom rack for at least 15 minutes. Perform a water drop test (see page 172) to ensure the baking steel is properly heated.

Fill a small bowl with water and place it on your work surface. Before shaping the dough, gently use your hands to lift the dough to make sure it is not stuck to the parchment paper. Take one egg yolk in your fingers and break it over the top of one of the dough balls, using your hands to spread it evenly. Wet your fingers in the water and then, starting at the top of the dough round, hold your fingers in a line and press firmly into the dough to create lines 1½ inches apart. Turn the dough 90 degrees and repeat to create a checkerboard pattern. Repeat the shaping process with the other egg yolk and dough ball. Sprinkle white and black sesame seeds over the top.

Lightly stretch one dough round and transfer to the hot baking steel. Repeat with the other dough round. Add 7 to 10 ice cubes to the hot cast-iron pan.

Bake until golden brown, 13 to 15 minutes.

Transfer to a cooling rack. Serve while warm.

Notes

♦ *If you are going to use the Ramadan pidesi for İskender Kebabs (page 249), I recommend not using sesame seeds to dress the top.*

♦ *Once cool, store in an airtight storage bag at room temperature and use for kebabs on the second day. You can also store the pidesi in the freezer for up to 3 months. To serve, allow to thaw at room temperature and then warm in a 350°F oven for 3 to 5 minutes.*

♦ *You can use Ramadan pidesi for delicious grilled cheese and other sandwiches. It's similar to Schiacciata (page 65) or focaccia.*

İskender Kebabs

Each recipe in this book was created with immense love and joy. But when it came to Turkish recipes, I felt an added layer of responsibility. I wanted to share them in their original, most delicious form. Döner, one of the most popular Turkish foods globally, is a perfect example. It involves thinly slicing whole pieces of raw beef, marinating them overnight, and then cooking them on a large rotating spit. American interpretations often don't do justice to the original recipe—for instance, the authentic version never uses ground meat. My aim was to bring you a recipe as close to the authentic Turkish döner as possible, a versatile dish that can be served in several delicious ways: with lavash, rice, pita, or as it is here, over pide (Turkish flatbread) with a tomato sauce for a dish called Iskender. Iskender is named for Iskender, the man who created the original at his restaurant in Bursa in 1867. It's not just a dish; it's a feast for the senses.

DÖNER

2 pounds sirloin or bottom round steak

1 large onion, peeled and quartered

1 garlic clove, minced

2 tablespoons whole-milk yogurt

1 tablespoon buttermilk

3 tablespoons extra-virgin olive oil

½ teaspoon dried thyme

1 teaspoon dried basil

1 teaspoon hot paprika

1 teaspoon kosher salt

½ teaspoon freshly ground black pepper

TOMATO SAUCE

2 tablespoons extra-virgin olive oil

2 garlic cloves, minced

¼ cup tomato paste

3 tablespoons mild Turkish red pepper paste

1 cup canned tomato sauce

½ teaspoon kosher salt, plus more as needed

½ teaspoon freshly ground black pepper

2 cups water

ASSEMBLY

3 tablespoons extra-virgin olive oil

3 to 4 tomatoes, cut into wedges

3 to 4 jalapeños or other small chile peppers, quartered

2 Ramadan Pidesi (page 247), cut into 1-inch cubes

1 stick (4 oz) butter

1 cup whole-milk yogurt, plus more if desired

2 sprigs fresh mint, chopped, for serving (optional)

Prepare the döner: If your steaks are thicker than ¾ inch, use a meat tenderizer to pound them to ½ to ¾ inch. Set aside.

In a food processor, process the onion to a puree. Set a fine-mesh sieve over a small bowl. Add the onion puree and press with a wooden spoon to strain the onion liquid—it should be about ⅓ cup.

Transfer the onion liquid to a large bowl. Add the garlic, yogurt, buttermilk, olive oil, thyme, basil, hot paprika, salt, and pepper. Mix well and add the steaks to the marinade. Using your hands or a wooden spoon, coat the steaks evenly with the sauce. Cover a large work surface with overlapping plastic wrap. Layer the pieces of steak in two stacks in the center of the plastic with the edges overlapping. Starting from one end, roll the steaks into a log. Cover with plastic wrap and twist the ends tightly so the log resembles a giant wrapped candy. For best flavor, let marinate in the fridge for at least 3 to 4 hours or overnight and then move to the freezer. If you don't have time to refrigerate, immediately place in the freezer and let freeze at least 3 hours or overnight.

If the meat has been in the freezer overnight, move the meat from the freezer to the fridge at least 2 hours before cooking and prepare the rest of your ingredients.

continued

continued

İskender Kebabs

Make the tomato sauce: In a medium saucepan, heat the oil over medium heat, add the garlic, and sauté for 10 to 15 seconds. Add the tomato paste and pepper paste, cooking for another 30 to 40 seconds. Add the tomato sauce and cook, stirring constantly, for 2 to 3 minutes. Add the salt, black pepper, and water and mix to incorporate. Reduce the heat to medium-low, cover, and continue to cook, stirring occasionally, until slightly thickened to the texture of store-bought tomato sauce, 7 to 10 minutes. Remove from the heat and set aside.

Assemble the dish: In a large nonstick skillet, heat 1 tablespoon of the olive oil over medium-high heat. Add the tomato wedges and chile pieces and cook until the outsides are seared, 2 to 3 minutes. Remove from the heat and set aside.

Remove the meat from the fridge and unwrap. Using a sharp knife, run it along the length of one side of the log to shave off thin (¼ inch or less) slices of the beef.

In the same large nonstick skillet, heat 1 tablespoon of the olive oil over medium heat. Add half of the sliced marinated meat and increase the heat to high. Do not overcrowd the pan or it will release too much liquid and the beef won't caramelize well. Cook the meat, stirring constantly, until lightly browned, 5 to 7 minutes. Using tongs, remove the meat from the skillet and place on a plate, keeping as much of the drippings in the pan as you can. If your kitchen is chilly, keep the cooked meat warm on top of the stove or in a 170°F oven. Cook the other half of the meat with the same process.

In the same skillet with the beef drippings, add the pide pieces and cook for 2 to 3 minutes to warm through.

Divide the pide cubes among serving plates. Top each with the cooked beef and pour about ⅓ cup of the tomato sauce over the top of each plate.

In a small saucepan, melt the butter and continue to cook until beginning to foam and lightly browned. Remove from the heat and immediately pour 2 tablespoons evenly over each plate. Add the roasted tomato and chile slices along the edges of the plates. Spoon ¼ cup plain yogurt on one side of each plate. Serve immediately with fresh mint, if desired.

Notes

♥ *This beef is what I use to make döner wraps. Serve it with Grandma's Lavash (page 241), Flour Tortillas (page 206), or Pitas (page 55), adding Cacık (page 64), onion salad, and your favorite toppings for a delicious wrap.*

♥ *Keeping the beef in the freezer makes it easier to get the thin slices required. You can keep the beef in the freezer for up to 3 months and then place in the fridge 2 hours before you are ready to cook.*

♥ *I generally prefer to use bread that is at least 1 day old.*

♥ *In Türkiye, it's common to add lots of melted butter over the top to fully soak the bread cubes. I prefer to use just a few tablespoons, but you can use more on each plate if you want.*

Adana Kebabs with Acılı Ezme, Sumac Onion Salad, and Ayran

Serves 4

I come from a family of culinary maestros: uncles and cousins who are restauranteurs and chefs, reigning over their kitchen kingdoms. Growing up, I feasted on the legendary Adana kebabs conjured by my uncle's skilled hands. Juicy and unforgettably flavorful, those kebabs provide a vivid memory on my palate.

Traditionally, lamb meat and sheep's tail fat are meticulously chopped and threaded onto skewers before being tenderly cooked over a charcoal or wood fire. The tail fat lends the kebabs their signature, delectable flavor—a characteristic feature of many Turkish kebabs.

However, living away from the homeland means tail fat is a rarity. So, to capture a taste resonant of the original, I prefer to craft my Adana kebabs with ground lamb. Understanding that everyone's palate is unique, I've experimented and created a harmonious blend of fatty ground beef and lamb. This fusion not only appeals to a wider audience but also maintains the delicious integrity of the recipe. However, for those who share my preference for ground lamb, feel free to prepare these kebabs with lamb alone. You're in for a treat that will make you fall in love with the exquisite flavors of Turkish cuisine!

ADANA KEBAB
½ large red bell pepper

2 garlic cloves, peeled

1 pound ground lamb

½ pound ground beef (80/20)

1 tablespoon kosher salt, plus more if needed

1½ teaspoons hot paprika

1½ teaspoons Aleppo pepper or red pepper flakes

1 teaspoon freshly ground black pepper

SUMAC ONION SALAD
2 small onions, thinly sliced

¼ cup chopped fresh parsley

1 tablespoon fresh lemon juice

2 tablespoons extra-virgin olive oil

1 teaspoon ground sumac

¼ teaspoon kosher salt, or more if needed

½ teaspoon freshly ground black pepper

1 teaspoon pomegranate molasses

2 tomatoes, julienned

FOR SERVING
6 to 8 Grandma's Lavash (page 241)

Acılı Ezme (recipe follows)

Ayran (recipe follows)

Make the Adana kebab: In a food processor, combine the red bell pepper and garlic and blend until finely minced. Transfer the bell pepper mixture to a fine-mesh sieve and press to lightly remove excess liquid.

In a medium bowl (or the bowl of a stand mixer), combine the pepper mixture, ground lamb, ground beef, salt, hot paprika, Aleppo pepper, and black pepper. Mix with your hands (or with the mixer's paddle attachment for 4 to 5 minutes on medium-low speed) until the mixture has broken down into a moist paste. Ensure the mixture is very thoroughly mixed, no longer resembling ground beef, or the kebabs will separate and break during cooking. Cover with plastic wrap and let rest in the fridge for at least 2 hours or overnight.

Make the sumac onion salad: In a medium bowl, combine the onion and parsley. In a small bowl,

continued

continued

Adana Kebabs with Acılı Ezme, Sumac Onion Salad, and Ayran

stir together lemon juice, olive oil, sumac, salt, black pepper, and pomegranate molasses. Add the sauce mixture to the vegetables and use your hands or a wooden spoon to combine well. Add the tomatoes just before serving and lightly toss to combine. Set aside.

Remove the meat mixture from the fridge and divide into 8 portions, about 100g each. Place a small bowl of water next to your workstation. Wet your hands periodically while handling the meat to ensure easy shaping without sticking. Using a 7-inch kebab skewer (see Notes), wrap a ball of meat around the skewer. Press and shape the meat with your hands to create a 5-inch-long and 1½-inch-thick kebab. Make sure the meat is secure on the skewer; it is traditional to see some of your handprint on the meat. Repeat for each piece of meat.

Preheat a grill over medium-high heat until nice and hot. Place the skewers on the heat and cook until the outside is caramelized and nicely browned, 4 to 5 minutes on each side, and registering an internal temperature of 145° to 155°F. (You can also cook the kebabs on the stovetop; see Notes.) Be careful not to overcook or the meat will be dry and hard.

Serve wrapped in fresh lavash and top with sumac onion salad and acılı ezme. Serve ayran as a beverage on the side.

Notes

♦ *For the kebab skewers, use the thickest metal skewer you can find—generally, the skewers will be flat and wide. I prefer to order mine from Amazon as the ones you find in stores are usually too thin to hold the meat securely. You can also use bamboo skewers and soak them for 30 minutes before shaping the meat. This will ensure they do not burn while cooking. If you can't find thick skewers, shape the kofta without the skewer and cook in a skillet.*

♦ *To cook on the stovetop, heat a cast-iron grill pan over medium heat. Before cooking, test to make sure the pan is hot by drizzling it with water. The water should immediately sizzle away. Once hot, add the kebabs and cook each side for 3 to 4 minutes, until caramelized.*

Acılı Ezme

Makes 2 cups

1 small onion, quartered

2 garlic cloves, peeled

½ red bell pepper, quartered

½ green bell pepper or 1 large Anaheim pepper, quartered

2 to 4 small fresh or dried red chile peppers

4 medium tomatoes, halved

¼ cup extra-virgin olive oil

1 tablespoon pomegranate molasses

2 tablespoons mild Turkish red pepper paste

1½ teaspoons kosher salt

1½ teaspoons ground sumac

1½ teaspoons crushed Aleppo pepper or red pepper flakes

In a food processor, combine the onion, garlic, red bell pepper, green bell pepper, chile peppers, and tomatoes. Process until finely chopped. Transfer the mixture to a fine-mesh sieve and press to lightly drain the excess liquid. Transfer the mixture to a medium bowl.

In a small bowl, stir together the olive oil, pomegranate molasses, red pepper paste, salt, sumac, and Aleppo pepper. Add the sauce mixture to the vegetable mixture and mix until fully incorporated. Store in the fridge in a clean jar and serve it as a sauce alongside omelets, burritos, or kebabs.

Ayran

Makes 8 cups

2 cups whole-milk yogurt

½ cup full-fat sour cream

1 cup buttermilk

1½ teaspoons kosher salt, plus more if needed

3 cups cold water

Ice and fresh mint, for serving

In a pitcher, whisk together the yogurt, sour cream, buttermilk, and salt until smooth. Add the water and continue to whisk until foamy. Adjust salt to taste and store in the fridge until ready to serve. Serve with ice and fresh mint.

Turkish-Style Phyllo

*Makes 4 large
börek sheets*

A robust concoction of just a few ingredients, this exquisite phyllo dough is kneaded vigorously until it develops a sturdy texture. Next, it's immersed in a mixture of butter and olive oil for a few hours, a process that imparts an unparalleled elasticity. With no fancy tools in sight, the dough is stretched by hand until it resembles fine tulle. The result? A finished product that outshines any store-bought phyllo—crisper, fresher, more delicious, and downright perfect.

I cannot stress enough the need for you to experience this creation firsthand. It might appear daunting at first glance, but rest assured that each step is straightforward and easy to follow. Please don't hesitate. In the wise words of culinary icon Julia Child, "Cooking is one failure after another, and that's how you finally learn!"

DOUGH

3 cups (390g)
all-purpose flour,
plus more for dusting

1 cup (220g) water,
at room temperature
(75° to 80°F)

1 tablespoon (14g)
extra-virgin olive oil

¼ teaspoon (1g)
granulated sugar

1½ teaspoons (9g)
kosher salt

FOR ROLLING

1 stick butter, at room
temperature

6 tablespoons extra-virgin
olive oil

Make the dough: In a medium bowl, mound the flour and make a well. Add the water and olive oil to the well and top with the sugar and salt. While in the bowl, use your hand as a claw to combine the ingredients. Scrape the ingredients from the bottom of the bowl and fold them over the top, pressing them into the middle. Continue to knead the dough in this way for 4 to 5 minutes. The dough will not be smooth and will still be a little bit dry, but don't worry. Wrap the dough with plastic wrap and let rest at room temperature for 45 minutes to 1 hour.

Transfer the dough to a lightly floured work surface. Using your hands, perform the basic kneading technique (see page 22) and knead for 5 to 7 minutes, until fully smooth and velvety. Roll the dough into a log and use a sharp knife or bench scraper to cut it into 8 equal portions. Round each piece of dough into a smooth ball (see page 22) and place on a plate or baking sheet. Cover with plastic wrap and let rest at room temperature for 5 to 10 minutes.

Roll the dough: In a small bowl, beat the butter until perfectly smooth and creamy. One at a time, use a rolling pin to roll the balls of dough into 6-inch rounds. Place 4 dough rounds in front of you and top each with 2 tablespoons of the creamy butter. Using a knife or an offset spatula, spread the butter evenly over each piece, leaving a ½-inch border around the edges. Carefully lay an unbuttered round of dough on top of a buttered round, so you have 4 stacks of 2 rounds with butter sandwiched between the rounds. Pinch the edges of each stack together firmly to seal well, so you end up with four pieces of butter-filled dough.

Add 1½ tablespoons of the olive oil to a plate and place the first dough sandwich on top. Spread another 1½ tablespoons of olive oil over the dough and top with the next sandwich. Repeat with each dough sandwich, ending with olive oil. Cover with plastic wrap and let rest at room temperature for at least 3 hours and up to 5 hours. At this point, the dough is ready to use for your favorite börek recipes.

Note

♥ *Don't be intimidated by the rolling process. This dough is much easier to stretch and handle than many other doughs.*

♥ *You can cover unused dough with plastic wrap and store in the fridge for up to one day. Before using, leave at room temperature for 3 to 4 hours so that the dough stretches easily when ready to assemble.*

Sarıyer Böreği

*Makes 4 large böreks
(serves 4 to 6)*

Turkish-Style Phyllo
(page 256)

POTATO FILLING

4 medium russet potatoes

1 teaspoon kosher salt

2 tablespoons extra-virgin
olive oil

1 onion, diced

1 teaspoon freshly ground
black pepper

1 teaspoon garlic salt

½ cup chopped fresh
parsley

2 scallions, chopped

1 tablespoon chopped
fresh basil

I make this with a potato filling, but the traditional filling is made with feta cheese, like the one used for Su Böreği (page 265). You can use that filling instead or stuff it with your preferred vegetable filling. Serve the börek with Ayran (page 255) or Turkish tea.

Make the phyllo dough as directed.

Meanwhile, make the potato filling: Peel the potatoes and cut each into 4 to 6 equal pieces. In a saucepan, add the potatoes and enough water to just barely cover them. Set over medium heat, add the salt and 1 tablespoon of the olive oil to avoid boiling over, and bring to a boil. Once boiling, reduce the heat to medium-low and cook until the potatoes are tender and will smash easily, 10 to 12 minutes. Drain off the water and cook the potatoes for 1 to 2 minutes over low heat just until all additional moisture is soaked up. Let cool to room temperature.

Using a fork or potato masher, mash the potatoes until chunky.

In a large skillet, heat the remaining 1 tablespoon olive oil over medium heat. Add the onion and cook until lightly golden brown, 5 to 6 minutes. Add the potatoes, pepper, and garlic salt. Stir and let cook for 1 minute until everything has come together. At this point, taste and season additionally if desired. Remove from the heat and let cool completely.

Add the parsley, scallions, and basil and stir until everything is fully incorporated. Set aside.

Line two baking sheets with parchment paper. Clean a large work surface, such as a table, that is at least 32 inches square and where you can access each side of the work surface comfortably. Uncover the plate of dough and pour about one-quarter of the leftover oil from the plate onto the large work surface to oil it. Gently place one of the dough sandwich rounds in the middle of the work surface. Using your hands or a rolling pin, gently press or roll the dough into a 12-inch round. Starting from one side, gently lift and stretch the dough, using the back of your hand to support the middle of the dough and stretch it

continued

continued

Sarıyer Böreği

evenly. Move around the edges of the dough so the whole thing is stretched evenly; don't worry if it tears slightly. Continue this process until the dough is 26 to 32 inches in diameter. Fold in the left and right sides of the round 2 to 3 inches. Then, fold the top and bottom sides in about 2 inches to form a rectangle with a long edge before you.

Divide the potato filling into 4 equal portions. Place one portion of the filling in a line about 1 inch from the bottom edge of the dough. Starting from the bottom, roll the dough around the filling and up to the top edge of the dough, creating a long potato-filled rope. Holding the ends, gently bounce and stretch the rope and place it on one of the baking sheets. Then roll the two ends into the middle to create the sarıyer börek shape. Cover loosely with plastic wrap to avoid drying out. Repeat to make 4 böreks, with 2 böreks per baking sheet.

Preheat the oven to 400°F.

Bake until golden brown, 30 to 35 minutes. Remove from the oven and let cool for 5 to 10 minutes. Use a sharp knife to slice and serve while warm.

Notes

❦ *Store the cooled börek in an airtight storage bag in the fridge for 3 to 5 days or in the freezer for up to 3 months. To reheat, transfer to a baking sheet and let sit at room temperature for 15 to 20 minutes. Place in a cold oven and preheat the oven to 350°F. Once it reaches temperature, the börek should be warm and ready to eat.*

Spinach Triangle Böreks

Makes 28 to 32 pieces
(serves 6)

These delicious pastries filled with spinach and cheese between layers of featherlight dough will remind you of Greek spanakopita. The difference lies in the filling; the Turkish version carries its own unique charm and will make you forget the store-bought triangle böreks from your freezer. This is a really great starter or option for your special-occasion menus, especially for Sunday brunch. Serve with Ayran (page 255) or Turkish tea.

Turkish-Style Phyllo
(page 256)

2 tablespoons extra-virgin olive oil

1 yellow onion, diced

16 ounces baby spinach

1 teaspoon garlic salt

1 teaspoon freshly ground black pepper

½ teaspoon grated lemon zest

¾ cup crumbled feta cheese

1 cup shredded mozzarella cheese

White and black sesame seeds, for topping

Make the phyllo dough as directed.

Meanwhile, in a medium saucepan, heat the olive oil over medium heat. Add the onion and sauté until lightly golden brown, 4 to 5 minutes. Reduce the heat to medium low and add the spinach. Continue to cook, stirring occasionally, until the spinach is wilted and the liquid has cooked out, 7 to 10 minutes.

Add the garlic salt, pepper, and lemon zest. Stir to combine and cook for 1 minute. Remove from the heat and let cool completely. Add the feta and mozzarella and stir until well combined. Set aside.

Line two baking sheets with pieces of parchment paper. Clean a large work surface, such as a table, that is at least 28 inches square and where you can access each side of the work surface comfortably. Uncover the plate of dough and pour about one-quarter of the leftover oil from the plate onto a large work surface to oil it. Gently place one of the dough sandwich rounds in the middle. Using your hands or a rolling pin, gently press or roll the dough into a 12-inch round. Starting from one side, gently lift and stretch the dough, using the back of your hand to support the middle of the dough and stretch it evenly. Move around the edges of the dough so the whole thing is stretched evenly; don't worry if it tears slightly. Continue this process until the dough is 24 to 28 inches in diameter. Holding the edge closest to you, gently fold in half lengthwise. Using a sharp knife or pizza cutter, cut 2 inches off the rounded and pointed sides to form a rectangle. Then cut the dough lengthwise into 3-inch-wide strips.

continued

continued

Spinach Triangle Böreks

With a short side facing you, add 1 full tablespoon of the filling 1 inch away from the bottom of the first strip. Starting from the bottom left corner, fold the dough to the opposite side to form a small triangle. Flip the triangle up over the next few inches of dough and then fold so the new bottom right corner reaches the left side. (This is like folding a flag.) Repeat until the triangle is fully wrapped with the dough. Place the package on the prepared baking sheet and cover with plastic wrap. Repeat with each strip of dough, leaving 1 inch between them on the baking sheet. Repeat the rolling and filling process with the remaining dough sandwich rounds and filling. Top the triangle börek with sesame seeds.

Preheat the oven to 400°F.

Bake until lightly golden brown, 20 to 25 minutes.

Let cool for 5 to 10 minutes before serving warm.

Note

♦ *Store cooled börek in an airtight storage bag in the fridge for 3 to 5 days or in the freezer for up to 3 months. To reheat, transfer the pastries to a baking sheet and let sit at room temperature for 15 to 20 minutes. Then place in a cold oven and preheat it to 350°F. Once it reaches temperature, the böreks should be warm and ready to eat.*

Su Böreği (Water Börek)

Serves 12

The crown jewel of Turkish cuisine, this recipe is a part of every celebration, wedding, and holiday. Rolling out each piece by hand using a Turkish *oklava*—a long and thin rolling pin—is a labor of love, so much so that many in the younger generation choose to buy the finished dish rather than make it. But fret not, for this recipe uses a handy pasta roller. After numerous trials, I've made sure this version is as close to traditional as can be while simplifying the process for you.

DOUGH

7 large eggs

2 tablespoons (28g) water

5 cups (650g) all-purpose flour, plus more for dusting

2½ teaspoons (15g) kosher salt

¼ teaspoon (1g) granulated sugar

1½ teaspoons (7g) extra-virgin olive oil

ASSEMBLY

Kosher salt

14 tablespoons butter

¼ cup heavy cream

2 tablespoons extra-virgin olive oil

1 cup chunk feta cheese

1 cup shredded mozzarella cheese

½ cup chopped fresh parsley

1 large egg

Make the dough: In a medium bowl, beat together the eggs and water. Add 4¾ cups of the flour, the salt, and sugar. Using your hands or a bowl scraper, stir and squeeze the ingredients until they begin to come together. Add the olive oil and continue to mix until just combined. Turn the dough out onto a work surface. Using your hands, perform the basic kneading technique (see page 22) and knead for 4 to 5 minutes, adding the remaining ¼ cup of the flour as you knead, until it is elastic and no longer sticky. (Alternatively, place all the ingredients in the bowl of a stand mixer and use a dough hook on medium speed to knead the dough for 4 to 5 minutes, until everything comes together. Periodically use a silicone spatula to scrape the sides of the bowl and add the bits of dough back into the middle.) It will not look perfectly smooth at this point, but don't worry. Cover the dough with plastic wrap and let rest for 20 to 30 minutes.

Unwrap the dough and continue to use the basic kneading technique to knead the dough for 5 to 7 minutes, until smooth and velvety.

Roll the dough into a rope and use a sharp knife or bench scraper to cut it into 14 equal portions. Fill a shallow bowl with all-purpose flour. Round each piece of dough into a smooth ball (see page 22). Place the balls in the flour and coat evenly. Transfer the balls to a plate or baking sheet. Cover with plastic wrap and let rest at room temperature for 1 to 2 hours.

On a lightly floured work surface, roll a ball of dough into a 3 × 5-inch oval. Using a pasta roller, start at a thicker setting (3 on a KitchenAid) and

continued

continued

Su Böreği (Water Börek)

roll the dough through once at each setting, decreasing in size each time. In the middle of the rolling process, sprinkle flour over the sheet and spread it evenly with your hands. Continue to roll until you reach the thinnest setting (8 on a KitchenAid). Roll through three times at setting 8, gently stretching the dough to widen as it exits the roller. The dough at this point should be 24 to 25 inches long and 6 inches wide.

Place two large kitchen towels or 3 or 4 pieces of parchment paper over a table or surface that is around 3 × 4 feet. Place the first sheet of dough on the lined surface and cover with another towel or parchment paper. Repeat with all pieces of dough, keeping them under the cover to keep them from drying out but making sure they don't touch each other.

When ready to assemble: Fill an extra-large bowl with cold tap water and set near the stove. In an extra-large pot, bring at least 5 quarts of water to a boil. Once it comes to a boil, add 2½ to 3 tablespoons salt and reduce the heat to medium.

Meanwhile, in a medium saucepan, melt the butter. Remove from the heat and stir in the heavy cream and olive oil. In a medium bowl, use a fork to mash the feta. Add the mozzarella and parsley and stir to combine, then set aside.

In a 9 × 13-inch baking dish, drop in 2 tablespoons of the butter mixture and use a pastry brush to spread it evenly around the sides and bottom of the pan. Take the first sheet of dough and cut it in half so you have two 12-inch pieces. Lay the 2 pieces next to each other in the pan, overlapping slightly to cover the entire base with a little up the sides. Using a spoon, add 1 to 1½ tablespoons butter mixture evenly over the top. (Note that the first layer of dough is not boiled, and that is intentional.)

Turn the boiling water up to high heat. Hold a full 24-inch sheet of dough and carefully feed it into the boiling water, making sure it doesn't stick to itself. Using two wooden spoons, turn the dough in the water for 10 to 20 seconds to make sure it cooks evenly. Lift the sheet with a strainer spoon and place in the cold water. Hold the cooled sheet with one hand and use the other hand to squeeze out any excess water. During the cooking process, the sheets may tear slightly, but don't worry as any tear will be inside the börek. Tear the sheet in half with your hands and layer the two pieces in the baking pan over the first uncooked piece of dough. The pieces should be wrinkled rather than stretched flat. Drizzle

Notes

❧ *To roll the dough the traditional way, by hand rather than with a pasta roller, roll each of the 14 dough balls into 14- to 15-inch rounds. As you work, arrange the rounds in two stacks under a kitchen towel to make sure they don't dry out. Follow the rest of the recipe as directed, beginning with When ready to assemble.*

❧ *This will be most delicious the first day, but you can store leftovers in an airtight storage container in the fridge for 2 to 3 days. Heat until warmed through in a dry skillet before serving. You can also store the börek in the freezer for 1 to 2 months. Cut it into slices and store in an airtight storage bag with parchment paper between the pieces. Let thaw at room temperature before heating until warmed through in a dry skillet and serving.*

1½ to 2 tablespoons of the butter mixture evenly over the top. Repeat this process with 4 more full sheets of dough. Once you have 6 layers of dough, distribute half of the feta mixture evenly over the dough. Repeat the cooking and layering process with 2 more full sheets of dough and then top with the remaining cheese filling. Continue to cook and layer the remaining dough sheets until you have 14 layers of dough. Using a sharp knife, poke at least 20 holes through the layers all the way to the bottom of the pan. Beat the egg into the remaining butter mixture and drizzle it over the top. Use a brush or your hands to evenly spread the mixture. It should mostly soak into the dough.

Preheat the oven to 450°F.

Bake until the top is crispy and golden brown, 30 to 35 minutes.

Let rest for 10 to 15 minutes before cutting into 3-inch squares and serving while warm.

Feta Hand Pies

Makes 12 to 14 hand pies

These hand pies are a customary treat in a Turkish tradition called Altın Günü, or Gold Day/Session, a gathering of neighborhood women and friends who each gift the hostess a small piece of gold. Essentially, it's an afternoon tea party with delectable Turkish pastries and salads, including these hand pies. The dough includes eggs and yogurt for a delightful texture—crispy and flaky outside, buttery and fluffy inside.

DOUGH

2¼ cups (293g) all-purpose flour, plus more for dusting

1 tablespoon (12g) granulated sugar

1 teaspoon (6g) kosher salt

1 tablespoon plus ¼ teaspoon (13g) baking powder

1 stick (4 oz/113g) unsalted butter, at room temperature

1 large egg

1 large egg white

¼ cup (55g) extra-virgin olive oil or neutral oil

¼ cup (62g) whole-milk yogurt

2¼ teaspoons (10g) apple cider vinegar

¼ cup (10g) chopped fresh dill

FETA FILLING

5 ounces feta cheese

2 tablespoons chopped fresh dill

2 tablespoons chopped fresh parsley

1 tablespoon minced green onion

Egg wash: 1 egg yolk beaten with 1 teaspoon water

Make the dough: In a medium bowl, stir together the flour, sugar, salt, and baking powder until well combined. In another medium bowl, combine the butter, whole egg, egg white, oil, yogurt, and vinegar and whisk to combine. Slowly pour the flour mixture into the wet ingredients, using your hands to combine. While the dough is still in the bowl, use your hands to perform the basic kneading technique (see page 22) and knead for 4 to 5 minutes, until it is elastic and no longer sticky. Add the fresh dill and continue to knead for 2 to 3 minutes, until fully incorporated. At this point, the dough should be soft and buttery. Cover with plastic wrap and let rest in the fridge for 2 to 3 hours.

Make the feta filling: In a medium bowl, use a fork to mash the feta into small crumbs. Add the dill, parsley, and green onion and use the fork to mix until well combined.

Preheat the oven to 350°F. Line 2 baking sheets with parchment paper.

Place the dough on a lightly floured work surface. Roll the dough into a log and use a sharp knife or bench scraper to cut into 12 to 14 portions (50g each). Round each piece of dough into a smooth ball (see page 22). Use your hand to press a dough ball into a 3-inch flat disc. Add 1 heaping tablespoon of filling to the middle of the bottom half of the disc. Fold the dough over into a half-moon and press the edges together. Place the pie on the baking sheet. Repeat with each piece of dough, leaving two inches between each on the baking sheet. Brush the top of each hand pie with the egg wash. Using a fork, press the tines around the half-moon's edge.

Bake until golden brown, 27 to 32 minutes.

Let cool for 20 to 30 minutes before serving.

Notes

❧ *While this recipe calls for a mix of feta cheese and dill, you can swap the fillings to match your tastes.*

❧ *Store the fully cooled hand pies in an airtight storage bag in the fridge for 5 to 7 days or in the freezer for up to 3 months. If frozen, allow to thaw at room temperature before warming. Place in a cold oven and preheat to 350°F. Once the oven is preheated, the pies will be ready to serve, preferably with Turkish tea or coffee!*

Pişi

Serves 4 to 6

The taste of pişi, a Turkish fried dough, is deeply ingrained in my childhood memories. Similar to a French beignet, these were a breakfast staple at our home, particularly during the summer months, when juicy apricots were abundant. With the scent of apricot jam wafting through the house, we would eagerly pack a picnic basket and head to the nearest green spot for a leisurely feast. The pişi—crispy on the outside and airy on the inside—are delightful, with a chewy dough and a neutral taste, so they can be eaten with sweet or savory toppings. Even though fresh apricot jam is not always at hand in the States, I do my best to keep this cherished tradition alive, pairing it with chocolate-hazelnut cream or cheese and tomatoes for a Turkish-style breakfast.

DOUGH

3 cups (390g) all-purpose flour, plus more for dusting

1 tablespoon (12g) granulated sugar

¼ teaspoon (2g) kosher salt

2¼ teaspoons (9g) baking powder

1 large egg

¼ cup (62g) whole-milk yogurt

¼ cup (55g) whole milk

½ cup (110g) water, at room temperature (75° to 80°F)

PIŞI

Neutral oil, for deep-frying

Powdered sugar, for serving

Apricot jam, for serving

Make the dough: In a medium bowl, whisk together the flour, sugar, salt, and baking powder until fully incorporated. In another medium bowl, whisk together the egg, yogurt, milk, and water. Add the dry ingredients to the wet ingredients. Using your hands or a bowl scraper, mix for 2 to 3 minutes, until the dough comes together.

Transfer the dough to a lightly floured work surface. Using your hands, perform the basic kneading technique (see page 22) and knead for 4 to 5 minutes, until the dough is almost smooth. Loosely cover with plastic wrap and a clean kitchen towel and let rest on the work surface for 15 to 20 minutes.

Knead the dough for another 2 to 3 minutes, until smooth. (Alternatively, you can knead the dough in a stand mixer on medium speed for 5 to 7 minutes, until smooth and no longer sticking to the sides of the bowl.) Cover with plastic wrap or a kitchen towel and let rest for 5 to 10 minutes.

Make the pişi: Line a plate with paper towels and set near the stove.

Uncover the dough and use a sharp knife or bench scraper to divide the dough into 2 equal portions. Cup your hands around both sides of one piece of dough and roll into a quick ball. Repeat with the other piece. Cover with plastic wrap to prevent drying.

continued

continued

Pişi

Pour 2½ inches of oil into a large pot and heat the oil over medium heat to 350°F.

Working with one ball at a time (and keeping the other one covered), place the dough on a lightly floured work surface and use a rolling pin to roll into an 8- to 9-inch round. Using a pizza cutter or sharp knife, cut into 2-inch squares, or cut into 3-inch squares and then cut on the diagonal for triangles. The squares don't have to be perfect, some edges will be rounded and that's totally okay.

Working in batches of 8 to 10 (to avoid crowding), carefully place the dough pieces in the hot oil and carefully swirl the pot lightly a few times to cover each piece with oil. This will ensure that your dough cooks more evenly and has a crispy outside and air-filled inside. Continue to fry for 3 to 4 minutes, stirring periodically with a straining spoon so each side is golden brown and cooked well. Remove to the paper towels.

Dust with powdered sugar and serve with apricot jam while warm.

Notes

♥ The oil-swirling process is very important to make the proper balloon-y texture, but it is also very important to be careful not to burn yourself. I always use a pot that has handles on both sides and leave the bottom on the burner as I carefully move the pot in a circle. When I was little, this step always felt like magic to me—watching my mom swirl the oil as the dough all of a sudden bloomed into a beautiful puffy pastry.

♥ You can also serve pişi without powdered sugar, as a savory dish with feta cheese and a tomato and cucumber salad, which is one of my favorite ways to eat this.

♥ If you have leftovers, I'm sorry, but you have to share—these are never as delicious the next day!

Kalburabastı

Makes 18 to 20 cookies

When we talk about desserts in Turkish cuisine, simple syrup desserts come to mind. From the Ottoman era, Türkiye inherited countless sweet treats, such as the globally beloved baklava. But there are numerous other syrup-soaked desserts made with a uniquely prepared cookie dough. These cookies are usually reserved for special occasions and served with Turkish tea or coffee. Among these, kalburabastı is a personal favorite of mine—as delightful as baklava but without the complexity. The name kalburabastı comes from an old Turkish kitchen tool, the *kalbur*, which was used to decorate this dessert. The indentation on the top can be made with a grater; it is traditional for this type of cookie but not necessary. This cookie is the perfect surprise for your guests at your next holiday gathering, offering them a unique texture and flavor, unlike many American desserts. I can't wait to hear your feedback!

SIMPLE SYRUP

2½ cups granulated sugar

2½ cups water

¼ teaspoon kosher salt

⅛ of a lemon

COOKIES

2¾ cups (358g) all-purpose flour

3 tablespoons (33g) semolina flour

1 teaspoon (4g) baking powder

½ teaspoon (2g) baking soda

¼ teaspoon (2g) kosher salt

1 stick (4 oz/113g) unsalted butter, at room temperature

½ cup (110g) peanut oil or neutral oil

1 tablespoon (12g) granulated sugar

½ cup (110g) whole milk

2 tablespoons (31g) whole-milk yogurt

½ teaspoon (3g) apple cider vinegar

½ teaspoon (3g) vanilla extract (optional)

1 cup (125g) coarsely chopped walnuts

¼ cup (25g) crushed pistachios, for sprinkling

Make the simple syrup: In a small saucepan, stir together the sugar, water, and salt. Bring to a boil over medium-high heat and, once boiling, squeeze the lemon juice from the wedge into the syrup and then add the spent lemon slice. Reduce the heat to medium-low and simmer for 12 to 14 minutes. Test for doneness by dipping a teaspoon into the syrup. Shake off the excess syrup, then hold the teaspoon above the saucepan. If the remaining syrup slowly drips off the spoon, the syrup is ready. If it falls quickly, continue to simmer for 2 to 3 minutes. Remove the syrup from the heat and let cool completely to room temperature while you make the cookies. Remove the lemon slice.

Make the cookies: In a medium bowl, whisk together the all-purpose flour, semolina flour, baking powder, baking soda, and salt. In another medium bowl, whisk together the butter, peanut oil, and sugar. Add the milk, yogurt, vinegar, and vanilla extract (if using) and continue to whisk until well combined. Add the dry ingredients to the wet ingredients. Using your hands, knead the dough by stirring and squeezing it together until the ingredients are combined, 2 to 4 minutes.

Preheat the oven to 350°F. Line a baking sheet with parchment paper.

continued

continued

Kalburabastı

Spoon out about 1½ tablespoons (30g) of the dough and roll into a ball in the palm of your hand. Flatten the dough into a 2½-inch round and fill with ½ tablespoon of chopped walnuts. Starting at the top, pinch the edges together over the filling to seal, creating a kayak shape. Press an extra-coarse grater against the top of the dough to mark the dough. Repeat to make more cookies, placing them 1½ inches apart on the prepared baking sheet.

Bake until lightly golden brown, 25 to 27 minutes.

Using a spatula, immediately and carefully transfer the cookies to a 9 × 13-inch baking dish. The cookies should be touching. Pour the cooled syrup over the hot cookies. It may look like too much syrup at first, but don't worry, it will soak into the cookies. Cover with plastic wrap and let rest at room temperature for 4 to 8 hours or overnight, until the dessert soaks up all of the syrup.

Sprinkle with the crushed pistachios to serve.

Notes

♥ *This dough will be very soft and fluffy when you finish kneading. This is okay! It will make for a soft cookie to soak up all the syrup.*

♥ *If you have a few cookies that cannot fit in the 9 × 13-inch dish, you can place them in a separate small dish with some of the syrup.*

♥ *This is a dessert that is even better the next day. Cover the baking dish with plastic wrap and store at room temperature for 2 to 3 days. If you can't finish it all, share with your friends and neighbors.*

ACKNOWLEDGMENTS

To my life's superhero, my husband: From the moment we met, you altered the course of my life with your unwavering support and inspired me to chase my dreams relentlessly. I am forever grateful for your profound understanding of me, which is often better than my own understanding, and for the trust you place in me. Thank you for being my chief taste tester, my sounding board, my steadfast supporter, and my constant companion, not just through the journey of this book but across the wonderful decade we've shared. I'm truly at a loss to imagine this journey without you.

To my cherished son, Kerem: Your boundless motivation and uncanny wisdom beyond your years have been a beacon throughout this endeavor. You are my greatest treasure.

To my dear family: Despite the miles that separate us, your unwavering support has been my pillar. Thank you for standing by me unconditionally, in every situation, with boundless love. I am immensely fortunate to have you in my life.

To my editor, Dervla Kelly: From our initial meeting, I was convinced that collaborating with you on my first cookbook was a pivotal and brilliant decision. Your warm demeanor and complete confidence in me solidified my intuition. Thank you for illuminating my path with your unparalleled expertise on this new journey, for your unwavering trust, and for your unfaltering support.

To my wonderful manager, Naomi Lennon: Your persistent dedication has made me feel truly valued. Thank you for always being present and perpetually advocating on my behalf since the beginning. It has been an absolute delight working with you. Thank you for tirelessly marching alongside me on this journey, and for never showing a hint of weariness or doubt.

To my assistant, Beka Olson: Thank you for being my indispensable right hand from day one. Your dedication through the long hours has been instrumental, from helping me write the recipes into their clearest form to restoring order in a kitchen turned upside down by photo shoots, readying it for the next day's tasks. Your insightful critiques, drawn from years of experience in the restaurant industry, your exacting palate, and your beautiful latte art in my cookbook's photography have been invaluable.

To Emma Campion, the designer of my book: Meeting you was meeting one of the kindest souls. Your exceptional talent and experience have transformed my first cookbook into the vision I always dreamed of, elevating it to a work of art. Your ability to know me so well, right from the start, has both amazed and delighted me.

To my new editor, Cristina Garces: Though you joined us later in the process, your embrace, guidance, and support have been a guiding light.

To the entire Ten Speed Press family: Bringing this book to life with your help has been an honor. The excitement is overwhelming, and my gratitude extends to everyone who played a part in this creation.

To the lifestyle photographers Andrea Gentl and Martin Hyers: My anticipation of the lifestyle photo shoots paled in comparison to the enjoyable and unforgettable experience you provided. Your professionalism and work ethic have taught me so much; your talent and discipline are truly admirable. My deepest thanks for your tremendous efforts.

A heartfelt thank you to Colonial Williamsburg for graciously opening up their stunning location for our lifestyle photo shoot. The backdrop of history and beauty added an unparalleled richness to our work. Additionally, my sincere gratitude to dear Kiri Franco for your unwavering help and support throughout our enchanting visit. Your contributions have been invaluable.

And to our huge Turkuaz Kitchen family: Writing these words brings a surge of emotion. Your trust, support, and incredible love have been the foundation of my journey. Without you, none of this would have been possible. From the deepest reaches of my heart, I regard you as an extended family, and my love for each of you knows no bounds. This book, into which I've poured my heart and soul, is for you. I hope you cherish it as much as I do and that it finds a place in your homes and hearts as you recreate my recipes in your kitchens.

INDEX

Note: Page references in *italics* indicate photographs.

Typefaces: Exljbris's Calluna, SilkType's Velour, and Monotype's Walbaum Ornaments

Library of Congress Cataloging-in-Publication Data
Names: Tunç, Bëtul, 1989– author. Title: Turkuaz kitchen : traditional and modern dough recipes
for sweet and savory bakes / Bëtul Tunç. Identifiers: LCCN 2023051848 (print) | LCCN 2023051849
(ebook) | ISBN 9781984862228 (hardcover) | ISBN 9781984862235 (ebook) Subjects: LCSH: Dough. |
Dough—Turkey. | LCGFT: Cookbooks. Classification: LCC TX769 .T863 2024 (print) | LCC TX769
(ebook) | DDC 641.7/109561—dc23/eng/20231221
LC record available at https://lccn.loc.gov/2023051848
LC ebook record available at https://lccn.loc.gov/2023051849

Hardcover ISBN: 978-1-9848-6222-8
eBook ISBN: 978-1-9848-6223-5

Background textures and decorative icons courtesy of Shutterstock.

Printed in China

Editors: Dervla Kelly and Cristina Garces
Production editor: Joyce Wong | Editorial assistant: Gabby Urena
Designer: Emma Campion | Production designers: Mari Gill and Faith Hague
Production manager: Dan Myers | Prepress color manager: Nick Patton
Copyeditor: Kate Slate | Proofreaders: Sasha Tropp and Lisa Lawley | Indexer: Elizabeth Parson
Publicist: Natalie Yera-Campbell | Marketer: Monica Stanton

10 9 8 7 6 5 4 3 2 1

First Edition